# John & Joséphine
## The Creation of The Bowes Museum

Caroline Chapman

Epilogue written by Adrian Jenkins

Published by The Bowes Museum
Barnard Castle, County Durham DL12 8NP

© 2010 The Bowes Museum

Design by Red Square Design, Newcastle

ISBN: 978-0-9548182-96

# Contents

Chairman's Foreword iii

Acknowledgements iv

List of Illustrations v

Prologue 1

John Bowes: Early Years at Streatlam 5

Le Théâtre des Variétés 23

Life in Paris 41

Joséphine and the Paris Salon 57

Assembling the Collection 69

Life in England 91

The Collection in Peril 109

The Legacy Realised 121

Epilogue 141

Notes 149

Bibliography 158

Index 160

# Chairman's Foreword

John and Joséphine Bowes were an extraordinary couple who did an extraordinary thing: they created a vast collection of artefacts to be housed in a majestic building for the people of County Durham, entirely at their own expense.

John Bowes's curriculum vitae spanned a diverse range of interests: businessman, landowner, farmer, engineer, horse breeder and art collector.

Joséphine also displayed an array of talents – actress, painter and contemporary art collector – and it was her vision that inspired their incredible legacy. Their paths crossed at the Théâtre des Variétés in 1847. At the time, neither of them could possibly have envisaged what their future together would bring.

*John and Joséphine Bowes: The Creation of The Bowes Museum* tells that story.

Caroline Chapman, author of this wonderful book, has captured the age in which John and Joséphine lived, and the Trustees and Staff owe her a great debt for her painstaking research in The Bowes Museum's extensive archive and in the Durham County Record Office. The end result has been well worth the effort.

Lord Foster of Bishop Auckland, 2010
Chairman of the Trustees, The Bowes Museum

# Acknowledgements

My first thanks go to John Eccles (Chairman of the Trustees from 2000 to 2007) as it was his idea that the Museum should have a new biography of John and Joséphine Bowes, and suggested that I should write it. That his suggestion bore fruit is due to the support and firm commitment of the Director of the Museum, Adrian Jenkins, for which I am extremely grateful.

I would like to pay tribute to John Bowes's previous biographer, the late Charles Hardy. As I followed his footsteps through the Museum's archives, I grew to respect his accuracy and integrity as a biographer. Only once did he fail me and that was on the subject of John's youthful health problems, over which he chose to draw a discreet veil. The unpublished thesis by the late James Vernon Wilkinson, with its special emphasis on the Théâtre des Variétés, was also very useful.

I would particularly like to thank certain members of the staff at The Bowes Museum, all of whom had little time to spare from their demanding responsibilities: Howard Coutts for his patience and readiness to share his vast knowledge about the Museum and its founders; Jane Whittaker for her unfailing help and support; Emma House for answering my endless questions about objects in the Collection and for her work on the book's design and content. The Museum archivist Judith Phillips, and the two archive volunteers Jo Angell and Margaret Harley, have all been generous with their time and advice. Margaret's fluent French was essential when it came to some of the subtleties of the language. I am also grateful to Elizabeth Conran who read and commented on the biography's first draft.

I would especially like to thank Dr Michael Harford Cross, whose knowledge of nineteenth-century medicine was invaluable. I am indebted too to Marina Logan-Bruce whose delvings in the Library at St. George's, University of London produced Bowes's medical case notes. Wendy Moore, author of *Wedlock*, a biography of John's grandmother, was kind enough to answer a number of questions. Lastly, my thanks go to the staff of Durham County Record Office who guided me through John Bowes's correspondence among the Strathmore papers, and to Lord Strathmore for his permission for quotes to be used from these papers.

Caroline Chapman, 2010

# List of illustrations

## Abbreviations

TBM    The Bowes Museum

TBMA   The Bowes Museum Archive

## Front cover

Joséphine Bowes, *Château du Barry at Louveciennes*, c. 1862, oil on canvas (TBM, J.45)

## Back cover

*The Bowes Museum*, 2009, photograph by Mike Kipling (TBM)

## Endpapers

*Architectural Drawing*, 1869, J. E. Watson (TBMA)

1    Thomas Hearne, *Barnard Castle*, 1788, watercolour (TBM, B.M.1060)

2    Joseph Miller, *Streatlam Castle*, 1829, oil on canvas (Strathmore Estates)

3    John Jackson, *John Bowes*, 1826, oil on canvas (The Royal Collection © 2009 Her Majesty Queen Elizabeth II)

4    John Cox Dillman Engleheart after George Engleheart, *Mary Eleanor Bowes*, 1800, miniature (TBM, Min.86)

5    John Downman, *Andrew Robinson Bowes*, 1781, drawing (© Fitzwilliam Museum, Cambridge)

6    *after* Mather Brown, *John, 10th Earl of Strathmore*, c.1800-50, oil on canvas (The Royal Collection © 2009 Her Majesty Queen Elizabeth II)

7    English School, *Mary, Countess of Strathmore*, c. 1840, watercolour on ivory (TBM, Min.83)

8    Thomas Shotter Boys, *Regent Street, Looking Towards the Duke of York's Column*, from 'London As It Is', engraved and pub. by the artist, 1842, colour lithograph (Private Collection/The Bridgeman Art Library)

9    John Jackson, *John Bowes* (detail), 1826, oil on canvas (The Royal Collection © 2009 Her Majesty Queen Elizabeth II)

10   William Makepeace Thackeray, Cambridge student taken from *Etchings by the late William Makepeace Thackeray while at Cambridge, illustrative of university life*, 1878

11   Master of the Virgo inter Virgines, centre panel of a *Crucifixion* triptych, 1490s, oil on panel (TBM, B.M.168)

12   John Frederick Herring senior, *The Streatlam Stud*,1836, (Private Collection/Photo © Christie's Images/The Bridgeman Art Library)

13   Daniel Maclise, *William Makepeace Thackeray*, c. 1840, drawing (National Portrait Gallery, London)

14   Joseph Mathias Negelen, *John Bowes*, c. 1830-40, crayon on paper (TBM, B.M.1035)

15   William Wyld, *The Palais Royal*, c. 1835, lithograph (Musée Carnavalet, Paris)

16   Théâtre des Variétés, coloured postcard (TBMA)

17   Elevation and plan of Théâtre des Variétés, (TBMA)

18   Victor Darjou, *The Actor Hugues Bouffé in his Dressing Room at the Théâtre des Variétés*, Paris, 1848, oil on canvas (Musée Carnavalet, Paris)

19   Louis Desanges, *Joséphine Bowes*, c. 1852-1860, oil on canvas (TBM, B.M.529)

20   Decorative belt made in Hungary, c.1850 (TBM, X.5264)

21   George du Maurier, *A Happy Dinner*, taken from his book *Trilby* (1894), wood engraving (Private Collection)

22   Edward Morin, *The Dressing Room of Hortense Schneider at the Théâtre des Variétés*, 1873, watercolour on paper (Chateau de Compiègne/Lauros/Giraudon/The Bridgeman Art Library)

23   Constantin Guys, *The Foyer of the Variétés*, c.1860-92 (Walters Art Gallery, Baltimore)

24   Thomas Shotter Boys, *Boulevard des Italiens*, 1833, watercolour, (British Museum/The Bridgeman Art Library)

25   Nicholas Edward Gabé, *The Barricade at Porte St Denis, Paris, 1848*, 1849, oil on canvas (TBM, B.M.485)

26   Antoine Dury, *Joséphine Bowes*, 1850, oil on canvas (TBM, B.M.297)

27   Gustave Caillebotte, *Boulevard Haussmann in the Snow*, 1879 or 1881 (Private Collection/The Bridgeman Art Library)

28    Joséphine Bowes, *Château du Barry at Louveciennes*, c. 1862, oil on canvas (TBM, J.45)

29    A path in the garden at Château du Barry, Louveciennes, c. 1862, photograph by Pierre Rion (TBMA)

30    Invoices for dresses bought by Joséphine Bowes from Worth and Bobergh (TBMA)

31    François-Xavier Winterhalter, *Empress Eugénie surrounded by her Ladies-in-Waiting*, 1855, oil on canvas (Château de Compiègne, France /Giraudon /The Bridgeman Art Library)

32    The Orangery at Château du Barry, c. 1862, photograph by Pierre Rion (TBMA)

33    Monbro *fils aîné*, Armchair for the Salon Bleu at 7 rue de Berlin, Paris, 1855 (TBM, FW.93A)

34    'Lit à la duchesse', 1850s, gilt wood and silk brocade (TBM, FW.112)

35    Monbro *fils aîné*, One of a pair of candelabra, c. 1855 (TBM, X.4431)

36    Edouard Manet, *Musique aux Tuileries*, 1862 (The National Gallery, London)

37    Edouard Manet, *The Racing at Longchamp*, Paris, 1864 (Potter Palmer Collection, The Art Institute of Chicago)

38    Joséphine Bowes, c. 1860, photograph (TBMA)

39    Charles Chaplin, *Girl in a Pink Dress Sitting at a Table with a Dog*, c. 1860-1870, oil on canvas (TBM, B.M.392)

40    Gustave Courbet, *View at Ornans, France*, 1864, oil on canvas (TBM, B.M.351)

41    Delacroix jousting with Ingres, French, c.1828, engraving (Private Collection/The Bridgeman Art Library)

42    Carpentier's invoices for supplying artists' materials to Joséphine Bowes (TBMA)

43    Eugène-Louis Boudin, *Beach Scene at Low Tide*, 1867, oil on canvas (TBM, B.M.689)

44    A. Provost, *Salon of Painting and Sculpture of 1857, the Main Room in the Palais de l'Industrie Gallery, Paris*, 1857, engraving (Musée de la Ville de Paris, Musée Carnavalet, Paris/Lauros/Giraudon/The Bridgeman Art Library)

45    Tickets for the Paris Salon, 1868 and 1869 (TBMA)

46    George du Maurier, *Varnishing Day at the Royal Academy*, 1877, pencil on paper (Manchester Art Gallery/The Bridgeman Art Library)

47    Joséphine Bowes, *Landscape with Trees and Cattle*, c. 1860-1867, oil on canvas (TBM, J.3)

48    Joséphine Bowes, *Still Life with Cooking Utensils and Vegetables*, c. 1860-1874, oil on canvas (TBM, J.34)

49    Tapestry, *The Birth of Samson*, c. 1540, silk and wool weft on wool warp (TBM, Tap.6)

50    Stefano di Giovanni Sassetta, *A Miracle of the Eucharist*, c. 1423-1426, tempera and gold on panel (TBM, B.M.52)

51    Circle of Primaticcio, *The Rape of Helen*, 1533-1535, oil on canvas (TBM, B.M.76)

52    El Greco, *The Tears of St Peter*, c. 1580-1589, oil on canvas (TBM, B.M.642)

53    Francisco de Goya, *Interior of a Prison*, c. 1793-1794, oil on tin plate (TBM, B.M.29)

54    Antonio Pereda y Salgado, *Tobias Restoring his Father's Sight*, 1652, oil on canvas (TBM, B.M.34)

55    Doorplate, French, late 17th century, brass (TBM, M.159)

56    Needle lace (detail), French, 1690s (TBM, The Blackborne Collection)

57    Faïence plate from Nevers, France, 1757, one of a pair (TBM, X.4046.1)

58    Meissen tureen, c. 1750, hard-paste porcelain (TBM, X.2784)

59    J. P. Ledoux, Sèvres Teapot, 1758, soft-paste porcelain (TBM, X.1271)

60    François Boucher, *Landscape with Watermill*, 1743, oil on canvas (TBM, B.M.486)

61    Giovanni Battista Tiepolo, *The Harnessing of the Horses of the Sun*, c. 1731, oil on canvas (TBM, B.M.51)

62    Adolphe-Joseph-Thomas Monticelli, *Landscape with Figures and Goats*, before 1866, oil on panel (TBM)

63    Emile Gallé, Engraved glass vase, 1871 (TBM)

64    Workshop of James Cox, Mechanical Silver Swan, c. 1773, silver with glass and metal fittings (TBM, X.4653)

65    Possibly Swiss, Mechanical mouse, c. 1810, gold with seed pearls and garnet eyes (TBM, X.5447)

66    Oval dish from Moustiers, France, c. 1750, tin-glazed earthenware, painted with the arms of Madame de Pompadour (TBM, X.1261)

67    J. E. Feyen, *John Bowes*, 1863, oil on canvas (TBM)

68    Streatlam Castle, late nineteenth-century, photograph by Elijah Yeoman (TBMA, 1998.31.28)

69   Antoine Dury, *Bernardine*, c. 1850, oil on canvas (TBM, B.M.911)

70   Joséphine Bowes, *Squally Weather, A Sketch near Boulogne-sur-Mer, France*, c. 1860-1870, (TBM, J.44)

71   J. Greenwood, *William Hutt*, etching (TBM)

72   Joseph Mallord William Turner, *Gibside from the South*, c. 1817, watercolour (TBM, 1983.35)

73   Martha Davidson, *The Palladian Chapel at Gibside*, early nineteenth century, sketchbook (TBM, 2005.1)

74   Arms of John Bowes, watercolour (TBMA)

75   Arms of the Countess of Montalbo, watercolour (TBMA)

76   Entwined initials of John and Joséphine Bowes, c.1876, plaster design (TBM)

77   English School, *John Scott*, c.1845-55, watercolour (TBM, 2006.1)

78   John Frederick Herring junior, *Mr. John Bowes's Bay Colt 'Cotherstone', by 'Touchstone' out of 'Emma', in a Loosebox*, 1844, oil on canvas (TBM, 2006.14)

79   Thomas Creswick, *A Relic of Old Times (Barnard Castle from the River)*, c. 1860, oil on canvas (TBM, B.M.967)

80   French School, *View of the Fires in Paris during the Commune on 24th and 25th May, 1871* (detail), colour lithograph, (Musée de la Ville de Paris, Musée Carnavalet, Paris/Lauros/Giraudon/The Bridgeman Art Library)

81   Jules de Vignon after François-Xavier Winterhalter, *The Emperor Napoléon III*, 1867, oil on canvas (TBM, B.M.1052)

82   *after* William Rainey, 'Chairs were brought that Napoleon and the Minister might sit out of doors', from *The Story of France Told to Boys and Girls by Mary Macgregor*, 1920, colour lithograph (Private Collection/The Stapleton Collection/The Bridgeman Art Library)

83   *Queue for rat meat*, lithograph after drawing by Cham, c. 1870

84   Jules Didier and Jacques Guiaud, *The Departure of Léon Michel Gambetta in the Balloon 'L'Armand-Barbes', 7 October 1870*, oil on canvas, (Musée de la Ville de Paris, Musée Carnavalet, Paris/Giraudon/The Bridgeman Art Library)

85   Hall of Mirrors, Palace of Versailles, converted into a German hospital, photograph, c. 1870

86   Edouard Manet, *La Barricade, scène de la Commune de Paris*, lithograph, 1871 (The British Museum)

87   French School, *View of the Fires in Paris during the Commune on 24th and 25th May, 1871*, colour lithograph, (Musée de la Ville de Paris, Musée Carnavalet, Paris/Lauros/Giraudon/The Bridgeman Art Library)

88   The Picture Galleries, The Bowes Museum c. 1900, photograph by Elijah Yeoman (TBMA, 1998.31.42)

89   'Mrs. Bowes's Mansion and Museum, Barnard Castle, Durham', from *The Builder*, 14 January 1871 (TBMA, 1998.31.42)

90   Emile Gallé, *Faïence jug depicting King Stanislas*, 1872 (TBM, X.4121)

91   In Memoriam card for Joséphine Bowes (TBMA)

92   Sedan chair bearing the arms of the Bourbon dukes of Parma, 18th century (TBM, FW.366)

93   Chelsea plate with botanical illustration, c.1750, (TBM, X.3373)

94   Alphonsine de Saint-Amand, Comtesse de Courten, photograph (TBMA)

95   John Bowes on the terrace at Streatlam Castle, n.d., photograph (TBMA)

96   Detail of letter from John Bowes to Ralph John Dent, 2 March 1884 (TBMA)

97   The Entrance Hall, The Bowes Museum, 1914, photograph by Friths (TBMA 2000.1.188)

98   Entrance Doors, The Bowes Museum, 2010, photograph by Syd Neville (TBM)

99   Chelsea pot-pourri vase and cover, c.1765 (TBM/The Lady Ludlow collection, gift of the Art Fund, 2004.101.2)

100  The Bowes Museum under construction, c. 1875, photograph (TBMA)

101  Fashion and Textile Gallery, The Bowes Museum, 2010, photograph by Syd Neville (TBM)

102  View from The John Eccles Reading Room, The Bowes Museum, 2010, photograph by Syd Neville (TBM)

# Prologue

1
John Bowes's home town of Barnard Castle in County Durham, where he and his wife Joséphine decided to build their Museum. Thomas Hearne's watercolour of 1788 shows the bridge over the River Tees and the ruins of the twelfth-century castle.

To the unwary traveller approaching the ancient town of Barnard Castle from the south, a sudden glimpse of three lofty slate-grey pavilions floating improbably above the treetops comes as a complete surprise. A dip in the road briefly hides this unexpected vision. But no sooner has the traveller satisfied himself that it was an illusion than a remarkable edifice swims into view. Standing boldly on its grassy mound, part French town hall, part Renaissance château, The Bowes Museum seems wildly out of scale and out of place amidst the lowering skies and muted colours of a windswept dale in County Durham.

Entering by the fine wrought-iron gates, the visitor approaches the Museum by a semi-circular drive, passing *en route* the jagged limbs of a giant monkey-puzzle tree, planted there by the Museum's founders in 1871. Once standing on the wide terrace which fronts the Museum, the visitor feels dwarfed as much by the building's soaring façade as by the massive iron entrance doors built, it would seem, to withstand a prolonged siege.

Beyond this formidable barrier the hall within is on the same grand scale, the ceiling rising to some thirty feet in height. A wide staircase of pink granite leads to the upper galleries where the principal collections are displayed. As the visitor wanders from room to room, the polished boards creaking beneath his feet, he passes cases of glowing porcelain, a vast faïence stove from Sweden, Salviati glass from Venice, richly veneered *boulle* furniture from France, engraved glass by Émile Gallé, a rich assortment of examples of French decorative arts, and one of the largest and most significant collections of European textiles in the country. In the picture galleries hang paintings of subjects ranging from the sacred to the quotidian, and from landscapes by such masters as Boucher and Tiepolo to portraits of Napoléon Bonaparte and his family.

When the visitor enters a suite of rooms on the first floor he is suddenly confronted by two large portraits, hung side by side. One shows a dark-haired woman with a tight smile, dressed in the height of Second Empire fashion. At her feet lies a golden labrador with appealing eyes. The other portrays a benign-looking gentleman with mutton-chop whiskers, seated on a convenient rock, a shotgun cradled against one shoulder. Just visible in the top left-hand corner of the picture is a substantial edifice. The portraits represent Joséphine and John Bowes, founders of this remarkable museum; the edifice is Streatlam Castle, John Bowes's ancestral home.

Although he lived in Paris for most of his life, John Bowes never lost his love for Streatlam or for Barnard Castle and its people, and the Museum is tangible proof of this affection. The house, however, is no longer there; following a series of vicissitudes – which will be explained in the succeeding pages – it was finally demolished in 1959, a sad fate for a house that had been in the Bowes family for over six hundred years. But much of the five hundred acres that surrounded Streatlam in John Bowes's time would be familiar to him were he to drive through them today.

The Streatlam estate lies three miles north-east of Barnard Castle. Entering its precincts from the south, the drive takes you through gently undulating parkland studded with fine beech and oak trees until you see ahead a steep-sided little valley through which flows the Forthburn Beck. Looking across the classic stone bridge – now lacking its balustrade – you are confronted by an impenetrable clump of pines drawn up like a Roman phalanx

2
Three miles north-east of Barnard Castle lies
Streatlam Castle, the principal residence of the
Bowes family for over 600 years. Joseph Miller's
painting of 1829 shows the Castle set among the
wooded hills of its extensive park.

to hide the void once occupied by the Castle. Standing on rising ground to the left of this obstacle is the shell of a handsome Orangery, rebuilt in its present form by Bowes in the last years of his life. To the right is a tall archway, now a lone sentinel but which in Bowes's day guarded the entrance to a spacious courtyard.

Once across the beck, the road skirts the sullen pines and guides you up a steep hill towards the stable block – empty now and silent – where Bowes's Derby winners were bred. To the right of this road, the ground plunges into a deep vale. The land immediately beyond this defile is broken by several odd mounds and protuberances, said to contain either detritus from the Castle or the corporeal remains of some of Bowes's racehorses. These mute echoes from John Bowes's past continue to haunt you as you leave the Streatlam estate.

Bowes's other property, Gibside, came to his family by marriage at the end of the seventeenth century. Situated in the north of the county, forty miles from Streatlam, Gibside's setting was enthusiastically described by Robert Surtees in his *History of Durham* of 1820: 'Woods, venerable in their growth and magnificent in their extent sweep from the height of the hills to the brink of the Derwent, intersected by deep irregular ravines. The whole landscape, to use a painter's phrase, is sketched in a broad, free style.'[1]

Although Gibside House has not been erased from the map with the same finality as Streatlam, what survives is little more than a ruin. The outer walls still stand, revealing a long low Jacobean mansion, its length softened by numerous mullioned windows. What is left of the crenellations stand out against the sky like broken teeth, but a magnificent cedar planted in the lee of the house extends its graceful limbs just as it did in John Bowes's day. Other buildings on the estate, like the Orangery – where Bowes's grandmother pursued her passion for botany – have been partially restored by the National Trust. But the pride of Gibside is the Palladian Chapel, begun in 1760 by George Bowes, John's great-grandfather, and completed by John's father, the 10th Earl of Strathmore. This graceful building, with its unusual three-decker pulpit, looks out on to the Long Walk, a broad grassy avenue nearly half a mile in length, said to have been used by George Bowes to exercise his bloodstock. But following the death of John Bowes's father, George Bowes's direct descendants never used Gibside as their family home.

When John Bowes died in 1885 the Museum was not even finished, let alone open to the public. But for him much of the joy of creation had already evaporated when Joséphine died in 1874. Her spirit had informed the project from the moment of its conception, and without her inspiration, companionship and guidance, the last stages of the Museum's construction had become a burden to him. Today's visitor, however, unaware of the cost in both human and financial terms of realising such a massive project, sees a magnificent building filled to capacity with objects which range from the curious to the sublime. The following pages will describe how John and Joséphine Bowes not only built the Museum but furnished the majority of its contents – and at their own expense. To make such a vision a reality was an act of dedication, skill, and astonishing generosity.

CHAPTER 1

# John Bowes:
# Early Years at Streatlam

John Bowes was born in the early hours of 19 June 1811 at No. 13 South Street, Chelsea. His mother, a Miss Mary Millner, had been obliged to move from the house originally chosen for the birth because of the 'attitude' of the 'lady of the house'.[1] His father had paid frequent visits to Miss Millner during the lying-in. When he returned the morning after the birth he took his son into his arms, kissed him, agreed with the midwife that the child closely resembled him, then carried him next door to his mother. On 29 June the boy was christened John Bowes, the register of baptisms confusingly and incorrectly documenting him as the son of John Millner and Mary. In this unorthodox, even furtive, manner did John Bowes make his entry into the world.

The Bowes family of Teesdale can be traced back to the Norman Conquest. Its first recorded member, Sir Adam Bowes, married in about 1310 the heiress of Streatlam Castle, which was to remain the principal family seat until the late nineteenth century. The estate of Gibside, which lay among the highly productive coal seams of County Durham, came into the family with the marriage in 1693 of Sir William Bowes to its heiress, Elizabeth Blakiston. Following the deaths of Sir William and his two eldest sons, in 1722 the family estates passed to the third son, George.

'Handsome George', as he was known, was now head of one of the richest and most influential landed families in north-east England. He became a popular and energetic colliery owner, breeder of racehorses and Member of Parliament for County Durham. His first wife (another heiress) died within three months of the wedding – Horace Walpole's gossip was that the bride 'was said to die of the violence of the Bridegroom's embraces'[2] – and he did not marry again for nineteen years. By the time his only child, Mary Eleanor, was born he was nearly fifty. A friend, writing to him a week after the birth, proffered some sound advice: 'What tho' it be'ent a Boy, the same Material will produce one, be industrious & apply yourself closely to the Business, & I warrant your success', and reminded him that 'at least your blood if not your Name will be transmitted to Posterity.'[3]

It seems that George Bowes did apply himself 'closely to the Business' and Mary Eleanor grew to be a learned woman, a fine linguist and botanist, and the possessor of a bosom that was 'uncommonly fine'.[4] She was also spoilt and wilful. In 1760, George Bowes died, leaving his daughter 'the greatest heiress perhaps in Europe', according to Lord Chesterfield, 'and ugly in proportion.'[5] Seven years later, at the age of eighteen, she married John Lyon, the 9th Earl of Strathmore, whose family had owned Glamis Castle in Scotland since the fourteenth century (the family also owned land in County Durham). One of the conditions of George Bowes's will was that whoever married his daughter was required to take the surname Bowes.

3
John Bowes, aged fifteen, by
John Jackson. Painted in 1826,
the year he went to Eton, the
portrait shows a charming but
shy-looking youth dressed in
a mulberry-coloured coat with
slashed sleeves.

4

This miniature of John Bowes's grandmother, Mary Eleanor Bowes, by John Cox Dillman Engleheart was copied in 1800 from a portrait, since lost, by George Engleheart. When her father George Bowes died in 1760 she became one of the richest women in Europe.

The marriage was not a happy one, although it did produce five children, three boys and two girls. Mary Eleanor later confessed that she had harboured an 'unnatural dislike'[6] for her eldest son John, and had shamefully neglected him and his two brothers. In 1774 the Earl, aware that he was suffering from tuberculosis, appointed guardians for his children. Two years later, in the hope that the warm climate of Portugal might effect a cure, he set sail for Lisbon. Before leaving he wrote his wife a last letter in which he voiced his regrets that their marriage had been a failure and chastised her for her 'most unnatural prejudice' against their eldest son.[7] He died at sea in March 1776.

Shortly after the Earl left England, Mary Eleanor embarked on a liaison with a certain George Gray, 'an unscrupulous entrepreneur who had returned from India with an enviable fortune, largely accrued through bribes.'[8] Mary Eleanor became pregnant by Gray and was about to marry him, but then fell irretrievably and disastrously in love with an Irish adventurer by the name of Andrew Robinson Stoney, marrying him in 1777 (he too assumed the surname Bowes in accordance with George Bowes's will, but as the Earl of Strathmore's widow Mary Eleanor continued to use the title Countess of Strathmore). The jilted Gray had to be 'bought off' for the considerable sum of £12,000 (about £865,000 today).

Stoney's career, both before and after his marriage to Mary Eleanor, shows him to have been a dangerous, devious and cruel man with a voracious appetite for money and sex. He had bullied and starved his first wife – allegedly once locking her naked in a cupboard for several days – and when she died had contrived to retain her house and fortune. Mary Eleanor's fortune, however, was not going to fall so easily into his hands: just before her marriage she executed an Ante-Nuptial Trust which denied him any control over her income and estates.

In 1778 Mary Eleanor's five children were made Wards of Court. They seldom saw their mother, who was denied access despite her frequent appeals to visit them. Since marrying Stoney she had given birth to two more children; the first, Mary, born in 1777, was George Gray's child (she was to become the Aunt Mary much loved by her nephew, John). The second was Stoney's son William, born in 1782. He was lost at sea in 1807.

After six years of marriage to Stoney, Mary Eleanor's situation was described by Jessé Foot, the family's doctor, as 'enough to draw tears down Pluto's cheeks'.[9] Stoney abused her both physically and mentally, raped the servants and committed serial adultery. The meeker she was, the crueller and more violent he became. In his desperation to generate enough money to discharge his election expenses (he became Member of Parliament for Newcastle in 1780) and pay for his extravagant way of life, he sold her house in London and clear-felled the timber at Gibside.

By 1785 Mary Eleanor could stand it no longer: she sued for divorce, citing Bowes's repeated adultery. Her story now enters the realms of a Gothic novel. Faced with bankruptcy Stoney Bowes, aided by several accomplices, kidnapped the Countess in London, bundled her into a carriage and carried her off to Streatlam Castle, a journey which took thirty-three hours. At Streatlam he held a gun to her head and demanded that she should drop the divorce suit. With remarkable courage, she refused to do so.

Alerted to the fact that the Countess was imprisoned in the Castle, a crowd of some two hundred men – most of them pitmen from the Strathmore collieries – gathered

5
John Downman's depiction of Andrew Robinson Bowes (known as Stoney Bowes) as a person of handsome and distinguished appearance perhaps helps to explain why Mary Eleanor fell so disastrously in love with him.

outside. But Bowes escaped and, with the Countess riding bareback behind one of his accomplices, in one of the worst winters the country had experienced for decades, journeyed hither and thither across one of the most inhospitable moors in England. For eight days this madness continued. When Bowes was finally cornered by the authorities, the Countess was in a pitiable state, barely recognisable to those who knew her. Bowes was convicted and sent to prison. In 1789 Lady Strathmore was finally granted a divorce, and in return for a pension transferred the estate to her eldest son John, the 10th Earl of Strathmore. The terrible Stoney died in 1810, after twenty-two years in prison.

The young Earl's education had been typical for a boy of his birth: public school and Cambridge were followed by a brief spell in the army. In 1790 he came of age, inherited his father's estates at Glamis in Scotland and purchased his mother's life interest in Streatlam and Gibside. Despite a wretched childhood and a youth overshadowed by

6
This portrait after Mather Brown of John Bowes's father, 10th Earl of Strathmore, shows a romantic figure wearing the uniform of a captain in the 64th Foot. He was a fond and attentive father to his only child, but died when John was only nine years old.

7
Mary, Countess of Strathmore, John Bowes's mother.
John was already nine years old when his mother
married his father, who died the following day. This
portrait was painted c. 1840 when she was married
to her second husband, William Hutt.

his overbearing uncle Thomas Lyon, the portrait by Mather Brown shows a proud and confident young man, with fine features and an air of romance.

His romantic nature found a focus during the Christmas of 1790 when he was taken by a friend to Seaton Delaval in Northumbria to see a performance of the *Fair Penitent*, given by the family of Lord Delaval. The heroine was played by Lord Delaval's daughter Sarah, one-time mistress of Frederick, Duke of York and now wife of Lord Tyrconnel. John fell deeply in love with this beautiful woman, six years his senior, with an interesting past and 'hair of such rich luxuriance that when she rode it floated on the saddle'.[10] With apparently little objection from Lord Tyrconnel, the couple spent the next ten years in a state of intimate friendship. But Sarah was yet another sufferer from tuberculosis, and died at Gibside in 1800. Grief-stricken, Lord Strathmore found consolation in the restoration of Gibside after its years of destruction and neglect by his appalling stepfather. He also completed the chapel begun by his grandfather George Bowes.

In 1809, nine years after the death of Lady Tyrconnel, Lord Strathmore entered into a liaison with Mary Millner. She was twenty-two, eighteen years his junior. One version of her story maintains that she was a housemaid at Wemmergill Hall, the Earl's estate in Lunedale in upper Teesdale. *The Auckland Chronicle*, however, declared that when she met the Earl she was 'working in the woods of Streatlam... at the laborious occupation of stripping the bark off the trees which had been felled by the woodmen.'[11] The only known facts are that she was born in Stainton and lived for two years with Lord Strathmore at Wemmergill before moving with him to London.

Their son John was born in London two years later. Within a week of the christening, the Earl executed a codicil to his will bequeathing to his trustees and executors the sum of £10,000 in trust for 'an infant child, who is my son, or reputed son, by Mary Millner...'[12] After about a year in London the Earl moved Mary and their son to Wemmergill Hall, and thence to Streatlam. According to *The Auckland Chronicle*, Miss Millner, once established at Streatlam, 'became the companion of the earl, over whom she eventually exercised a considerable influence'.[13]

In 1817, at the age of six, John Bowes was sent to a school in Ealing, Middlesex run by the Rev William Goodenough. Judging by the few letters to his son which have survived, the Earl was devoted to the boy and pleased with his progress at school. 'My Dear Boy,' he wrote in November 1817, 'Your Letter... contained a good specimen of your Improvement in writing, and with Practice and Attention, you will, I have no doubt, write a very good Hand.'[14] In August 1819 he refers to a parcel he had sent the boy which contained 'six Pair of Cotton Stockings, a Silk Handkerchief, a Shoe Horn & some Paper'. He adds, 'I am happy to hear from Him [Dr Goodenough] so favourable an Account of you, & I trust that you will continue to merit his Approbation.'[15]

Dr Goodenough and his wife looked after the boy 'with almost parental concern'. (The haunch of venison later sent annually from Streatlam to the Goodenoughs testifies to John's sustained affection for the couple.) In his holidays John returned to his parents at Streatlam Castle. Apart from learning to ride, to fish and to shoot, there is no record of how he occupied himself while at home, but his intimate knowledge of the castle's every nook and cranny attests to long hours spent in exploration. This knowledge was to prove invaluable in the future when he had to administer the house and estate from afar.

John did have one companion in his boyhood: his cousin Susan Jessup. Her mother, Anna Maria, one of the daughters of the ill-fated Mary Eleanor, had married under wildly romantic circumstances. While living in London she had begun a secret correspondence with Henry Jessup, a penniless young lawyer who occupied a room in the house opposite. Although they had never been closer to each other than the width of the narrow street allowed, they fell in love and planned to elope. One night, Anna Maria walked along a plank laid on top of a ladder which had been pushed across the street until it connected their two windows. The couple were married at Gretna Green. But Jessup died young, leaving his widow with two daughters; they later moved to a house near Gibside, some forty miles from Streatlam. John and the younger of the two daughters, Susan, became very close, John regarding her more as a sister than a friend. When Susan later married John Davidson, they lived at Ridley Hall, near Gibside.

In January 1820 a letter from Lord Strathmore at Gibside to his son shows that he had been ill: 'My Dear Boy, Mr. Abbs yesterday took off the Blister and dressed the Part, since which I have found myself so much relieved...'[16] But by July the Earl was clearly dying. On 2 July he was conveyed by sedan chair to St George's Church in Hanover Square, London, where he and Mary Millner were married. Despite being close to collapse he was able to make the required responses at the ceremony, and declared it was one of the happiest moments of his life. He died the following day.

There are several reasons given for this precipitate marriage. Augustus Hare, the travel writer and raconteur (and a distant relative of Susan Davidson), maintained that early in their relationship Mary Millner and the Earl 'went through a false ceremony of marriage, after which, in all innocence, she lived with him as his wife.'[17] Not until he was on his deathbed did he confess to her that their marriage was false, whereupon she insisted that a proper ceremony should take place.

Another reason is given by Baron Henry de Gelsey in an article in *The British Racehorse* in 1955: 'It was well-known that the Earl's decision to marry his lady was strongly influenced by the child's exquisite qualities, his quickness of apprehension, his aristocratic appearance, his charming manners, his eagerness to learn, and last but not least by his boyish beauty, worthy of the brush of a Gainsborough, a Reynolds or a Lawrence.'[18]

The simplest and most likely explanation is that the Earl, aware that he was dying, hoped his marriage would legitimise the boy. He also took steps to ensure that his wife's position was legally secure; on the day he died he added a last codicil to his will making it clear that his bequests to her would now be hers as Countess of Strathmore.

Despite Lord Strathmore's efforts, his will was contested. As a result of two very public court cases in 1821 and 1825 – in which John was referred to as a bastard – the title passed to Lord Strathmore's younger brother Thomas, who became the 11th Earl of Strathmore (and it is from Thomas that the late Queen Elizabeth The Queen Mother, Patron of the Friends of The Bowes Museum, was descended). Thus John, while still a boy, lost not only his father but the title, Glamis Castle and the Scottish estates. However, his father's English property, collieries and estates ensured that he would still be a very rich man.

It is hard to imagine life at Streatlam for the young John and his mother following the Earl's death. Although she was legally Countess of Strathmore, the tenants on the estate, the household staff and the county as a whole all knew her as a local girl who had had an illegitimate child by the Earl. She had lived with him at Streatlam for the past seven years but, according to her evidence during the court case in 1821, she never dined with him when guests were present, only when they were alone. Thus it appears that Lord Strathmore himself had not fully acknowledged her as his official companion. His death had placed her in a still more ambiguous position and there are indications that some of the staff made her aware of it. One of John Bowes's first acts when he came of age in 1832 was to dismiss Richard Dobson, the estate agent at Streatlam, not only accusing him of being a swindler but also because 'his conduct with regard to Lady Strathmore and myself, till he found it was necessary to curry favour with me, was highly disrespectful and improper'.[19]

And yet, according to Augustus Hare, 'Lady Strathmore always behaved well. As soon as she was a widow, she said to all the people whom she had known as her husband's relations and friends that, if they liked to keep up her acquaintance, she should be very grateful to them, and always glad to see them when they came to her, but that she should never enter any house on a visit again; and she never did... She was a stately woman, still beautiful, and she had educated herself since her youth, but, from her quiet life (full of unostentatious charity) she had become very eccentric.'[20]

There is no record that the Countess was in touch with any members of the Earl's family – apart from the Earl's illegitimate half-sister, Mary – either before or after his death. When John Bowes died in 1885 his obituary notice in the *Darlington & Stockton Times* stated that the Earl and Mary Millner 'would have married but for the hostility of the Strathmore family'.[21] If this was true, it is perhaps understandable that a family able to trace its history back to the fourteenth century was reluctant to accept the girl from Stainton as one of their own.

Her awkward position at Streatlam may have prompted the Dowager Countess to seek refuge in the Strathmore house in London for part of John's school holidays. There she could live with relative anonymity and yet enjoy the benefits of a wealthy widowhood.

In the 1820s London already contained a population of one and a half million people. The smoke from their fires filled the air with smuts; sulphurous fogs frequently shrouded the city in darkness and the reek of overflowing cesspools was a constant reminder of the city's woefully inadequate drainage. While the Thames may have run softly, it stank like a sewer – which indeed it was. (In 1832 deaths from the cholera epidemic in London reached the almost unimaginable figure of eighteen thousand.)

But John Bowes and his mother could afford to turn their backs on the grinding poverty depicted by Dickens and Gustave Doré and retreat into the elegant streets and squares of Mayfair and Belgravia. The late Earl's residence was at 54 Conduit Street, a thoroughfare lined with gracious Georgian houses that extended (as it does today) from New Bond Street to the colonnades and fashionable shops of the newly-completed Regent Street. Cows still grazed in St James's Park, milk was delivered by milkmaids carrying pails suspended on yokes over their shoulders, and liveried footmen hurried through the streets on errands for their noble masters.

8
The Strathmore residence in London was in Conduit Street, a turning off Regent Street. This lithograph of 1842 by Thomas Shotter Boys, looks south down Regent Street to the Duke of York's Column in Waterloo Place.

9
This detail of John Jackson's painting confirms a description of the youthful John Bowes as possessing 'a boyish beauty, worthy of the brush of a Gainsborough, a Reynolds or a Lawrence.'

Social life during the Season was hectic and prolonged, some parties ending in the small hours. But although John's mother had a title and a house in Mayfair, she was a *parvenue* and would never have been accepted by Society. Judging by her conduct towards her husband's relations, she had the tact to know – and to accept – her position, although it must have been a lonely one. Introducing her son to the cultural delights of the city was permissable however, and she had taken John to the opera at least once before he was ten years old. Thomas Wheldon, the Bowes's family solicitor in Barnard Castle, was sometimes invited to share their box when he was in town. It was probably during these periods in London that John's passion for the theatre, which was to have such long-term consequences, was first aroused.

The English theatre had recently undergone a major revolution with the introduction of gas lighting in place of candles and oil lamps. 'The stage lamps are rising', wrote an excited spectator in 1837, 'flash goes the flood of light over the blinking multitude.'[22] Huge theatres, seating up to three thousand people, staged lavish spectacles and melodramas, complete with fabulous costumes and dazzling special effects. For the more literary-minded there was Shakespeare and Sheridan, performed by great actors like Edmund Kean, John Philip Kemble and William Charles Macready. Marie Taglioni, the divinity of Romantic ballet, appeared for the first time in London in 1829, and floated about the stage like a butterfly. The upper classes favoured the Italian opera, where the audiences were more select, better dressed and far less noisy.

In 1826, at the age of fifteen, John was sent to Eton, the school selected by his father soon after John was born. This rite of passage was marked with a portrait by John Jackson. Splendidly attired in mulberry satin, with flourishes of lace at throat and wrists, a slightly insecure-looking boy gazes pensively into space. Richard Dobson described him two years later as a 'Tall fine looking Young Man, very active & fond of field sports...'[23] While he may have looked tall to Dobson, according to John's passport he was 5ft 6in in height.

10
An etching by William Makepeace Thackeray showing a university student seated at a high desk. Thackeray and Bowes became friends when they shared a tutor at Trinity College, Cambridge.

John was at Eton during the reign of the legendary Dr Keate, known as the Flogging Head Master. Keate had inherited an unruly, rebellious school and had set about taming it with gusto – on one occasion he beat sixty boys in one batch and seventy-two in another.[24] The staff was inadequate in both quality and quantity, the classes absurdly large and the curriculum almost exclusively classical.[25] Apart from a few Latin exercises in The Bowes Museum Archive – some of them adorned with sketches of elegant, curly-haired youths – only one brief glimpse of John's years at Eton has survived. In a letter to Lady Strathmore, one of John's masters wrote: 'Ever since he has been my pupil, he has conducted himself most irreproachably, and has uniformly exerted himself so as to make very good Improvement, and progress in his studies.'[26] So much for John's diligence and model behaviour, but it is tempting to wonder how a boy of his sensitive nature and illegitimate birth fared among his contemporaries.

However, he did make a lifelong friend, Alexander Kinglake, who later wrote the classic travel book *Eothen*. (In his Introduction to the 1982 paperback edition of *Eothen*, Jonathan Raban wrote: 'If one remains alert to its tone and responsive to its architecture, it reveals itself as a brilliant acid comedy, a sly masterpiece, as full of tricks as an Egyptian magician.')[27] Kinglake followed *Eothen* with his eight-volume *History of the War in the Crimea*, one of the best known historical works of the nineteenth century.

After only two years at Eton John went up to Trinity College, Cambridge, the 'largest, wealthiest and the most distinguished of Cambridge colleges'.[28] Kinglake followed him five months later and together they shared a tutor with William Makepeace Thackeray. Thackeray and Bowes were both born in 1811 and both had lost their fathers in childhood, but they were very different in character. Even as an undergraduate John showed signs of being a thoughtful, steady young man, whereas Thackeray was something of a dandy and soon fell in with a crowd of dissolute young bucks and frittered his time away, leaving Cambridge without taking his degree. His real love was drawing – he was a brilliant caricaturist – and his only ambition at this stage was to become an artist.

While still at Cambridge Bowes spent one of his long vacations travelling on the Continent, possibly his first trip abroad. He travelled with the Rev Arthur Pearson, a friend of the family and also a student at Dr Goodenough's school and later at Trinity. In the Durham Record Office there are two little pocket-books in which John kept a brief record of this tour of 1830. Beginning with a visit to Brussels, the account ends abruptly among 'the glaciers of the Rhône'. The only points of note are his interest in paintings, his awareness of unpleasant smells, and his visit to the opera in Frankfurt where he saw Marie Taglioni in *La Muette de Portici*. It was during this trip that Bowes bought his first painting, *The Temptation of St Anthony* by Cornelis Saftleven, which is now in the Museum's collection.[29]

Little is known of John's academic career at Cambridge, but he spent some of his leisure hours shooting at the Cambridge Rifle Club and dining at the Cambridge Beef Steak Club. In 1832 he confessed to Wheldon that he 'had delayed getting up my subject for this confounded degree so long that I am obliged to read hard that I may be able to *scrape* through'.[30]

Scrape through he did, and at once began to canvass to become the Liberal Member of Parliament for the southern division of County Durham. (Two other candidates were nominated for South Durham, Robert Shafto and Bowes's friend Joseph Pease.) As early as April 1832 he had issued a long-winded address to the electors which concluded with a declaration of his support for 'every measure which has for its object the maintenance of our civil rights, the full and perfect security of religious freedom... the prompt and certain extinction of Colonial Slavery',[31] and affirmed his belief in Parliamentary reform. These 'liberal' views were 'years in advance of Liberal Party policy, particularly in his attitude to Roman Catholics and his advocacy of the secret ballot'.[32]

In June Bowes and Pease were elected, taking their seats in the first Reformed Parliament in February 1833. William IV was on the throne and Lord Grey Prime Minister. Bowes was to remain a Member of Parliament until 1847, a period of great political and constitutional reform. There is no record of his giving any speeches, but he was an assiduous lobbyist on behalf of his constituents. A year after he had taken his seat, both Houses of Parliament were destroyed by fire. The present building was not opened until 1852.

11
John Bowes was only nineteen when he bought his first painting while touring the Continent in 1830. Ten years later he purchased some twenty Old Masters, including a *Crucifixion* triptych painted in the 1490s by the Master of the Virgo inter Virgines. The central panel of the triptych shows Christ on the cross alongside the remorseful and unrepentant thieves.

On 19 June, six months before he entered Parliament, John had celebrated his twenty-first birthday. The church bells rang all day long at Barnard Castle and Staindrop and, at Streatlam, 'Two to three hundred of his tenantry were entertained in the old English style, with roast beef and plum pudding. Three Ayrshire bullocks, bred and fed upon his estate... were killed and distributed to the poor on his estates on the occasion.'[33] The scale of these celebrations demonstrates that John Bowes was already a force to be reckoned with in the county, not only because he owned vast estates, collieries and racehorses but because he had shown himself ready to act on behalf of its citizens.

Possibly the most far-reaching effect of Cambridge on John's life was the marriage of his mother to one of his tutors, William Hutt. Hutt was ten years older than John and fourteen years younger than Lady Strathmore. Years later, Augustus Hare wrote a trifle disparagingly about the marriage: 'Seeing no one but Mr Hutt, the agreeable tutor of her son, Lady Strathmore had married him, and by her wealth and influence he became member for Gateshead. He was rather a prim man, but could make himself very agreeable... I think he rather tyrannized over Lady Strathmore, but he was very well behaved to her in public.'[34] The Countess and Hutt were married in 1831 in St George's, Hanover Square, the same church in which the Countess had married the dying Earl in 1820.

The effect on John Bowes of his mother's marriage to Hutt seems to have been entirely beneficial: at one stroke he had acquired a stepfather who could almost double as an older brother, his mother was no longer dependent on him for company or protection, he was able to hand over the administration of Gibside to Hutt, who willingly accepted John's offer of the house as a country residence for himself and the Countess, and Hutt could manage the collieries in his absence. Following Hutt's election as Member of Parliament for Hull in 1832, he also had a friend in the House with whom he shared many of the same regional concerns. Relieved of so many responsibilities, Bowes was now able to concentrate on his parliamentary duties, the running of the Streatlam estate, and his racehorses.

The Streatlam Stud had been founded by his father. The horses were originally kept at Esher in Surrey, but in 1795 Lord Strathmore had decided to move five of them to Streatlam. These were the days before railway transport so the horses, accompanied by their entourage of stable boys and grooms, plodded gamely north to their new stables. It was the descendants of these five horses, together with others purchased by his father, that John had known since childhood.

Soon after he came of age John appointed Isaac Walker junior as stud groom and John Scott of Whitewall, near Malton, as his trainer. It was a winning combination: in 1835 the Stud came gloriously into its own when Mündig won the Derby. Not only was he the first northern horse ever to do so, but John's winnings temporarily relieved the strain on his finances. To celebrate this remarkable victory, Bowes commissioned John Frederick Herring senior to paint Mündig with his jockey, William Scott (John Scott's brother), in the saddle. A year later Herring painted a delightful picture of the Streatlam Stud, the mares and foals grouped together in the dappled shade of an ancient tree.

John's early letters to Thomas Wheldon, the Barnard Castle solicitor, betray a constant anxiety about money. The estate he had inherited was so encumbered with mortgages

12
Bowes inherited the Streatlam Stud, pictured here by John Frederick Herring senior, from his father. Although Bowes kept a comparatively small stable, he was remarkably successful, breeding no less than four Derby winners. The chestnut on the right is Emma, the stud's greatest mare.

and other liabilities that it required a quarter of the income from rents to pay the interest on the various loans.[35] As soon as John came of age he reduced the Streatlam staff by six and discharged the groom, Isaac Walker senior. Despite pathetic letters from the wives of two of the discharged staff, John refused to relent, exhibiting an almost ruthless streak for one so young. Yet throughout his life, his dealings with all his employees were scrupulously – almost clinically – fair. Provided they served him loyally and well, he treated them with kindness and consideration. Indeed, for most of his long-term employees he evidently felt great affection, often quoting their characteristic remarks in his letters.

It was also to Thomas Wheldon that John Bowes revealed – in a series of letters from July to November 1833 – that he was suffering from what he refers to either as an 'unfortunate little disease' or 'that confounded disease of mine'. Although the words 'not clap' (the standard English word for gonorrhoea in the nineteenth century) appear in a torn section of one the letters,[36] judging by his symptoms and the treatment he received, there is little doubt that it was indeed a severe case of gonorrhoea. In a letter to Wheldon, dated 25 July 1833 and marked 'Private', he wrote:

> I have been induced to consult Brodie as well as Vance, & as the plan they together have adopted with regard to my case is very violent, being the use of an injection of caustic strong enough to dislodge the devil himself, they wish to have me under their immediate inspection... You will please not mention [illegible] matter to any one... you will I daresay see my object & use secrecy.[37]

The 'Brodie' he consulted was Sir Benjamin Brodie, a specialist in diseases of the urinary organs and the joints, and one of the most outstanding surgeons of his day. The records of some of Brodie's patients have been preserved in the archives of St George's Hospital, where he held the post of Assistant Surgeon for fourteen years. Brodie's case notes present two problems: he identifies his patients not by name but by age and, true to his profession, his writing is barely legible. However, by comparing one set of Brodie's case notes with Bowes's accounts of the treatment of his disease to Wheldon, it is difficult to avoid the conclusion that Brodie's patient was indeed John Bowes.

Further confirmation comes from advice, given by a friend, that Bowes should consult Professor Claude François Lallemand 'as there is no man in Europe equal to Monsieur Lallemand of Montpellier for disorders in the urethra'.[38] There is no evidence that Bowes took this advice, but by then he must have been pretty desperate for a cure as he admits to having had the disease for three to four years, thus since the age of twenty-two or twenty-three. He had even fought the 1832 election while in the throes of it: 'If it had not been for the confounded Election last year,' he told Wheldon, 'I should have cured it then.'[39]

Despite spending several weeks of the autumn of 1833 at Bognor – sea bathing was considered efficacious for venereal disease – and undergoing a variety of ferocious remedies, he was not cured by November. Indeed, nine years later he told Wheldon, 'I am still suffering from my infernal complaint.'[40] There are even indications, this time in two letters from his stepfather William Hutt, that he was not yet clear of it in 1844.

This is hardly surprising as it was only the introduction of antibiotics in the 1940s that made any real impact on venereal diseases. Although the disease quite often burnt itself out in time, it is highly likely that it rendered the sufferer infertile. Since it has often been suggested that it was because they never had children that John and Joséphine Bowes poured all their money and energy into the founding of The Bowes Museum, John's 'infernal complaint' assumes considerable significance.

In September 1832, a year before these revelations, Bowes spent three months in Paris. This may not have been his first visit, but it is the first of which there is a record. If he went alone, it was a bold venture for a twenty-one-year-old. But Bowes was already showing a self-reliance, independence and clarity of purpose that were to prove fundamental characteristics. He was also a most stoical traveller, an attribute which was to serve him well in years to come.

'Nobody who has not personally experienced it,' wrote the banker Sir Edward Blount in his *Memoirs*, 'can imagine the intolerable nuisances of the Channel crossing in the thirties.'[41] The crossing itself could take up to eight hours. Bowes described one passage: 'I had to lie on the floor of the Cabin, not being able to get a berth, and the rain prevented my staying on deck; fellows *catting* round me in all directions.'[42] If the sea was too rough for the boat to dock, the passengers were dumped overboard into rocking dinghies and rowed ashore through the breakers. Once ashore they were met 'by a shoal of Custom House officers, who waylaid the wet, weary, and frequently seasick passengers. Examination in those days was carried to the length of bodily search' which, depending on the number of passengers, could last over an hour.[43]

Frances (Fanny) Trollope, when landing at Calais, was amused by an exchange she overheard between two travellers: '"What a dreadful smell!" said the uninitiated stranger, enveloping his nose in his pocket-handkerchief. "It is the smell of the continent, sir," replied the man of experience.'[44] The traveller, having survived the Channel crossing, still had the journey to Paris ahead of him. According to Thackeray, who made his first visit to France in 1829, it could take up to forty hours by coach.

Thackeray was also in Paris during the autumn of 1832, and his diary shows that he and John Bowes spent many hours together, indulging their mutual passion for the theatre. 'Spent a pleasant evening talking about Theatres with Bowes' is his diary entry for

26 October.[45] Described by a fellow undergraduate at Cambridge as 'a tall [6ft 3ins] thin large-eyed, full and ruddy faced man with an eye glass fixed *en permanence*',[46] Thackeray must have towered over his smaller, neater friend. Together they attended the first performance of Victor Hugo's *Le Roi s'amuse*, which was also its last as the play caused a riot and was promptly banned by the police.

Two years later Thackeray's diary entry for 1 November records that he spent the day 'chiefly in talking theatricals with Bowes & wandering through the town for exercise; dined with him in the evening.'[47] This companionship in Paris does not appear to have extended to England except on one notable occasion in 1841 when Bowes invited Thackeray to stay with him at Streatlam to help him campaign for re-election. Thackeray, now married and living in Paris, was in need of funds and the invitation was accepted with alacrity. Thackeray's article, which appeared in *Fraser's Magazine*, not only provides a lively account of electioneering in South Durham but also contains the only extant description of life at Streatlam in John Bowes's bachelor days, and is thus a valuable document.[48]

Thackeray wrote the article in the 'voice' of an imaginary American correspondent, Napoleon Putnam Wiggins of Passimquoddy, who had been sent to cover an English election. When 'Mr Wiggins' arrived at Britton Hall (Streatlam), Mr Britton (John Bowes) was out electioneering but had left orders that his guest should be well cared for. He was greeted on his arrival by the staff and 'half a score of household dogs', including a Newfoundland, a St Bernard 'and other hounds of smaller degree'. Thackeray settled gleefully into his stately abode: 'I was for a couple of days the lord of a grand house and park, of a stable full of horses, a garden full of good things, and a hall full of servants. Gods! how I rung the bells, and made the fellows run and scamper.'

Having been shown to 'a snug apartment', he went downstairs to dine. 'Fancy an old, lofty, black oak parlour,' he wrote; 'with tall windows looking into a park, and slim, dappled, rickety-looking deer, passing close by them... Fancy a great, stiff, shining, damask table-cloth, opposite which is placed a tall, red chair.' Before a blazing fire he drank some of 'the best ale that a human tap ever produced' and ate his dinner. 'It was', he declared, 'like an evening out of a novel. Every thing was so trim, so good, so abundant, so ready, that my young heart expanded with satisfaction; and for a little while, at least, I felt reconciled to the aristocracy.' Conducted upstairs by the old butler, he slept in a bed 'covered (for summer) with four blankets'.

In the morning, after a vast breakfast, he inspected John Bowes's domain. Streatlam Castle consisted of twenty-four bedrooms (with six spare blankets per room 'ready against the winter'), 'two oak drawing rooms, the yellow drawing-room, the great dining-room... the billiard-room, the study, the gentlemen's room, &c.' He then visited the garden where he saw hothouses, 'great, fat, red-cheeked nectarines... grapes... [and] a deal of flowers', and was given a pineapple for his dinner by the gardener.

It was not until 2 a.m. that Thackeray, dozing over his cigar, heard John Bowes gallop up to the house in a chaise. His host had been up since six o'clock, 'had canvassed a score of villages, driven a hundred miles, had not dined until ten o'clock, and proposed to be off at seven the next morning...' A reluctant Thackeray was obliged to roll out of bed at 'the horrible hour of six' to find Bowes 'fresh up, and dressed, and smiling', and after another

13
Daniel Maclise's drawing shows Thackeray in about 1840, the year before John Bowes invited him to Streatlam to help him with his election campaign. Thackeray's subsequent description of this visit provides a vivid and amusing insight into life at the Castle.

huge breakfast they were carried through the park by two 'galloping greys' on their way to a tumultuous reception by the electorate of Darlington.

Posterity reaped an unexpected benefit from Thackeray's visit to Streatlam: 'I have in my trip to the country,' he told the publisher James Fraser, 'found materials (rather a character) for a story...'[49] The 'character' was none other than the appalling Stoney Bowes, and his bizarre and cruel behaviour to his wife (John's grandmother) had either been described to Thackeray by John Bowes, or Bowes had lent him a copy of Jessé Foot's *Lives of Andrew Robinson Bowes and the Countess of Strathmore*. The result was Thackeray's first successful novel, *The Luck of Barry Lyndon*, published in 1852.

Thackeray remained with Bowes throughout the three weeks of what he referred to as 'the cursed racket of this infernal election'. The picture he paints of Bowes reveals a cool, self-possessed, highly organised, energetic and conscientious young man (he was thirty) who was in command of himself, his household and his vast properties and yet could still find the resources to fight a tough election – and win. A Leader in *The Durham Chronicle*, written at the time of the election, adds to this picture: 'A more unassuming and amiable gentleman than Mr. Bowes doesn't exist; he is an honour and an ornament to his native county; and the better he is known the more will he be admired and cherished by all who can prize a cultivated mind and a manly spirit, and the sure offspring of those when united with frankness and honesty and an independent and uncompromising character.'[50]

For any young woman whose family was willing to overlook his illegitimacy and focus instead on his character, wealth and prospects, John Bowes was a highly eligible young man. Marriage, however, appeared to hold little attraction for him. On hearing of a friend's forthcoming nuptials, he remarked to Thomas Wheldon: 'If ever I chance to be spliced, from which the Lord defend me, I trust it will be with a fairer prospect of happiness than young Ellice has before him.'[51]

# CHAPTER 2

❦

# Le Théâtre des Variétés

Negelon

John Bowes's first visit to Paris in 1832 had a fundamental effect on his life. It was perhaps not just the city's charm, its theatres and art collections which captivated him, but a sense of freedom from a society which found it hard to forget the circumstances of his birth. Paris had other attractions, some of them of a kind which Bowes would have hesitated to enjoy in London for fear of damaging his reputation. But in Paris he could be plain Mr Bowes, a rich, good-looking young Englishman who loved the theatre and bred successful racehorses.

Bowes was still in his twenties when he developed the habit of spending every Christmas in Paris. Fresh from university, where he and his fellow students would have talked into the small hours, putting the world to rights, he still needed the companionship of young men like himself. In Paris he could enjoy a way of life soon to be made famous by Henry Murger's *Scènes de la Vie de Bohème* (1845). Thackeray, who was living in Paris training to be an artist, described life as an art student as 'the easiest, merriest, dirtiest existence possible',[1] and recalled how he and his friends 'used to meet in each others little rooms and talk about Art and smoke pipes and drink bad brandy & water.'[2] Associating with Thackeray, John Bowes could join in similar pursuits.

Unlike Thackeray, however, Bowes had a foot in two camps: as a member of both the Jockey Club and the Cercle de l'Union, two of the most exclusive clubs in Paris, he mixed with the élite of both English and French society. The Cercle de l'Union accepted only diplomats and the highest aristocracy. 'Wealth does not give access to it,' wrote Charles Yriarte in *Cercles de Paris* in 1864. 'Talent, even genius... count as nothing, there.'[3] The club was remembered by one of its members, Lord Palmerston, as 'a great convenience to a casual visitor at Paris, and gives one a *Pied à Terre* immediately for news and society and knowledge of who is here and what is going on.'[4] Bowes nearly always stayed at the club, until he took a house in the rue de Rougemont. It was possibly at l'Union that he learnt of the death in March 1842 of the 3rd Marquess of Hertford, the great collector, and promptly reported the news to Wheldon: 'Lord Hertford died last evening. He had been paralyzed, and speechless for some months, but the night before he died he slept as usual with two French Whores.'[5]

Gaining admission to the French Jockey Club would have presented no difficulties for Bowes as he was a member of the English Jockey Club, his admission following automatically when his horse Mündig won the Derby in 1835. Besides, the Anglomania which flourished in Paris in the early part of the century sprang in part from an admiration of the British Turf. The journalist Albert Vandam, a close observer of French society, related how even 'some of the fashionable *habitués* of the Café de Paris, though not knowing a fetlock from a pastern, were but too pleased to join an institution which, with the mania for everything English in full swing, then conferred as it were upon its members a kind of patent of "good form", and, above all, of exclusiveness, for which some, even amidst the fleshpots of the celebrated restaurant, longed.'[6]

14
A smiling, confident John Bowes in his
mid-twenties, executed by the Swiss artist
Joseph Mathias Negelen. Bowes has already
adopted the mutton-chop whiskers which he
was to retain throughout his life.

In the 1830s Paris was still a medieval city, its warren of narrow, tortuous and unlit streets surrounded by high walls. If London was odoriferous, the air of Paris was positively pestilential. There was no centralised system for collecting rubbish so it was dumped on the streets. Even the Tuileries Palace had no proper sanitation, water being brought to the rooms in buckets. Richard Wagner, who went to Paris with his wife in 1839, described it as a 'city of infinite variety, brilliance and filth'.[7] But among the city's many charms were the boulevards, wide tree-lined streets where people congregated in the cafés, browsed in the fashionable shops or strolled in the cool of the evening. For the poet Alfred de Musset, they were 'one of the points of the earth where the pleasure of the world is concentrated.'[8] For more forbidden and decadent amusements, there was the notorious Palais Royal, an inevitable attraction for a youthful and curious John Bowes, although an entry in Thackeray's diary for October 1832 records his surprise at meeting him there. But it was predominantly Bowes's love of the theatre that fuelled his friendship with Thackeray in Paris.

From his early days Bowes had been a keen theatre-goer and, according to his obituary in the *Newcastle Daily Chronicle*, possessed an exceptional 'histrionic talent'.[9] The Durham County Record Office has a cast list for *Bombastes Furioso, a Burlesque Tragic Opera* in which John played Distaffina – presumably a female role. There are also scripts for two plays written by John when he was about eighteen: *The Devonshire Heiress, a Farce in Two Acts* and *The Old Maid of Barbrous [sic] Love, a Comedy in Two Acts*. The latter begins hilariously. Sir Andrew Boreum, having apparently not seen his son for twelve years, greets him at breakfast:

Sir A:    Well Jack my Boy, I'm glad to see you once again in old England, "England Europe's glory", ha! ha! it does my old heart good to look at you give me your hand ha! ha!

Young B: Thank'e, Sir, thank'e, I've not been so long afloat, but that I enjoy myself ashore, shiver my topsails but 12 years hard service makes one look gladly on old messmates & a snug birth [sic].'[10]

15
From the late eighteenth century to the 1830s the Palais Royal boasted the most enticing cafés, shops and brothels in Europe. In William Wyld's lithograph of c.1835 it is thronged with fashionable Parisians enjoying a summer afternoon.

By the middle of the nineteenth century – when Bowes himself became heavily involved in it – the theatrical industry in France was thriving. One of the most significant events in its recent revival had been the visits to Paris between 1822 and 1832 of three companies of British actors which for the first time had exposed French audiences to authentic English language versions of some of Shakespeare's plays.[11] In particular, the tour in the autumn of 1827 'finally established Shakespeare as a timeless classic... and set new standards which were generally adopted in France after a very short while.'[12]

One of the principal actors involved in this tour was the famous William Charles Macready, who later became a friend of John Bowes. Macready was a morose and sometimes violent man – characteristics that were alien to Bowes's pacific nature – and yet, according to Macready's diary, they were already corresponding in 1837: 'Wrote to Bowes about the *Domino Noir* and to Dickens, thanking him for his present of *Pickwick Papers*.'[13] During another tour to Paris in the winter of 1844-5, Macready and Bowes dined together and 'talked over the drama and other matters...'[14] Seven years later, when Macready was performing *Hamlet* in Paris, his diary entry for 9 January 1851 reveals his respect for his young friend (Bowes was eighteen years his junior): 'Bowes, a critic far beyond the many who write here, observed to me, "Yours is the only intelligible Hamlet I ever saw".'[15] Despite this close association, there is no evidence that Macready had any influence on Bowes's decision to buy the Théâtre des Variétés.

Situated in the boulevard Montmartre, the Variétés is the oldest theatre building in Paris still in use today. It was described by Texier in his *Tableau de Paris* of 1852 as 'the temple of coarse-grained humour, of puns, of bawdy witticisms and of outrageous dialogue.'[16] In 1846, when John Bowes became involved with it, the Variétés was the most fashionable and popular *comédie-vaudeville* theatre in Paris, its success largely due to the skilful management of its colourful proprietor, Nestor Roqueplan, and to two of the leading players, the comedian Bouffé and the celebrated Virginie Déjazet. (Jules and Edmond Goncourt, whose journals give a fascinating insight into Parisian society, describe visiting Roqueplan and finding him dresssed 'all in red and wearing embroidered slippers or moccasins, so that he looked like a cross between a public executioner and an Ojibway Indian.'[17]) By the middle of 1847 the theatre was in profit, the ideal moment for the wily Roqueplan to dispose of it.

Having decided to buy the Variétés, Bowes requested his solicitor Thomas Wheldon to provide the funds but without disclosing what for. In their ensuing correspondence, Bowes became increasingly irritated not only by Wheldon's inability to raise the money but also by his apparent lack of effort in doing so. 'You have really put me in a complete fix', he wrote in July 1847, 'by not answering my letters...'[18] These are unusually harsh words for Bowes, and indicate his absolute determination to get what he wanted.

This correspondence makes unhappy reading: Wheldon's association with John's family went back a long way; he was almost twice Bowes's age and there were times when he seems to have been more of a father figure than a solicitor to his young client. Furthermore, it later transpired that Wheldon's anxiety over the state of his own finances had seriously affected both his health and his ability to work. However, the money was finally raised, and in July 1847 Bowes became the proud owner of the Théâtre des Variétés.

Bowes was always prudent with his money, and what might appear to have been a risky undertaking was based on his knowledge that in 1846, when he first became interested in the theatre, the weekly income could be as much as £1,000 while the annual expenditure was some £25,000. However, during the last six months of Roqueplan's management the average weekly takings had dropped to £600.[19] In 1847 the theatre's personnnel included forty stage artists, an orchestra, a chorus and numerous individuals ranging from dressers and lamplighters to the box office attendants, bringing the total number of employees to one hundred and fifty one.[20]

The *comédie-vaudeville* is difficult to define, but in general it consisted of anything from one to five acts of humorous dialogue with songs and dances, the songs being modern or topical lyrics set to well-known tunes. 'Each evening's entertainment consisted of a

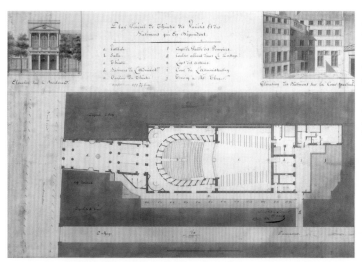

17
The audience entered the Théâtre des Variétés from boulevard Montmartre (left), walked through the foyer and into the auditorium, which could seat 1500 people. Lit by gas throughout the performance, the atmosphere in the theatre was suffocatingly hot, especially in summer.

18
Wearing the costumes of his numerous
principal roles, the actor Hugues Bouffé is
shown in his dressing room at the Théâtre
des Variétés. Victor Darjou painted it in 1848,
a year after Bowes bought the theatre.

minimum of three vaudevilles'; thus in 1851 the Variétés put on fifty-nine different works, of which thirty-seven were new.[21] These figures demonstrate that life within a theatre like the Variétés was one of frenzied and relentless activity.

Since theatre-going was probably the principal form of entertainment in Paris, every theatre faced stiff competition from its numerous rivals. For Bowes to fill the Variétés every night of the week for an entire year 'would have meant a *weekly* audience of some 8,500; and over the year the extraordinary number of around 440,000 spectators.'[22] It was a challenge that John Bowes was to find it difficult to meet.

One of the stars of the Variétés, the comedian Bouffé, later recalled his four years at the theatre during Nestor Roqueplan's management as his 'honeymoon' period. His view of John Bowes's era was somewhat different: 'My succession of fresh sorrows began with the departure of Nestor... after having sold the Variétés to a M. Bans [sic], an English millionaire, who understood nothing about running a theatre and only wanted to be director so that he could produce Mlle Delorme on the stage, whom he later married.'[23] Bouffé was no doubt right about Bowes knowing nothing about running a theatre, but he was wrong about him buying the Variétés purely as a vehicle for Mlle Delorme. Her reign as a star of the Variétés was to begin later – but only by a few months.

Throughout his life Bowes kept a record of when and to whom he wrote letters, jotting them down in minute letter-diaries. (The majority still exist and are housed in the Durham County Record Office.) From 1842 to 1846 these diaries reveal that when he was in England he corresponded with a certain Mlle Ernestine in Paris, the letters regularly enclosing the sum of £20 or more. If she is the 'Souris' – 'Mousie' – who appears in the diaries in 1840, their relationship had existed for even longer. In 1842 Bowes had persuaded John Mitchell of the French Theatre in London to give Ernestine a part in one of his plays, which shows that he was bold enough to maintain his mistress in London as well as in relatively anonymous Paris.

There is another possible reference to Ernestine in Macready's diary during his Paris tour of 1845. Macready had just completed a performance of *Macbeth*: 'Bowes returned, and sat long. He said that his wife was disgusted with the audience for lavishing so much applause on Miss Faucit [Helen Faucit, a fellow actor], but they know best what they like.'[24] If this is indeed Ernestine, then Bowes was passing her off as his wife.

19
Louis William Desanges has shown Joséphine Bowes, aged about thirty, dressed at the height of fashion and wearing a diamond necklace given to her by her husband. Her kittenish smile may explain why Bowes always called her 'Puss'.

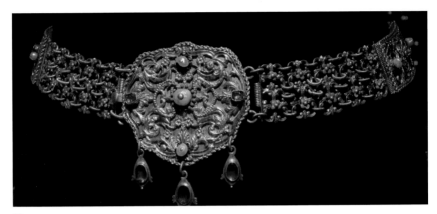

20
The decorative belt worn by Joséphine in the
portrait (left) is made of gilt-bronze and silver,
inlaid with enamel, turquoise, garnets and pearls.
The belt is on display in the Museum.

In April 1846 a letter to Wheldon from Paris shows John Bowes again in amorous vein:
'I arrived here on Thursday afternoon. I had a very pleasant journey as I fell in with a little
French actress of my acquaintance going the same road. There was a sober-minded
English Gentleman in the Coupé of the Diligence with us – Boulogne to Paris – who
understood just enough French to be evidently extremely astonished at the rather *lively*
nature of our conversation.'[25] Was this Ernestine? Or yet another of Bowes's young
actresses? Either way, Richard Wagner, for one, would not have been surprised. 'Never
mind what circles he moves in,' he wrote, 'a self-respecting man owes it to himself to
keep a mistress... the Britons... are remarkably well-adapted to it, and there is not one of
them who has not within a day of his arrival formed a blissful, if fleeting, relationship with
a ballet dancer at the very least.'[26]

But Ernestine's days were numbered: in April 1847, Mlle Delorme makes her first
appearance in the letter-diaries. For a brief period Bowes wrote to them both, but the
entry 'Wte Ern' in the diary on 30th April proves to be the end of Ernestine.

Mlle Delorme was the stage name of Joséphine Benoîte Coffin-Chevallier, the daughter
of a clockmaker who, though a native of Lyons, had lived most of his life in Paris. Born
on 26 April 1825, Joséphine was twenty-two when she met John Bowes, fourteen years
his junior. She may have taken her stage name from the play *Marion Delorme* by Victor
Hugo, first staged in Paris in 1831. Hugo had based his play on the life of a seventeenth-
century courtesan who numbered among her lovers George Villiers, Cardinal Richelieu
and the Marquis de Cinq-Mars (who was executed for plotting to kill Richelieu). After a
life of fantastic adventures and a brief marriage to an English lord, Marion Delorme died
in poverty in Paris. It is a romantic story, and one that would have appealed to an aspiring
young actress like Joséphine.

Bowes's letter-diary for 1847 shows that by July Mlle Delorme had become 'Puss', a
sobriquet she was to retain until her death. The diaries also show that during his brief but

21
George du Maurier's engraving of *A Happy Dinner* captures the convivial café life enjoyed by the likes of the Goncourt brothers and Nestor Roqueplan, the previous owner of the Variétés. Du Maurier had studied art in Paris in the mid-1850s and later wrote the hugely successful book *Trilby*.

frequent absences in England, Bowes wrote to Joséphine every other day; he had fallen deeply and irrevocably in love with her.

There are two portraits of Joséphine in The Bowes Museum, one painted by Antoine Dury in 1850, and another attributed to Louis William Desanges. The latter shows a young woman with long dark ringlets, holding a book. Her rather kittenish expression perhaps explains Bowes's pet name for her. The pink silk dress garlanded with pearls is caught at the waist by a distinctive belt (the belt survives and is in The Bowes Museum). Around her neck is a diamond necklace, given to her by John Bowes.

Bowes's purchase in 1846 of a house at 8, rue Rougemont marked the beginning of a crucial change in his life. This was followed by his decision not to stand for Parliament in the 1847 election. 'The Town is full of electioneering,' he cheerfully informed Wheldon from London in July. 'What a luxury it is to see all this, & know one has not to pay for it!'[27] With his presence in London no longer required, he let the house in Conduit Street. By the end of 1847 he can be said to have more or less taken up permanent residence in France.

He had now created a little world for himself in Paris. The house, situated in a quiet street, was only a few minutes' walk from the Variétés and his two clubs, the Cercle de l'Union and the Jockey Club. In the boulevard des Italiens, just across from the Cercle de l'Union, was the Café de Paris. It is inconceivable that a rich young man like Bowes would not have become an *habitué* of the most elegant restaurant in Paris. Also in the boulevard des Italiens was the Café Anglais, opened in 1854. When the Café de Paris closed in 1856, the Café Anglais became the zenith of fashion. 'It was generally agreed that the food was exquisite,' wrote Boutet de Monvel. 'It was incomparable, so much so indeed that Dugléré, the *chef de cuisine*, was one day christened by Rossini "the Mozart of French cooking".'[28] One of the Anglais' chief attractions was the private rooms where ladies of the night could be discreetly entertained. Within a stone's throw of the Variétés was Tortoni's, famous for its ices and much frequented by the actors and clientèle of the theatre.

Thus, at the age of thirty-six, in love with Joséphine Delorme, the owner of a popular theatre and living at the heart of the most vibrant city in Europe, John Bowes was in his element.

England, however, still made its demands on his time. The collieries, the racing stables at Malton and his properties at Streatlam and Gibside constantly required his attention. The thousands of letters in The Bowes Museum Archive and the Durham County Record Office attest to his close supervision, his remarkable memory and his intimate knowledge of every aspect of his business affairs and possessions. But such control could not always be exercised by letter and he had to make frequent visits to England.

In May 1847 Bowes hurried back to Paris from England in time to attend Joséphine's début performance in *Mademoiselle Grabutot*, a one-act vaudeville in which she played the lead, a role which required her to impersonate her brother. The subsequent review of her performance by Charles Matharel de Fiennes, the theatre critic of *Le Siècle*, was withering:

> As for a poor vaudeville which they played on Sunday at the Théâtre des Variétés, and which is called *Mlle Grabutot*, we hope we may be excused analysing it, for we could not understand it. A young lady called Delorme, dressed as a man, made her first appearance in this play; she seemed to us to be equipped with plenty of self-assurance but very little talent. We shall see whether she improves when she condescends to appear in the garb of her own sex.[29]

De Fiennes's opinion of Joséphine's abilities as an actress never altered. At times, his criticisms seem verging on the vindictive: 'It is not possible to be bad so superbly,' he said of her role in *Le Foyer des Acteurs* in August.[30] He complained about her 'nasal twang and ungraceful bearing'[31], of her 'killing' every role she played, and accused her of trying to imitate, if not parody, the established star of the Variétés, the divine Déjazet. 'Do you know Mlle Delorme?' he enquired innocently of his readers, and then let rip with terrible gusto: 'An impossible voice, impossible figure, sings down her nose, infernal conceit, the easy self-assurance of a star performer sure of herself and her audience. She chatters on stage, she gazes at the audiences and speaks, gesticulates and sings in a way that is not allowed even among barnstormers.'[32] He was the only critic to be so consistently savage about her and it is difficult to explain why, unless he took exception to Bowes's promotion of his protégée at the expense of other more talented actresses – a view expressed both by de Fiennes and by others connected with the Variétés.

It is curious that Bowes, the most fastidious of men, should have been so bewitched by the theatre that he was able to ignore the squalor and decadence of so much that went on at the Variétés. The Goncourt brothers recount a conversation with an acquaintance, a theatre proprietor, in March 1861: 'He spoke... about the incurable disease of the theatre which, once you have caught it, always brings you back to the stage – a disease like prostitution or beggary.'[33]

This correlation between prostitution and the theatre was not wide of the mark. The actress Nana, heroine of Émile Zola's novel *Nana* – and coincidentally the leading actress at the Théâtre des Variétés – spends much of the novel juggling with her numerous and predominantly aristocratic lovers, most of whom 'contributed' in some way or another to her maintenance. Even Zola's fictional manager of the Variétés refers to the theatre as his 'knocking-shop' and one, if not more, of the principal actresses in Bowes's day was a courtesan. Alice Ozy, one of Mlle Delorme's co-stars at the Variétés, happily combined the two occupations, numbering among her lovers Victor Hugo and his son, the Duke of Aumale and Louis Napoléon Bonaparte. Zola had based his research for the book (the ninth in his series of twenty novels which trace the history of a family under the Second Empire) on the Variétés itself, and his descriptions of life within its walls are too vivid not to be authentic.

Behind the scenes the Variétés was a maze of rickety stairs, narrow passages and chaotic dressing rooms. One of Nana's would-be lovers, in search of her during the interval, was 'stifled by the heavy, overheated, backstage atmosphere, with its strong underlying stench of gas, stage-set glue, squalid dark corners, and the smell of the female extras' unwashed underwear' – an environment which he found both intoxicating and erotic.[34]

22
Edward Morin's watercolour shows Hortense Schneider in her dressing room at the Théâtre des Variétés. Although a star at the theatre some years after Joséphine's day, the two actresses may well have used the same dressing room.

A later scene in the novel depicts the 'Prince-of-Scotland' lounging at his ease in Nana's dressing room, 'surrounded by a vulgar entourage of dressers, tarts, stage hacks, showmen, and exhibitors of women'.[35] Zola's Prince-of-Scotland is based on the Prince of Wales (the future Edward VII), who had an affair with the actress Hortense Schneider when she was starring in Offenbach's *La Grande Duchesse de Gerolstein* at the Variétés in 1867. Apparently her dressing room was a rose-coloured room with Turkey carpets and an enormous mirror stretching the length of one wall, although this description bears little resemblance to Edward Morin's watercolour, painted in 1873. As a star in some of the theatre's productions, Joséphine may well have been an earlier occupant of Miss Schneider's dressing room.

The Variétés' auditorium – described by Zola as 'white and gold picked out in a delicate green'[36] – could seat fifteen hundred people, all jammed together thigh-to-thigh on red plush seats. (Zola's research at the Variétés was carried out some twenty-five years after Bowes's tenure of the theatre, but apart from a major redecoration instituted by him in 1851 there is no reason to suppose that it had altered much in appearance.) By the time Bowes owned the theatre, lighting by gas of both the auditorium and the stage was well established. (One of the stars of the French ballet, Emma Livry, was burnt to death when she stood too close to a wing-light and her dress caught fire.) The auditoria of all theatres remained lit throughout the performance for the simple reason that many people were there less to see than to be seen. As a result, the heat was suffocating. Zola describes the state of an audience at the Variétés after a long performance: 'People were gasping, their hair was sticky with sweat. They'd been there for three hours, and the atmosphere was stuffy from their breath and the smell of their bodies. In the glare of the gas-jets you could see a thick haze of dust hovering under the chandelier.'[37]

The audience represented a cross-section of Parisian society: the *demi-monde* (made up of women who fell midway between respectable society and prostitution); the *haut monde* (fashionable society), the Parisian *bourgeoises*, who were fanatical theatre goers. 'They love to enumerate what they have seen,' wrote Octave Uzanne.'"We went on Monday to the Variétés, on Wednesday to the Français, Thursday to the Nouveautés".'[38] Then there were artists, writers, wits, journalists, actors, stockbrokers, a liberal sprinkling of the aristocracy and members of the Court and diplomatic corps – 'a strangely mixed bunch, comprising every kind of genius and corrupted by every kind of vice...'[39]

The trick was to know where the *demi-monde* and the *haut monde* crossed over – a task that became increasingly difficult as the century progressed and all but impossible during the Second Empire. The Goncourt brothers, attending the première of *Rothomago*, were outraged to find themselves in a box next to one occupied by the mistresses of a horse-dealer in the Champs-Élysées, one of them a 'famous sometime bare-back rider at the Hippodrome'. These ladies were joined by Napoléon III's latest mistress: 'What a farce!', exclaims Jules Goncourt. 'This prince's mistress, chatting with circus artistes in a box full of whores, arranging for sealed envelopes [from Napoléon] to be delivered to her in public, for policemen with despatches to knock at her door!'[40]

How did John Bowes, with his English county background and part aristocratic parentage, fit into this sex-obsessed society? And how did he manage to steer the theatre through the numerous difficulties that beset it? His various managers (one of whom, Morin, had been

Mlle Delorme's private drama tutor) would have been in charge of the actual day-to-day running of the theatre, but the ultimate responsibility rested with Bowes. How, for instance, did he cope with that most insidious of Parisian theatre practices, the *claque? Claqueurs* were members of the audience who were paid by management to attend a performance and ensure its success by loudly applauding it. They could equally well destroy it by booing and hissing its first performance, a fate which befell the Goncourts' play.

To some observers of the Parisian theatrical scene, John Bowes would always be an outsider. Roger Boutet de Monvel, a later administrator of the Variétés, described him as 'A pompous Englishman, renowned for his racehorses and his considerable riches which he used to restore the Château de Luciennes [which Bowes bought in 1852]. Not content with possessing the ancient abode of la Dubarry [mistress of Louis XV], M. Bowes wanted to own a theatre and, to satisfy his wish, bought the Variétés. Much good it did him as from that day on began a period of obscurity and disaster for the theatre on the Boulevard Montmartre.'[41] One disaster, however, that was utterly beyond Bowes's control was the revolution which broke out in Paris in February 1848.

'There was', wrote the English historian Philip Guedella, 'a sound of breaking glass in every continental capital west of the Russian frontier.'[42] On 22 February there had been trouble in the air and the Variétés had only a quarter of its usual attendance. The following day a 'villainous-looking mob', ranging along the boulevard des Capucines – just round the corner from the theatre – came face to face with government troops. One of the mob was shot and panic ensued. At the end of three days, three hundred and fifty people were dead and the King, Louis-Philippe, had abdicated, fleeing Paris for England dressed, allegedly, 'in an old hat, shabby coat, blue spectacles, a toupee and carrying a cotton umbrella.'[43] Thus ended the thousand-year-old French monarchy. The Tuileries was sacked by the mob, the throne set on fire and a republic proclaimed.

This extraordinary turn of events was neatly summarised by an American resident in Paris: 'We dined under a Monarchy, supped under a Regency, went to sleep under a Provisional Government, and woke up under a Republic – not to mention about two hours when we had just no government at all.'[44]

John Bowes wasted little sympathy on the King: 'Louis-Philippe richly deserves his fate,' he wrote to the Gibside agent, Ralph Dent. 'He attempted to carry through a system of falsehood, & humbug, & failed...' This letter was written from Boulogne to which Bowes had prudently removed himself, though not without some difficulty, as he explained to Wheldon: 'I had to follow a succession of Will o'the Wisps in the shape of burning stations along the Northern line, and was at last obliged to strike across the Country in such conveyances as I could find to Abbeville.'[45]

Bowes told neither Dent nor Wheldon that he took Mlle Delorme with him when he left Paris. Leaving her in Boulogne, a town which was to become very familiar to them both, he returned to Paris 'to arrange some matters of business', which presumably included the Variétés, which had been closed during the revolution. Ten days later he was back in Boulogne and the couple sailed for England. Bowes stayed at Arthur's Club while Mlle Delorme was settled into a quiet hotel in Leicester Square where she was joined for three months by her mother, Madame Coffin-Chevallier. Since Bowes was adept at

23
Composed of everyone from stockbrokers, artists and writers to members of the aristocracy and prostitutes, the audience gathers in the foyer of the Variétés. The drawing is by Constantin Guys who was famous for his depictions of the *demi-monde*.

concealing his actions when he wished to do so, it comes as no surprise that absolutely nothing is known about how the two women passed their time in London.

Bowes and Mlle Delorme did not return to Paris until early August. This long absence may have been caused by a fresh revolution which broke out in Paris in June, resulting in the death of more than two thousand people and the arrest and transportation of thousands more. For a month following these terrible events troops were bivouacked in the boulevards, including outside the Variétés in the boulevard Montmartre.

During the five months Bowes remained in England, the Variétés had limped along under Morin's management. With the theatre playing to half-empty houses, Bowes was obliged to put in more money to keep it afloat. The popular Bouffé, upset by circumstances in the theatre, took leave of absence with '*une maladie nerveuse*'.

In September 1848 Mlle Delorme played the lead in *Candide*. The play was judged 'a merry little extravaganza' by the critic of *Galignani's Messenger*, a daily paper circulated among English residents throughout Europe. De Fiennes, however, was not impressed: while praising attempts by the other actors to be funny, he added, 'But can one be funny playing opposite Mlle Delorme?'[46]

Criticism of the involvement of John Bowes and Mlle Delorme in the theatre even surfaced in England: in August 1850 a paragraph which had appeared in the Paris newspapers was picked up by *The Globe, Durham Chronicle* and the *Newcastle Journal*. The gist of it was that Bowes had bought the Variétés for £50,000 in the name of Mlle Delorme, 'an actress in the theatre, who has contrived to empty the house of its old *habitués* in an unhappy attempt to imitate the celebrated Mlle Déjazet.'[47]

24
The fashionable boulevard des Italiens lay at the heart of John Bowes's life in Paris. A short walk north took him to his house in Cité d'Antin; an even shorter walk east and he was at the Théâtre des Variétés in boulevard Montmartre.

Even Thackeray, in Paris in early 1849, was not above taking a swipe at his old companion: 'He has 40,000 a year and palaces in the country,' he wrote to a friend, 'and here he is a manager of the Théâtre of Variétés – and his talk about actors and coulisses all the time of the interview – I wish it could be the last: but he has made me promise to dine with him and go I must to be killed by his melancholy gentlemanlikeness.'[48] This seems a little unfair of Thackeray, who had disported himself in considerable style in one of the 'palaces', had been lent money by Bowes (which he did not repay until 1858), and seems to have forgotten the hours they had spent together discussing the theatre. In about 1835 Bowes had even financed a publication of Thackeray's entitled *Flore et Zéphyr*. Perhaps if the author had known what a strain the Variétés imposed on Bowes's finances, he might have been more charitable.

Mlle Delorme did not appear on the stage of the Variétés throughout 1849. Her absence may have been a bid to quell the persistent criticism of her talent and to assuage the wounded feelings of her fellow actors who – if de Fiennes is to be believed – resented the favouritism shown her by Morin and Bowes, as well as her involvement in the theatre's administration. Bowes's purchase of a house for her in Auteuil, a village near the Bois de Boulogne, would have filled the void left by the Variétés. Tucked away in this rural retreat, Mlle Delorme could indulge her love of the country and for animals, which at various times included cats, canaries, rabbits, pigeons, goats, a cow, and her beloved dogs Palette and Bernardine.

Morin's position at the theatre was also no longer tenable and he left in late 1849. In his wake followed other managers, none of whom seemed able to restore the theatre's fortunes. However, the Variétés did have one resounding success with *La Vie de Bohème*, based on Henry Murger's book, which was premiered in late November 1849. 'Here, for the first time, sophisticated Paris [was] introduced to Latin Quarter life, with its humour and pathos, its miseries and simple joys.'[49] All Paris flocked to see the play, and on the boulevards and in the salons the talk was of little else. (Murger's book was the basis for Puccini's famous opera *La Bohème*, first staged in 1887.)

In January 1851 Mlle Delorme made what proved to be her last appearance at the Variétés and then retired from the stage. But for Bowes there was to be no respite. Pressing business in England obliged him to make frequent trips to London, sometimes for only a few days at a time, while at the Variétés, directors continued to succeed one another with little success. Bowes twice took over the direction himself, remaining as sole director from January 1854 to June 1855. In an attempt to stave off disaster he had poured in

25
This painting by Nicolas Edward Gabé shows fighting in the streets during the revolution which broke out in Paris in February 1848. All the city's theatres were closed and John Bowes fled to England, accompanied by Joséphine.

more money, funds he could ill afford as in 1852 he had purchased a small château in a village to the west of Paris. He had also taken the lease of 7, Cité d'Antin, 'an area of Paris notorious as a haunt for bankers and kept women' and within easy reach of the boulevard des Italiens.[50] The Variétés had ceased to be the focus of either his life or Mlle Delorme's and he decided to sell it.

In 1854 the theatre staff received three months' notice of the termination of their contract, and on 26 May 1855 the Variétés was closed. Despite the many problems and the loss of their employment, twenty-six of the theatre's personnel, including the actress Alice Ozy, signed a letter addressed to John Bowes testifying to 'their recognition of the kindness' he had shown them. To Bowes, who was always a scrupulously fair and generous employer, the last sentence must have been extremely gratifying: 'We treasure the memory of your paternal administration...'[51]

Bowes soon found a lessee for the theatre, but selling it was to take another three years, even though he was prepared to let it go at a loss. In 1857 he offered it to the 4th Marquess of Hertford, who was known to be purchasing property in Paris, but his offer was politely declined. The Variétés was at last sold in April 1858.

It is impossible to put a figure on the losses John Bowes incurred as the owner of the Variétés, but they were considerable. He had been defeated not only by some poor directors, bad reviews and discontent among the actors, but by riots, revolutions, cholera epidemics and a loss of morale during the Crimean War, all of which had adversely affected the theatre-going public. His dream of owning a theatre had degenerated into a nightmare and he must have been profoundly relieved to get rid of it. Besides, long before he actually sold the theatre his life had taken another course entirely.

# CHAPTER 3

❧

# Life in Paris

The portrait of Mlle Delorme painted in France in 1850 presents a very different young woman from the one who cavorted, flirted and sang on the stage of the Variétés. The artist, Antoine Dury,[1] has portrayed a lady dressed in the height of fashion seated in a luxurious interior with her favourite dog, Bernardine, at her feet. The chair is a *bergère* in Louis XV style, the table is *boulle* marquetry, the Japanese Imari vase a type that became much sought after in the nineteenth century. All these pieces reflect the flamboyant style of the Second Empire which was so much to her taste.[2]

Her expression is difficult to read: were her lips often compressed into that tight line, or has her smile frozen after being too long seated in the same position? There is a stubborness about the mouth and chin, a sharpness to the hazel eyes beneath the straight eyebrows – and yet contemporary accounts record that in conversation her face became animated, even radiant, when she smiled.

The artist has caught her at a moment of metamorphosis: the scripts of some of her plays on the table beside her signify her wish to be depicted as an actress, but her dress and the setting foreshadow a new phase in her life. Turning her back on the raffish, decadent world of the theatre she was to become a society hostess, patron of the arts, a talented amateur artist, the wife of John Bowes and the official owner of the Château du Barry.

France, too, was undergoing momentous change. When John Bowes told Wheldon in late 1848 that he believed that 'almost all the *thinking* people are heartily sick of the Republic, but I do not see how they are to get out of it',[3] he cannot possibly have foreseen that by 1852 there would be another Bonaparte seated on the imperial throne of France. Elected president of the Second Republic after Louis-Philippe's abdication, Prince Louis Napoléon, nephew of Napoléon I, executed a skilful *coup d'etat* in 1851 and exactly a year later was proclaimed Emperor Napoléon III.

One of Napoléon's first acts on becoming emperor of the Second Empire was to appoint Baron Haussmann as Prefect of the Seine. With a map of Paris pinned to the wall of Napoléon's study in the Tuileries, and armed with a battery of coloured pencils, the Emperor and Baron Haussmann began their transformation of the city. 'We ripped open the belly of old Paris, the neighbourhood of revolt and barricades,' Haussmann recalled in his *Mémoires*, 'and cut a large opening through the almost impenetrable maze of alleys...'[4]

26
Antoine Dury's portrait of Joséphine in 1850 shows a fashionable woman seated in a luxurious interior. Yet at the time she was still a vaudeville actress appearing in lead roles at John Bowes's theatre. She would not become Mrs Bowes for another two years.

27
Under Napoléon's rule, Paris was transformed into the most magnificent city in Europe. The medieval alleys were swept away to be replaced by broad tree-lined streets like boulevard Haussmann, painted after a heavy fall of snow by Gustave Caillebotte in around 1880.

Work began in 1853 and for years the city shook to the sound of falling masonry and the thump of pile-drivers. Out of this vast building site gradually emerged the public parks, the wide tree-lined boulevards and the apartment buildings, linked one to another by a filigree of wrought-iron balconies, that are such distinctive features of Paris today. Other less glamorous but more basic changes were made, such as the laying of a new drainage system and improvements to the city's water supply. Captain Gronow, who lived in Paris for some forty years, was lost in admiration: 'A beautiful, fairy-like city has replaced the crowded heaps of dingy, dark dwellings; the blind alleys and the fetid courts have been exchanged for lofty and elegant mansions, wide and well-paved thoroughfares, and spacious open places.'[5]

Some Parisians felt disoriented by the changes. 'I am a stranger to what is coming and to what is here,' Goncourt mourned. 'It is silly to come into the world in a time of change; the soul feels as uncomfortable as a man who moves into a new house before the plaster is dry.'[6]

The Second Empire was to last only eighteen years, but it was an age of luxury and brilliance, of frivolity and excess, of extravagant fashions and sexual liberation, all set to the lilting music of Offenbach's operettas. At night the centre of Paris blazed with light from the new gas lamps. In 1855 and 1867 Paris staged vast exhibitions which brought visitors from all over the world to marvel at the glittering new city.

It is typical of John Bowes that his correspondence gives no indication of these great changes. The majority of his letters to have survived are addressed to his business associates, his agent Ralph Dent, and his solicitor in Barnard Castle. They contain requests, politely-expressed orders and information about his movements. Only occasionally did he comment on the weather, his health and, later, the health of his wife. Of his private correspondence very little remains, whether by chance or by design is unknown.

Bowes's letters to Ralph Dent are the most informative about his whereabouts, and those of 1852 reveal that during that year he crossed the Channel no fewer than eighteen times. In addition to his usual trips to England, he returned to be 'pricked' as High Sheriff of the County of Durham, to see his horse Daniel O'Rourke win the Derby and to attend the launch of a steam collier, the *SS John Bowes*. In June he crossed to Calais to meet Joséphine, returning with her to London where – it is assumed – she met her future mother-in-law, the Countess of Strathmore. In July he was back in England for the Summer Assizes and to attend a Parliamentary Election. When in Paris he wrestled with problems at the Variétés and completed complex negotiations to buy the Château du Barry at Louveciennes (or Luciennes), and in August he and Joséphine Coffin-Chevallier signed a contract of marriage, followed by a civil marriage ceremony. The couple then went on honeymoon for six weeks. (The civil ceremony was followed by a religious one two years later, on 3 August 1854 in St Marylebone Parish Church in London.)

28
In 1852 John Bowes purchased Château du
Barry at Louveciennes, a village outside Paris,
and gave it to his wife as a wedding present.
This view of the Château was painted by
Joséphine, a talented amateur artist.

The single factor – apart from the constitution of an ox – that enabled Bowes to make these journeys was the development of the railways, which in Britain began in the late 1820s. Seemingly overnight, human beings were able to travel at thirty miles an hour, twenty miles faster than the average stagecoach. Many travellers were unnerved by such speed: '... it is really flying,' reported Thomas Creevey in 1829, 'and it is impossible to divest yourself of the notion of instant death to all upon the least accident happening. It gave me a headache which has not left me yet.'[7]

But the railways transformed Bowes's life. The journey from Calais to Paris by public coach, which had taken anything up to forty hours, by 1850 took him about six, while the journey from London to Darlington had been reduced from some thirty-five hours to twelve and a half. It was also fortunate for the Boweses that the first of the Paris stations to be built was the Gare Saint-Lazare, which was within a few minutes' drive of their house in Cité d'Antin. The station was also perfectly situated for the Château du Barry, enabling them to make the journey there by train in under half an hour.

The Château had been given by Louis XV to his mistress, Comtesse Jeanne du Barry, in 1769. Du Barry had added an orangery and an enchanting neo-Classical pavilion where she gave magnificent parties. When Bowes bought the Château (as a wedding present for Joséphine and in her name), the Orangery was included in the purchase but the Pavillon du Barry was already a separate property and not for sale.

The Château stands in a twenty-acre park on the left bank of the Seine in the village of Louveciennes, described by the artist Mme Vigée Le Brun, a friend of Mme du Barry, as 'one of the most charming places to live outside Paris'[8] (she was ahead of her time in her appreciation of the village; in the 1870s it became a favourite haunt of some of the Impressionists, including Sisley and Pisarro). Vigée Le Brun had last seen the Pavilion in 1789 'at the height of its splendour', but when she revisited it in 1812 she found that all was desolation and decay. In the wake of the Revolution and du Barry's execution, the Pavilion had been stripped of its contents. Allegedly the Countess had buried her jewels in the grounds of the Château, and they have never been found.

29
The Château stands in a twenty-acre park, set with mature trees, a lake and a summer house. The Boweses added many new features, including a second lake, shrubberies, a rock garden and 350 rose trees.

Although the Boweses twice visited their new home in the summer of 1852, it was not until the following year that any redecoration was carried out. To furnish the Château, they employed the fashionable Parisian firm Monbro *fils aîné*. The large number of Monbro's beautifully-written invoices in the Museum's archives attest to the scope of the service the firm provided for their clients: everything from fine pieces of furniture and copies of antiques, to curtains and doormats, and from spring-cleaning to reupholstering. The bills indicate the huge sums spent by the Boweses to achieve the luxurious softness of Second Empire interiors. Many of the pieces bought from Monbro can be seen in the Museum today.

The Monbro invoices for decorating and furnishing were an invaluable aid to Charles Hardy when he reconstructed the appearance of the Château for his biography *John Bowes and the Bowes Museum*, first published in 1970. On the ground floor there were the vestibule and ante-room, the small drawing room and the 'grand salon', the dining room and the billiard room. The salon was a symphony of blues – blue curtains and blue upholstery – and furnished with fine eighteenth-century pieces and a plethora of chairs of various shapes and sizes.

On the first floor were John and Joséphine's bedrooms, the smoking-room and the library. There is mention of a bathroom for Madame, which is surprising as few French châteaux boasted either baths or water-closets in the nineteenth century (when a certain *vicomte* brought his English wife to his château in the 1860s, 'she found one bathroom, no water-closets and sixty chamber pots'[9]). On the second floor were bedrooms for guests and their servants, and for the Boweses' own domestic staff. The kitchens and day rooms for the domestics were in a two-storey building which can be clearly seen in Joséphine's painting of the Château, now in the Museum.

Part of the contents of their library has survived and reveals an eclectic taste: books on natural history, horticulture, agriculture, Denon's massive work *Voyage dans la Haute et Basse Egypte*, guide books to Versailles, and a very battered copy of *Souvenirs de Londres en 1814 et 1816*. All rub shoulders with the novels of Dickens, Sterne, Scott, Pope and George Sand and entire sets of the prolific French novelist Paul de Kock. English literature was extremely popular in France during the early part of the century; in 1830, when the vogue was at its peak, '111 English novels were published in France, compared to only 109 French'.[10]

In front of the Château was a large lawn with a small artificial lake at one end. Distributed about the grounds were a vegetable garden, a fountain, a *temple d'amour* and a thatched summerhouse. Avenues of tall trees afforded fine views of the Pavilion or across the Seine to the countryside beyond. The place had what William Hutt, John's stepfather, once referred to as a 'quiet beauty'.

During their ten-year ownership of the Château the Boweses carried out a number of changes to the grounds, including the addition of another lake, fed by a stream enlivened by waterfalls and pools and crossed by a little stone bridge. Extensive shrubberies, a rock garden, quick-set hedges, rhododendrons, herbaceous borders and three hundred and fifty rose trees were planted. The orchard was extended and the Orangery was, appropriately, filled with orange trees. There was even a small vineyard, which often produced more wine than the household could consume, and of sufficiently good quality for Hutt to ask John to include a bottle of the 1856 vintage in his portmanteau when he next came to England.[11]

With their town house at Cité d'Antin – also furnished and decorated by Monbro – and their 'place' in the country, the scene was set for the Boweses to enter Society. Their timing was perfect: the Second Empire with all its hedonism, gaiety and style was gathering pace. Napoléon and his beautiful Spanish wife Eugénie were installed in the Tuileries Palace. Every winter they threw four lavish State Balls at the palace, to which between four and five thousand people were invited. In the autumn they gave a series of house parties at Compiègne, their château some fifty miles north of Paris.

Again, John Bowes gives no clue as to whether he and Joséphine attended any of these social occasions, although an article on Bowes by Baron de Gelsey in *The British Racehorse* asserted that Bowes was a friend of the Emperor.[12] This could be true, as there is concrete evidence that he presented a picture to Napoléon. As it was not in Bowes's nature to curry favour, there must have been a connection of some kind between them. Besides, John Bowes's nationality (Napoléon was an ardent Anglophile), French wife, reputation as a breeder of Derby winners, wealth, ownership of the Variétés theatre and membership of the most exclusive clubs in Paris were surely sufficient reasons to gain him a seat at the Imperial table.

The Empress set the tone for the entertainments, exhibiting a preference for the style of her heroine, Marie-Antoinette. She also set the fashion in dress (a pair of her evening shoes can be seen in the Museum), aided by the remarkable skill of the English dressmaker Charles Frederick Worth, who measured and cut his patterns with such exquisite accuracy that they seldom required more than one fitting (he once made a dress for her in under four hours). According to Albert Vandam, Worth 'became the absolute autocrat in matters of feminine apparel. It was not even an enlightened despotism. His will was law.'[13]

30
Joséphine Bowes spent lavishly on her wardrobe. These bills are for dresses supplied by the leading fashion designer of the day, the Englishman Charles Frederick Worth, who also designed clothes for Empress Eugénie.

Edmond de Goncourt gives this delightful description of the arduous life of a society lady and of the range of functions for which different oufits were required:

> The life of a Parisian élégante is far from being an idle one; it is, on the contrary, a prodigiously active and frightfully exhausting life... The cares of the toilette, the daily succession of visits, receptions and fêtes, the theatres, the flower and picture shows, races, lectures, attendance at church, with many other duties and pleasures, form a cycle absorbing every hour and moment of this rushing, fluttering, *froufroutante* existence. In short, a Parisian woman of fashion lives in a perpetual whirl, which allows her no graceful intervals of leisure in which to retire within herself and indulge in dreams and reverie. Dress alone constitutes an intolerable tyranny – one, however, to which she slavishly submits.[14]

In 1853 the crinoline made its first appearance, the fashion rapidly spreading through France, then to Britain and America. It was uncomfortable and expensive, the simplest taffeta dress requiring over fifty metres of material. To the basic skirt was added every conceivable kind of trimming: embroidery, frills, ruches, elaborate bows, lace, even fresh flowers. Women no longer walked but glided, their feet invisible beneath their rustling draperies. In his massive study *Fashion in Paris*, Octave Uzanne made his view of women's fashions abundantly clear: 'With the Second Empire we reach the most hideous period in female dress that has ever vexed the artistic eye'; he described the crinoline as a 'diseased fashion'.[15]

The German artist François-Xavier Winterhalter immortalised these flouncy confections in his painting of the Empress and her ladies-in-waiting, the picture sometimes irreverently referred to as *au rendez-vous des grisettes*.[16] Not everyone was charmed by the ladies' appearance. 'Their hair is dragged off their faces so tightly that they can hardly shut their eyes,' declared the Earl of Malmesbury, returning from an Imperial function in 1862, 'and their scarlet accoutrements, jackets, cloaks, etc., as they happen to be very fair, make an *ensemble* indescribably unbecoming.'[17]

Joséphine Bowes was among the many fashionable women who bought her clothes from Maison Worth in rue de la Paix, despite their exorbitant cost. On 19 March 1869 she celebrated her fête-day by buying seven dresses from Worth. Two of the most expensive are described as: 'Dress, gauze, embroidered white satin £43: dress, pink taffeta £43.' The bill amounted to £234 (£10,530 today). In 1872 she outdid her previous record by spending 11,184 francs at Worth, equivalent to almost £500 at the time or £22,500 today.

She also possessed some fine jewellery. Bills from the Paris jeweller Briquet show that she was particularly fond of earrings. In 1865 John Bowes paid Briquet the sum of 37,990 francs for items of jewellery purchased over a period of two years.[18] An English journalist resident in Paris circulated the story that he had seen Madame Bowes wearing on her head a diamond bird-of-Paradise said to have cost £120,000, but this story appears to be quite untrue.

The first ball to be given by the Boweses – and the only one known to have taken place at the Château – was on 18 June 1856, the eve of John Bowes's forty-fifth birthday. Some one hundred guests were invited, many of them driving down from Paris in their carriages, a journey of less than an hour. Turning through the gates they caught their first glimpse of the Château, framed by tall trees and gilded by the light of the evening sun.

As the dining room was too small for so many guests, refreshments were served in the Orangery, empty now of the orange trees, which were always moved on to the terrace during the summer. The indispensable Monbro supplied the chairs, plates, glasses and cutlery, carpeted the Orangery with green canvas and illuminated it with hundreds of candles. The Grand Salon was furnished with a further one hundred chairs.

There were more parties at their town house in Cité d'Antin, and the occasional visit from English friends. One such, Henry Morgan Vane, wrote to thank Bowes for his hospitality and asked to be remembered most kindly to Madame Bowes 'who has, I hear, been giving some most beautiful and agreeable reunions.'[19]

This view of Joséphine as a gracious and accomplished hostess is confirmed by Bowes's old school friend Alexander Kinglake, who had just returned from the Crimea and was in the throes of writing his monumental history of the war. 'I don't know', he wrote in January 1855, 'when I have passed three or four hours so pleasantly as those few which I passed in my way through Paris. It cheered me to find you kind and cordial as ever... & somehow Madame Bowes exercised some kind of conversational spell which made me absolutely voluble.'[20]

In 1855 the Boweses sold the house in Cité d'Antin and rented a larger one at 7, rue de Berlin (now rue de Liège) which was to remain their home for the rest of their married life (Bowes bought the house outright in 1862). It was some distance north of Cité d'Antin and thus further from Bowes's clubs, the Variétés and his other old haunts, but much closer to Gare St Lazare. The house required about ten staff, including the gardener and the coachman. Possibly due to the Boweses' concern 'as to the minute cleanliness of the apartments in the House',[21] or because of Mrs Bowes being 'very hasty in her temper',[22] there were frequent problems with the servants. (It is alleged that during the Boweses' sojourns at Streatlam, Joséphine would hide money about the house to see if it was stolen, and that she required the carriage to be ready and waiting at the front door every day in case she might want to go for a drive.[23])

For some reason, the Boweses chose to employ a number of English servants. As Joséphine spoke little English the task of securing them fell to John, who bombarded Ralph Dent with letters asking him to find yet another housemaid or footman, or a lady's maid for Joséphine. The latter should not be 'a *Dressy* or fine Person like most English maids are [but] a plain respectable Person.'[24] A female servant must be prepared to wear 'short gowns so as not to trail on the ground, & carry the dirt after her.'[25] Male servants were required to be intelligent, quiet and sober. Once the long-suffering Dent had found a suitable individual, his or her journey to Paris required a further series of letters from John containing detailed travel arrangements. Very young or female servants would be safe on the train as there was a guard whose 'special business is to attend to Ladies, & young Persons.'[26]

In 1860 the Boweses decided to sell the Château. If they had bought it partly as an ideal place to bring up children, Joséphine's age (she was now 35), her increasingly frail health and John's possible infertility, all combined to make child-bearing progressively unlikely. It took two years to complete the sale but long before the contract was signed, the livestock had been sold and some of the furniture moved to the Paris house. The orange trees, however, and some of the furniture and objects were crated up and sent by barge down the Seine to Le Havre. There the crates (one of which contained Joséphine's donkey) were loaded on to Bowes's steam collier, the *Marley Hill*, which took them to Middlesbrough. The last part of the journey to Streatlam was by rail.

From 1862 onwards the house at rue de Berlin became the focus of their lives in France and the setting for numerous social occasions. In 1865 the Boweses threw a large dinner party in January and a supper dance in February. In late March a supper dance to celebrate Joséphine's fête – the main event of every year – took place. Analysis of the bills for the party shows that the house was filled with spring flowers, potted geraniums and rhododendrons. The guests consumed copious amounts of *paté de foie gras*, truffles, lobster and salmon, then moved on to the beef, two hams – one from York and one from Bayonne – turkeys, chickens, and thirty-six larks. For dessert there were Russian macaroons, plum cake, rum babas, crystallised fruits, two hundred and seventy-five assorted ices and fifty water ices. Wine would have come from Bowes's well-stocked cellar, but in addition there were a hundred bottles of champagne. Music for dancing was supplied by a quartet.

33
The Salon Bleu at the Boweses' house in rue de Berlin was hung with dark blue damask and furnished with chairs like this one made by Monbro *fils aîné* in 1855. The eighteenth-century tapestry is from Beauvais.

34
This carved and gilded bed, known as *lit à la duchesse*, was part of a bedroom set belonging to Joséphine Bowes. A superb example of Second Empire furnishing, it still preserves its original curtains and canopy of woven silk brocade.

35
One of a pair of candelabra supplied by Monbro *fils aîné* for the Château du Barry.

A special feature of some of the parties at rue de Berlin was the game pie made by the Streatlam housekeeper, Mrs Dixon, which always took pride of place in the centre of the table. The arrangements for the making and dispatching of the pie entailed a lengthy correspondence between Bowes and Ralph Dent. In 1866 Bowes asked for 'another Christmas Pie this year, but not so much Pepper as in that of last year', and added a plea that the 'Crust had better be a good deal stronger than the last which was broken.'[27] In view of all this entertaining, it is hardly surprising that in 1865 Bowes told his solicitor John Dickonson Holmes (who had succeeded Thomas Wheldon on his death in 1850) that Mrs Bowes was 'pretty well but rather fatigued having been out to a good many parties lately'.[28]

Due in part to Bowes's compartmentalising of his life – letters were for communicating information and instructions, not for idle gossip – and in part to a woeful lack of any letters to friends and family in the archives, very little is known about the identity of the guests who attended these functions. The few names that have survived would be meaningless to today's reader. An English journalist who claimed to know John Bowes well stated that Bonapartists 'predominated at his table.'[29] If so, it was perhaps more by accident than design, for Bowes had no admiration for Bonapartism.

That Joséphine wished to be seen as a society hostess and patron of the arts is confirmed by her subscription to a monthly magazine called *La Revue Critique* which chronicled its subscribers' activities in artistic and social circles. In its late 1868 issue, under the heading 'The Fashionable World and the Salons', appeared the following:

36
Twice a week, when the band played, Parisian society gathered in the gardens of the Tuileries. Edouard Manet's *Musique aux Tuileries*, painted in 1863, brilliantly captures the sparkling atmosphere of Second Empire Paris. This was one of Manet's first paintings to show a scene from contemporary life.

Elegant and cultured society has reopened its salons. Paris appears lively and gay. One entertainment follows another, the season is in its full splendour. The return to Paris of Mme Bowes [from a trip round northern Europe] is a fortunate event for the aristocratic world, of which she is one of its finest ornaments. Besides the liking which she inspires in the upper echelons of society, Mme Bowes is very favourably thought of in the world of the arts.[30]

For the wealthy, like the Boweses, life in Paris during the Second Empire was sweet. Artists like Renoir and Manet portrayed a city vibrant with movement and colour: ladies in their billowing crinolines and pert little bonnets lean on the arms of their top-hatted escorts, dance cheek to cheek at the Moulin de la Galette or listen to the band of the Garde Impériale in the Tuileries gardens. Other artists depict the bustling life of the grand boulevards with their pavement cafés, the trotting hackney cabs or *fiacres*, the crossing sweepers in their clogs, the horse omnibuses, and everywhere the vivid reds and blues of soldiers' uniforms.

Charles Augustus Cole, who produced *The Imperial Paris Guide*, extols this life of pleasure: 'To smoke a cigar on a summer evening, on a chair, before one of the cafés on the western boulevards, observing the full tide of life streaming past, is not an unpleasant way of passing an hour or two. The scene witnessed there will not easily be forgot.'[31] Another, less enthusiastic observer comments in 1860: 'We are in the Parisian paradise, or the Parisian hell. Every night, since 1 January, has been spent in festivities, spectacles, concerts and dances. It is a perpetual coming-and-going, a constant toing-and-froing, a continual volcano.'[32]

The writer Henry James, who lived in Paris from 1875 to 1876, described dining on a summer evening in a restaurant near the Bois de Boulogne, where 'stately trees picturesquely grouped... make long evening shadows on a lawn, and irreproachable tables, and carriages rolling up behind high-stepping horses, and depositing all sorts of ladies. The drive back through the wood at night is most charming, and the coolness of the air extreme...'[33]

For the Boweses there were visits to the public art galleries – the finest in Europe – the great Sarah Bernhardt at the Odéon, their six-seater box at the Opera and drives in the Bois de Boulogne in the barouche upholstered in blue cloth and with devices emblazoned on both doors.[34] For a compulsive shopper and bargain hunter like Joséphine, the advent of the great Paris department stores in the 1850s must have provided hours of happy browsing.

During lulls between social engagements, the exhausted socialite could curl up with the novels of Flaubert, Dumas *père*, Victor Hugo, Mme George Sand, the creator of science fiction Jules Verne, and the poetry of Baudelaire, Verlaine and Théophile Gautier.

In 1857, when a new racecourse was inaugurated at Longchamp, the Boweses made regular visits. Thousands of Parisians arrived by road, some in elegant landaus and *calèches* (the most sought-after carriages were made in England), some in dogcarts, large omnibuses, or perched on the roof of mailcoaches while their servants guarded the crates of champagne inside. Others came by rail or by *bâteau-mouche* (excursion boat) down the Seine. Depending on their station in life, people gathered either in the public enclosure or in one of the five grandstands in the private enclosure. The women were

37
The French were heavily influenced by the British passion
for horses and racing, and in 1857 inaugurated a racecourse
at Longchamp in the Bois de Boulogne. Manet's painting
catches the excitement of a race in progress.

lavishly dressed and carried little parasols to ward off the sun. (Bowes's horse Nobleman was to run, unsuccessfully, in the first Grand Prix in 1870.) 'It is from England', explained Gustave Claudin, 'that we have borrowed the passion for racing. Races have become an institution for us...'[35]

Anglomania extended to other aspects of life in the capital: French women adopted English fashions such as plaids, tweeds, leather belts and dresses trimmed with leather, while men wore their 'whiskers *à l'anglaise*, their suits *à l'anglaise*, their bearing and jargon and carriages *à l'anglaise*.[36]

In 1867 the feverish brilliance of the Second Empire reached a climax with the opening of the Paris International Exhibition. An enormous oval building, made of glass set in a filigree of ironwork – similar to London's Crystal Palace in 1851 – was erected on the Champ-de-Mars and filled with exhibits from all the leading nations. In the area surrounding the dome, countries as diverse as Egypt, Russia and Mexico presented before an astonished public exhibits such as Kirghiz yurts, an Inca temple, and the exposed and blackened flesh of an Egyptian mummy.[37] 'At the English buffets in the Exhibition', wrote the Goncourts, 'there is a fantastic quality about the women, with their splendid beauty, their crude pallor, their flaming hair; they are like whores of the Apocalypse, something terrifying, frightening, inhuman.'[38]

A staggering fifteen million visitors[39] from all over the world attended the Exhibition, including the Emperors of Russia and Austria, the Prince of Wales (his mother, Queen Victoria, had attended the Paris Exhibition of 1855 as guest of the Emperor and Empress), King Wilhelm of Prussia (who asked for a map of Paris's new boulevards), his formidable Chancellor Count Otto von Bismarck, and General von Moltke – and, of course, John and Joséphine Bowes. Albert Vandam, writing with the benefit of hindsight, declared that 'The journey to France of Moltke and his royal master in 1867 was not a pleasure trip, but a downright military reconnaissance.'[40] (The 'reconnaissance' Vandam refers to was for the war which erupted between France and Prussia three years later.)

In April this constellation of foreign royalty attended the first ever production of Offenbach's *La Grande Duchesse de Gérolstein* at the Théâtre des Variétés – surely a high point in the theatre's existence. Together with the flower of Parisian society, these illustrious monarchs rocked with laughter at the antics of General Boum, commander of the army of a fictitious German principality whose Chancellor, Baron Puck, had engineered a war as a way of diverting attention from his domestic difficulties. Hortense Schneider triumphed as the amorous Duchess and entertained everyone from the Prince of Wales to the Viceroy of Egypt in her dressing room.[41] (During the six weeks that he was in Paris, the Viceroy patronised the Variétés forty times.[42]) Typically, John Bowes makes no mention of this event, but he was in Paris at the time and it seems inconceivable that he and Joséphine would have missed it.

The Paris Exhibition lasted for six months. 'A picture lingers on of a vast, cosmopolitan party given by France for the entire world', wrote Pierre de la Gorce, one of the Second Empire's great historians. He adds, however, that those who saw it 'remember two feelings, a feeling of dazzling brilliance and a feeling of fear... Never have people enjoyed themselves more frenziedly or more uneasily.'[43]

CHAPTER 4

Joséphine and the Paris Salon

Joséphine was a woman of many talents: she had achieved some success as an actress, had then established herself as a society hostess and was soon to prove a major collector of works of art. But she cherished another ambition: to gain recognition as an amateur artist. And she was in the right place at the right time to pursue such an ambition.

In the mid nineteenth century, Paris was the centre of the art world. It had the finest galleries, the best art schools and a rapidly developing art market. Above all, it was the centre for the art of the moment. In the mid sixties Benjamin Champney, an American artist who had been travelling in Italy, described his pleasure on returning to Paris 'to be surrounded by the interests of today, to see what the greatest artists of the greatest modern school were doing... it was with delight that I turned from the musty old galleries [of Italy] to find so much freshness and nature here.'[1]

Thackeray was in no doubt that Paris was the ideal place to study art: '... the painter's trade, in France, is a very good one; better appreciated, better understood, and... far better paid than with us. There are a dozen excellent schools in which a lad may enter here... In England there is no school except the Academy, unless the student can afford to pay a very large sum...' Even the city itself was an inspiration: 'the streets are filled with picture-shops, the people themselves are pictures walking about; the churches, theatres, eating-houses, concert-rooms, are covered with pictures...'[2]

These views were enthusiastically shared by Henry Murger in his *Scènes de la vie de Bohème* and by George du Maurier in his highly successful novel *Trilby*, both of which described in authentic detail the life of poverty-stricken art students living with their *grisettes* in chilly attics in the city's Latin Quarter. (A *grisette* was a girl who would willingly share the lot of an artist or student). Despite Murger's definition of Bohemia as 'bordered on the North by hope, work and gaiety, on the South by necessity and courage; on the West and East by slander and the hospital'[3] (Murger was to die at the tragically early age of thirty-nine), these romantic tales of student life immediately captured the popular imagination.

Thackeray began his short-lived attempt to become an artist by copying Old Masters in the Musée du Louvre, although he confessed to his mother that 'studying these great old painters puts one sadly out of conceit with one's mean little efforts.'[4] The Louvre was rare in that it also allowed women to copy paintings. This was an important concession as obtaining a training in art was a constant struggle for any woman who wanted to make art her profession; wherever she turned, she found herself up against restrictions imposed by the male art establishment. Until later in the century there were no art classes for women, nor were they allowed to attend men's art classes. Thus, to study life drawing from a live nude model – essential training for any serious artist – was not only impossible but forbidden. Instead, women had to be content with copying plaster casts of classical statues.

38
Having abandoned the stage and become a wife and society hostess, Joséphine Bowes nursed a further ambition: to succeed as an amateur artist. This photograph was taken c. 1864, three years before her first painting was accepted by the Salon.

However, for a cultured middle-class woman to paint and draw simply as a congenial pastime had long been considered acceptable in polite society since it could be combined with her real purpose in life, which was to marry and produce children. The most favoured subjects were flowers and landscapes. At the same time, a wide range of artists' materials were now available over the counter, and private drawing masters – many of them established artists who needed to supplement their incomes – were plentiful.

By the 1860s it was at last possible for a woman to study with one of the male artists who held classes exclusively for women. One such was the fashionable portrait painter Charles Chaplin. 'His was the only *atelier* at that time where all students were women,' declared Louise Jopling, an English artist who attended his classes in Paris in 1867, 'so that careful mothers could send their daughters there without any complications arising between the sexes.'[5] Chaplin also allowed one of his ex-students to provide a nude model, but only at seven o-clock in the morning.[6] (Joséphine later bought five of Chaplin's paintings, all of which are now in The Bowes Museum.) The Académie Julien was another school which offered classes for women and, according to the Russian artist Marie Bashkirtseff, nude male models were available to the students by 1877, but whether they were with or without drapery is unknown.[7]

Cushioned by her husband's wealth, Joséphine did not have to rely on public art classes but instead took private lessons from the well-known landscape painter Karl-Josef

39
Among the many obstacles facing women artists in the nineteenth century was their exclusion from male art classes. By the 1860s, however, Charles Chaplin, painter of this *Girl in a Pink Dress*, was offering classes exclusively for women.

40

Gustave Courbet's *View at Ornans* of 1864 catered to a more popular taste than the scenes of peasant life which earned him recognition as leader of the Realist School. Joséphine was a great admirer of his work and some of her paintings reflect his influence.

Kuwasseg. Her style owes much to his influence, and also to that of Gustave Courbet, for whose work she had the greatest admiration. Courbet's realistic treatment of rural subjects and scenes from everyday life placed him at odds with the two giants of the art world of the Second Empire: Ingres, the great painter of classical subjects, and his rival Eugène Delacroix, the major painter of the French Romantic movement.

Courbet's rural subject matter had emerged from the Barbizon School, a mid-nineteenth century group of landscape painters centred on the village of Barbizon in the Forest of Fontainebleau. The group were pioneers of painting *en plein air* – sketching out of doors directly from nature. Joséphine's paintings are not overtly Barbizon in style, but the majority of her oils were developed from sketches she made from nature.

In The Bowes Museum Archive there are some bills for the materials Joséphine ordered for a painting expedition she made to Fontainebleau in 1866. They show that she took with her '10 tubes couleur'. It had not been until the 1840s that the messy business of painting in oils was greatly facilitated by the introduction of metal tubes. Previously, dry pigment had been stored either in little glass jars or in strips of pig's bladder, tied up like miniature suet puddings. The bladder had to be pierced by a tack, then resealed after the paint had been squeezed out – a hazardous process for women already hampered by the voluminous skirts and furbelows of the fashion of the day. The tubes were not only much easier to use but safer to transport, enabling artists to take their equipment out of the studio.

In the same period, prepared canvases stretched to standard sizes became readily available; Joséphine's order included an assortment. She also took with her a parasol, which was 'essential for judging the correct overall tonality of a picture painted in full sunlight'.[8] Other pieces of equipment were a mahlstick with which to steady the hand holding the brush, and a walnut box for the paints. The bills also included charges for a porter to transport the easel and a carriage to convey the paintings, both proof that Joséphine's sketching expeditions were carried out in a very different style to that of the many artists who were obliged to make their forays into the countryside either on foot or on horseback.

In 1849 the English firm of Winsor & Newton was advertising a combined sketching seat and easel, described in their catalogue as 'a new and very clever arrangement and the most convenient and pleasant apparatus ever introduced for the use of the lady sketcher.'[9] Whether Joséphine availed herself of such a piece of equipment is unknown, but she must have sat on something.

One disadvantage of painting *en plein air* was the unwanted advice proffered by passers-by. Charles-François Daubigny, a leading member of the Barbizon group, recorded the remarks of an officious bystander: 'All the time I was working he was asking "Why are you using yellow? Ah! Now there's a lovely blue! You should use violet for the background! With talent like that one need never be alone, etc."'[10]

There were other difficulties peculiar to women with sketching in the open. Berthe Morisot had to abandon a painting expedition she made with her husband to the Isle of Wight, explaining to her sister: 'I found the wind was frightful, my hat blew off, my hair got in my eyes. Eugène was in a bad mood as he always is when my hair is in disorder...'[11] Women, if alone, were also vulnerable to approaches from men. The animal painter Rosa Bonheur solved the problem by obtaining permission from the Paris police to wear men's clothes when she was working in a public place.

Joséphine was seldom alone as John Bowes always accompanied her on her painting excursions unless he had to return to England on business or to attend race meetings. In the summer of 1865 the couple spent two months at Cernay-la-Ville, a secluded village 'principally frequented by Landscape Painters',[12] on the edge of the Forest of Rambouillet, some thirty miles west of Paris. They took long walks together, which were good for Joséphine's health, but Bowes had to amuse himself somehow while she painted. When Joséphine became ill at Cernay, he complained to Ralph Dent that it was 'a great bore to

41
French caricature illustrating the rivalry between the two colossi of art, Ingres and Delacroix. Here Delacroix, armed with a paint brush, jousts with Ingres, armed with a pencil. Behind them is the French Academy.

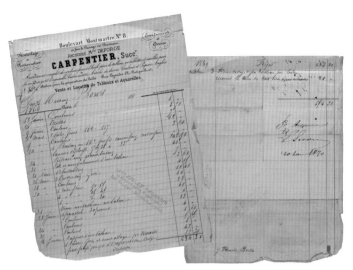

42
The art dealer Carpentier,
conveniently situated opposite
the Théâtre des Variétés, also
supplied artists' materials.
This invoice for 1869,
addressed to Mme Bowes,
includes paints, canvases,
brushes and a parasol to
protect Joséphine from the
sun while painting *en plein air*.

be laid up in a lodging in such a place',[13] which is perhaps why they later bought a small house in the village which Joséphine continued to use regularly for several years. One of the paintings she produced at Cernay, *Landscape with Trees and Cattle*, was her first to be accepted by the Paris Salon – the public display of new works of art held annually in the Louvre – in 1867. The same painting was exhibited the following year in London at the Royal Academy.

Another area much favoured by artists was the coast of Normandy. By the 1860s the fishing villages of Trouville and Deauville had become fashionable destinations for wealthy French tourists. Trouville alone attracted an annual influx of some 20,000 visitors, including the august personage of Empress Eugénie herself.[14] Boudin's poetic seascapes, with their luminous skies and distant figures promenading along the shoreline, are among the most memorable images of the region (the Boweses bought four of his works).

It was, however, the bleaker coastline around Calais and Boulogne which became the principal inspiration for several of Joséphine's paintings. This was not so much out of choice as because she was so afraid of the sea that she refused to cross the Channel until she considered it calm enough to risk boarding one of the packet boats bound for England. As a result she spent days, sometimes weeks, sketching stormy skies, fishermen's huts, and the sea in its various moods. One of her most advanced works, *Squally Weather: A Sketch near Boulogne*, was shown at the Salon of 1870.

For any budding artist, acceptance at the Salon (its official name was The Exhibition of Living Artists) marked a turning point in his or her career. 'It was both the exhibition place and the market place for modern art, especially for art that might appeal to the general public.'[15] Its importance can be measured by the number of artists exhibiting, which rose from 258 in 1801 to 3,190 in 1880.[16] During this period the Salon's location had changed several times, finally settling in the Palais de l'Industrie in the Champs Elysées following the International Exhibition of 1855.

43
By the 1860s the Normandy coast had become a fashionable destination for wealthy French tourists. Eugène Boudin's *Beach Scene at Low Tide* portrays this new trend while capturing the shifting light and scudding clouds.

The 'artistic excitement' during the days appointed for artists to deliver their work to the Salon jury was described by the American artist May Alcott Nieriker (immortalized as Amy in the novel *Little Women* by her sister Louisa May Alcott). 'Then pictures literally darken the air, borne on men's shoulders and backs, packed in immense vans, or under an arm of the painter himself, all going to the same destination...'[17] Large pictures trundled by in wheelbarrows or handcarts; marble statues and large bronzes teetered on trolleys. For days the streets surrounding the Palais were impassable and the local wine shops seethed with bearded, pipe-smoking artists.[18]

Having delivered his work to the Salon, the artist then had an agonising wait to see if his picture had been accepted and, if so, where it had been placed. This was vital as they were hung so thickly on the walls, and some of them at such a height, that an artist could wander for ages through the galleries trying to locate his precious exhibit. 'Corot, who had been hung in the worst positions for fifteen years, used to say: "Alas I am in the dungeons again this year."'[19]

The day before the official opening of the Salon was known as 'varnishing day: for the artists to have added a last coat of varnish to their paintings *before* they were hung would be to risk a possibly still-tacky surface becoming covered in the dust stirred up by the frenzied activities of the hanging committee.

In 1863, when over half the pictures submitted to the Salon were rejected, there was such an outcry that the Emperor (whose taste was known to be for pretty girls rather than pictures) intervened and ordered an exhibition of rejected pictures, called the *Salon des Refusés*. When the influential critic Théophile Thoré reviewed the exhibition he declared that it was as if the French school was reinventing itself.[20] While it attracted great attention and included artists such as Whistler and Manet – whose painting *Déjeuner sur l'Herbe* (originally exhibited under the title *le bain*) caused a furore – this experiment ended the following year, to be repeated again in 1873.

The annual Salon was hugely popular with Parisians. 'They come as they would to a pantomime or a circus,' wrote the historian and critic, Hippolyte Taine. 'They want melodrama or military scenes, undressed women and *trompe d'oeil;* and they get it: battles and *auto-da-fé*, scenes of slaughter in Roman arenas, Andromeda on the rocks, stories about Napoléon and about the Republic, illusionistic jugs and dishes.'[21] They came from all walks of life and all classes of society. Claude, the central character in Zola's *The Masterpiece*, was astonished by 'the truly staggering figure of 50,000 visitors on some fine Sundays. There was a whole army of them, the rearguard of the lower classes, ignorantly following their betters and filing wide-eyed through this great picture shop.'[22]

There is no evidence that Joséphine either sold or wished to sell her paintings in the 'great picture shop'. She wanted public recognition, not money. In the view of the *Revue Critique* – to which she subscribed – Joséphine deserved it. 'Among our most talented landscape painters she has gained a position of great distinction. Her works shine with a vivid awareness of the beauties of nature. She combines taste and skill with liveliness and inspiration.'[23] However, for the majority of exhibitors, selling their work was essential, and for this they had to rely on attracting attention from art critics and dealers.

The widespread interest in the Salon ensured that few newspapers and journals could afford to ignore it, some even devoting several pages to the exhibition. The opinions of certain critics carried great weight and could make or break an artist's reputation. The novelist and critic Edmund About, Joséphine's favourite author, once declared the painter Henri Fantin-Latour to be a 'true artist', and it would appear that this comment prompted Joséphine to buy one of his still-life paintings soon afterwards.[24] The painter Pierre Auguste Renoir was in no doubt about the influence of the Salon on prospective buyers. 'There are in Paris, at most, fifteen art lovers capable of appreciating a painter outside the Salon,' he told the dealer Durand-Ruel in 1881. 'There are 80,000 who would not buy so much as a nose if a painter is not [exhibited] in the Salon.'[25]

44
This engraving shows crowds thronging the painting and sculpture galleries in the Palais de l'Industrie in the Champs Elysées, the location for the 1857 Paris Salon. Exhibition at the Salon could make the difference between success and failure for an artist.

Exposition de peinture et de sculpture de 1857. — Le salon principal dans la galerie du palais de l'Industrie

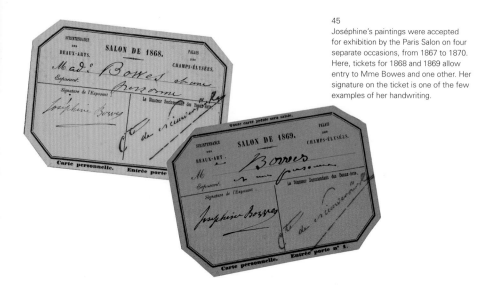

45
Joséphine's paintings were accepted for exhibition by the Paris Salon on four separate occasions, from 1867 to 1870. Here, tickets for 1868 and 1869 allow entry to Mme Bowes and one other. Her signature on the ticket is one of the few examples of her handwriting.

Another route to success for an artist was to be taken up by one of the rapidly growing number of picture dealers operating in Paris at that time. Many of them had begun trading not as dealers but as proprietors of shops selling artists' materials. They became acquainted with the artists and introduced their work to collectors. By 1845 it was estimated that there were a hundred art dealers in Paris.[26] Several of them, including the famous Durand-Ruel, had shops in the rue Lafitte, described by the critic Théophile Gautier in 1858 as 'sort of permanent Salon, an exhibition of paintings which lasts the whole year through'.[27]

Joséphine Bowes was to rely heavily on the advice of several dealers when she began to buy paintings for The Bowes Museum. They sold everything from watercolours to engravings, and from small landscapes to scenes of everyday life – in short, pictures which people could hang in their homes. The buyers of these small-scale pictures tended to be from the bourgeoisie, grown increasingly prosperous under the Second Empire. The days of the great collectors had passed, together with the grand classical paintings depicting historical, biblical or mythological events – painted by artists such as Jacques-Louis David and his pupil Ingres – which had dominated the art world for so long. 'Will they never understand', wrote Balzac in his novel *Les Paysans*, 'that great art is impossible without large fortunes, without large and secure private means.'[28]

As a painter, Joséphine may have been regarded a trifle warily by her fellow artists: not only was she an amateur – and a female amateur at that – but her husband's wealth ensured that painting for her could be a pleasant pastime whereas for them it was both a profession and a means to survival. And yet the fact that no fewer than four of her paintings were accepted by the Salon (from 1867 to 1870) must have commanded their respect. When she began to buy paintings by her Salon contemporaries for the Museum, she became not just a fellow artist but a potential patron – a subtle alteration to the way in which she was perceived.

46
In his *Varnishing Day at the Royal Academy*, George du Maurier takes a humorous view of the confusion caused by artists frantically varnishing or touching up their pictures immediately before the opening of an exhibition. The Carpentier invoice (p.63) shows that in 1869 they varnished Joséphine's painting for the Salon.

Joséphine was a talented and dedicated painter, but with her many social commitments and the constant pressure of building up the collection for the Museum – which she and John began in earnest in the early 1860s – there can have been little time for her to paint. One method of surmounting this problem was to do so whenever she and John Bowes went on holiday or on collecting trips. Hence there are 'souvenirs' of Hungary, the South of France, Savoy, Switzerland and the Black Forest, as well as numerous seascapes and views painted around Calais and Boulogne.

She also painted at Streatlam when she and John returned to England for their annual summer holiday. In 1865 Bowes instructed Ralph Dent to organise a room in the house – he identified the room exactly – as a studio for her. 'As Mrs. Bowes is rendered nervous by the least thing – the noise of Rats & Mice annoy her exceedingly' – he wanted the skirting board and cornice removed to 'prevent the possibility of Rats & Mice getting in there', the windows made to close properly to avoid draughts, and the top of the sash window to be a single sheet of glass to improve the light.[29]

The Bowes Museum possesses over sixty of Joséphine's paintings. The majority are small landscapes, with an occasional figure in the distance. Some of her early forest scenes – such as *Study of Birch Trees* – are reminiscent of a stage set for a romantic ballet like *Giselle*, and were no doubt influenced by her years as an actress at the Variétés. But her trees are clearly recognisable species and her clouds well observed. (In view of her love of animals, it is surprising that she appears rarely to have painted them.) In what are thought to be her earliest works she adhered to correct Academic technique and looked to the works of artists such as Claude Lorrain and Jean Honoré Fragonard but by 1865 her work had begun to show the influence of contemporary artists; her style had become freer and was based on observation of nature and colour.[30]

Between about 1865 and 1867 Joséphine painted a group of small pictures which are very extraordinary for their date. The paint is very thick in places, spread on with a palette knife – a favourite tool of Courbet's – and sometimes pared back again to show the weave of the canvas, then over-painted once more. In another mode, her *Study of Poplars*, which was probably painted at this time, shows areas of single colour placed side by side without gradation of tone, rather in the manner of pre-Impressionist painting. The lessons learned from these experiments were modified and used in later paintings.[31]

Joséphine's still-life paintings are thought to date from the last years of her life. By then her health was failing and travelling, even into the countryside, had become too much of an effort. Yet she continued until the end of her life 'to develop her technical skills, scale and colour harmonies, in response to the avant-garde of the 1850s and 60s.'[32]

# CHAPTER 5

❧

# Assembling the Collection

John Bowes always maintained that it was Joséphine who first conceived the idea of founding a museum. Such a massive project perhaps went some way towards filling the void caused by their lack of children, and also capitalised on Joséphine's passion for collecting things.

For one person to entertain the idea of not only building a museum but also assembling its contents is in itself astonishing. 'Relatively few public museums existed in Europe at that time, and most were funded by national governments bent on schemes of national or social improvement.'[1] Even the South Kensington Museum (which was later rebuilt and renamed the Victoria and Albert Museum) was not opened until 1857, its genesis a direct result of the Great Exhibition of 1851 which had initiated a movement in England to establish museums by which 'all classes might be induced to investigate those common principles of taste, which may be traced to the work of all ages'.[2] This idealistic approach would have appealed to John Bowes as it echoed his own view that a museum should be both popular and educational.

In the catalogue for the exhibition *In Celebration: The Art of the Country House* (held at the Tate Gallery in 1998), Giles Waterfield – joint curator of the exhibition – suggests another motive for the creation of The Bowes Museum:

> As museums and galleries were established in Britain during the nineteenth century, the landed classes distinguished themselves by founding almost no institutions themselves. Only aristocrats of illegitimate birth – such as Sir Richard Wallace of the Wallace Collection, or John Bowes of The Bowes Museum – appeared interested in commemorating themselves by establishing galleries.[3]

While the illegitimacy of Wallace and John Bowes may be a plausible motive, the process towards the creation of their two 'galleries' followed very different paths. The founders of the Wallace Collection (principally, the 3rd and 4th Marquesses of Hertford) 'were pleasure-seeking voluptuaries surrounding themselves with beautiful objects'.[4] Their combined collections, with additional works gathered by Richard Wallace (the illegitimate son of the 4th Marquess), were donated to the nation after Wallace's death and housed in the family's main London residence, Hertford House in Manchester Square, London. The Bowes Museum, on the other hand, consisted almost entirely of works purchased over a period of twelve years by John and Joséphine Bowes as museum exhibits to be housed in a building created for that purpose. Nor should it be forgotten that the Museum was allegedly Joséphine's idea, not John's.

Long before he met Joséphine, John Bowes had proved himself a collector in his own right. In this he was not unusual; acquiring works of art had become a conventional practice from the eighteenth century onwards, when rich young men were sent abroad on a Grand Tour to broaden their minds and steep themselves in the art and culture of Europe. The walls of England's great country houses are adorned with mementos of their travels: a romantic landscape by Poussin, a classical ruin by Piranesi or a portrait of the young tourist painted by the fashionable Roman artist Pompeo Battoni: 'The Grand Tour transformed English taste in art and enriched the nation's artistic wealth.'[5]

49
The Bowes Museum's tapestry collection is one of the largest in Britain. This superb sixteenth-century Flemish example depicts *The Birth of Samson*. Most of the figures are more than life size.

50
John Bowes bought
his first painting at the
age of nineteen, thus
long before he met
Joséphine. His taste
was for Mannerist
and fifteenth-century
works – like this panel
by Sassetta, *A Miracle
of the Eucharist.*

John's urge to collect may also have been influenced by his great-grandmother Mary, the second wife of George Bowes, who began to acquire Old Master paintings soon after her marriage in 1743. Among other works, she purchased one attributed to Rubens.[6] John would have known the painting well as it was at Gibside until 1873 when it was moved, probably by Bowes himself, to Streatlam.

It was works by Rubens that caught his eye when in 1830, at the age of nineteen, he himself made a brief 'Grand Tour' of the Continent, noting in his pocket book that he had seen some 'fine sacred pictures' by Rubens in the museum at Antwerp and others in a sale at Aix-la-Chapelle. Rubens, however, was already far beyond the means of all but the fabulously rich: in 1856 the 4th Marquess of Hertford bought Rubens's *The Rainbow Landscape* – outbidding the National Gallery – for the considerable sum of 4,550 guineas (over £200,000 today).

According to a list in Bowes's own hand, which included the purchase prices, he had acquired fifty-seven pictures before the end of 1844. His choice demonstrates the then popular taste for Italian High Renaissance or Dutch seventeenth-century works, but it also reveals a marked interest in fifteenth-century art.[7]

His first painting, bought in 1830, was *The Temptation of St Anthony*, then ascribed to Teniers the Elder but now attributed to Cornelis Saftleven. *A Boar Hunt* by Frans Snyders cost him £60 (roughly £2,400 today). A fine Solario of *St Jerome in the Wilderness*, which shows the artist's debt to his master, Leonardo da Vinci, was bought from the dealer Samuel Woodburn in 1841 for just under £10. In the same year a gentle *Nativity* by Jacques Stella, a close friend of Poussin, cost Bowes just over £2. The huge *Crucifixion* by the Master of the Virgo inter Virgines, purchased in 1840 for a mere £38, is the largest known work by this artist, famous for his powers of expressing grief.[8] *The Rape of Helen* from the circle of Primaticcio is one of the most important works from the School of Fontainebleau in Britain today. This painting was one of at least nine that Bowes bought through the distinguished collector and connoisseur Edward Solly. Solly had built up a spectacular private collection of fourteenth- and fifteenth-century Italian and Flemish paintings which was eventually purchased by the Berlin Royal Gallery.

A 'Fra Angelico', which Bowes bought from the Duke of Lucca's sale at Christie's in 1840, has since been identified as *A Miracle of the Eucharist*, part of the predella panel from the altarpiece painted by Sassetta for the chapel of the Arte della Lana (the Wool Merchants' Guild) in Siena around 1425. The painting shows a doubter of the True Presence of the Body of Christ struck dead as he is about to receive communion. A little black devil is depicted snatching the soul of the stricken figure. It has been suggested that the figure may be the English reformer John Wycliffe: Wycliffe had doubted the validity of the mass and was taken ill in a church and died. He is thought to have come from the tiny village of Wycliffe, which is situated only three miles from Barnard Castle.[9]

Although Bowes may have failed to buy many High Renaissance paintings he did purchase fifteenth-century and Mannerist works. 'At that time neither artistic period was given separate status and fifteenth-century works were dismissed as primitive. Bowes collected sufficient to be considered an early enthusiast.'[10] At that stage, of course, he was buying not for a museum but to enhance the family collections at Streatlam and Gibside.

When Bowes purchased the Château du Barry in 1852, he and Joséphine furnished it in the lavish style of the French nineteenth century, buying the majority of pieces from Monbro *fils aîné*. Again, these purchases were made for their own private use. But in 1859, at an auction of the stock of Monbro, they bought a large carved and painted fifteenth-century Flemish altarpiece by the Master of Ste-Gudule. It seems improbable that a work of this kind was intended for either the Château or the house in Paris, so its acquisition may be the first sign that they had begun to buy for a museum.

51
John Bowes bought *The Rape of Helen* in 1841 from Edward Solly, a notable collector, who believed it to be by Francesco Primaticcio. It has since been reattributed to the circle of Primaticcio.

Further signs came in 1861 when they purchased a number of portraits and landscapes, which included *Cybele Beseeching Saturn to Spare her Child* by the Circle of Jan Gossaert (called Mabuse) and *Victory of the Risen Christ* by Jacob de Backer. They bought most of these works from an art dealer, Benjamin Gogué, who put them into store in his atelier in the rue du Cherche-Midi. When the Château du Barry was sold in 1862, the furniture and decorative objects that were not required for rue de Berlin were stored at Streatlam. In these two storehouses the Boweses now had a worthy nucleus for their museum.

Benjamin Gogué was to play an important role in the lives of John and Joséphine Bowes. He was an astute judge of paintings, especially of Old Masters, and he had some valuable contacts in the art world. It was Gogué who was to negotiate the purchase of more than seventy Spanish paintings from the collection of the Conde de Quinto, an acquisition which ensured that The Bowes Museum now owns the most important collection of Spanish paintings in Britain outside London and Glasgow.

John and Joséphine's interest in Spanish art was probably aroused by the appearance in France of Spanish paintings confiscated by Napoléon and his brother Joseph (King of Spain from 1808 to 1813), during the Peninsular Wars. Most of the paintings were returned to Spain at the end of the Napoléonic Wars in 1815, but other works looted by Napoléon's generals, especially by Marshal Soult, remained in France.

Interest in Spanish art received fresh impetus when the Spanish Gallery of Louis-Philippe was opened in the Louvre in 1838. The French king had purchased some five hundred paintings when the Spanish government's nationalisation of provincial monasteries and convents in 1835 released a flood of works onto the market. The Gallery received a further bonus in 1851 in the form of a private collection of Spanish paintings bequeathed to Louis-Philippe by an Englishman, Frank Hall Standish, as a token of his 'great esteem for a generous and polite nation'.[11] It seems likely that John Bowes was aware that Standish had been born within seventeen miles of Barnard Castle and had inherited a fortune and estates, but not the baronetcy – an early history very similar to his own. The Louvre's collection of Spanish paintings, which included works by El Greco and Goya, was to have a great influence on the young Edouard Manet.

Some of the paintings released in Spain in 1835 were used to furnish newly-created museums. One such was the Museo de la Trinidad in Madrid (later integrated into the Prado). Its director from 1847 was the Conde de Quinto, a colourful character who amassed a substantial private collection of paintings before voluntarily following Queen Maria Christina into exile in France – allegedly dressed as a woman and carrying a doll. The Conde settled in Paris, where he died in 1860. The Conde's widow was a client of Gogué and instructed him to sell the entire collection as soon as possible as she was in great need of money.

Gogué prepared a catalogue of the collection, a difficult task given the condition of some of the paintings. He was instructed by the Condesa to offer some to private buyers before the collection went on sale at public auction. In the spring of 1862 negotiations began between the Condesa and John Bowes, with Gogué acting as agent for both sides. In June, Gogué sent Bowes a proof of the catalogue. 'We have a lead over the others,' he told him. 'You can have what you like... only Mme la Cse de Q wants you not to delay in replying.'[12]

Gogué's letters to Bowes during the negotiations were gathered together by Elizabeth Conran for the second edition of Eric Young's *Catalogue of Spanish Paintings in the Bowes Museum*. In a prefix she noted that: 'Gogué wrote at great speed. His handwriting is difficult, his punctuation minimal, his construction colloquial and his spelling terrible.'[13] She is correct on all counts!

By early July Bowes had bought twenty-four pictures, including a Murillo (which was later attributed to the Circle of Zurbarán) and Antonio de Pereda's *Tobias Restoring His Father's Sight*. Gogué reminded Bowes that while the Condesa had authorised him to give Bowes first choice, he had already received offers from other collectors. He went on to recommend certain artists, including Goya and El Greco. 'I have sold several pictures by these two masters. Although these two do not appeal to you as masters, I think you might well take one of each of them for your collection...'[14] On 10 July he returned to the subject: 'As for the Greco and the Goya, I would be happy for you to see them yourself.'[15]

By the end of July the Boweses had bought several more paintings. 'This time the Condesa has done very well,' Gogué told Bowes. 'I shall remind her of this every time the opportunity arises and for those pictures at a higher price, we will have substantial reductions...'[16]

52
On advice from their principal dealer, Benjamin Gogué, in 1862 the Boweses bought more than seventy paintings by Spanish artists from the Conde de Quinto's collection. One of their most important purchases was *The Tears of St Peter* by El Greco.

While the Boweses were in England for their annual holiday at Streatlam, Gogué continued negotiations. In early September he gave Bowes a resumé of the situation, including a description of the improvement to one of the paintings he had been restoring. He ended his letter with an interesting observation: 'Forgive me for writing at such length – it is because I look on your pictures as your children and because I am convinced that you like people to talk to you about them.'[17]

By October, with the Boweses still in England, the Condesa was becoming impatient. Gogué informed Bowes that she had implored him to 'see your art lovers, complete the sale, make some money'.[18] During some tough bargaining, Gogué undertook to buy several more paintings at the Condesa's price on condition that she throw in a few extra ones. She expostulated but eventually agreed. One of the make-weight pictures was the *Tears of St Peter* by El Greco. However, when the Boweses returned to Paris in mid November, they insisted on substituting two different paintings for two of the make-weights – one of which was the El Greco!

Their reluctance to buy the El Greco may seem strange today, but in 1862 the artist had fallen out of favour and was not being collected. Nor can the Boweses have been encouraged by Gogué's comment that the *St Peter* had 'all the qualities, all the faults of this master'.[19]

53
Francisco Goya's haunting *Interior of a Prison* is one of the treasures bought by the Boweses from the Conde de Quinto's collection. Its message – man's inhumanity to man – was a theme to which the artist repeatedly returned.

54
The beckoning finger of the archangel Raphael invites the viewer to witness *Tobias Restoring His Father's Sight*, painted by Antonio de Pereda in 1652. This is one of over seventy paintings bought by the Boweses from the Conde de Quinto's widow.

But the Boweses were to be given a second chance; it seems that when the remainder of the de Quinto collection was auctioned Gogué bought some of the paintings for his own stock, one of them the El Greco. On a list of purchases made by John Bowes in April 1869 appears this item: 'St Peter by El Greco with oak leaf frame 200 [francs]' (£8, or £350 today). Gogué finally had his way.

Fortunately for the Museum, Gogué also overcame the Boweses' lack of interest in Goya, persuading them to buy from the Condesa two fine paintings by the artist, the moving *Interior of a Prison* and an intimate portrait of *Don Juan Antonio Meléndez Valdés*. When The Bowes Museum opened to the public in 1892, even the National Gallery in London owned nothing by Goya.

By the end of 1862 the Boweses had collected nearly two hundred paintings. The problem of where to store them was solved by Gogué agreeing to a proposal by John Bowes that he should act as curator of a gallery which was to be built on land purchased by Bowes in the rue Blomet. Monsieur Auguste Pellechet, the architect who had supervised the alterations at the Château and at rue de Berlin, designed the building which was to include a flat for Gogué and a workshop in which he could clean and restore the pictures. When the gallery was almost completed, responsibility for it was taken over by Pellechet's son, Jules, who was later one of the joint architects of The Bowes Museum. The Temporary Gallery, as it was always called by Bowes, was an ideal half-way house for the collection before it was moved to England.

There has been much speculation as to why the Boweses chose to build their museum on the outskirts of a small market town in a relatively unknown and sparsely-inhabited corner of northern England. Despite the ever-increasing scope of the railway network, even by the late 1870s – when the Boweses must surely have hoped their museum would be completed – Barnard Castle remained a complicated and time-consuming destination for all but the most ardent museum visitor. The notion that the Boweses had considered building it at Calais but rejected the idea on the grounds that France was so politically unstable, is unsupported by any written evidence (though it was France's political instability that persuaded Richard Wallace to bring his family's collection to England). To build it at Barnard Castle, however, would satisfy John's wish to bring a new dimension into the lives of the people of his native County Durham, a wish that was obviously fully supported by Joséphine.

As further proof of their intentions, in 1864 Bowes instructed John Dickonson Holmes, his Barnard Castle solicitor, to take steps towards the purchase of some fields occupying most of the area which now forms The Bowes Museum park. It appears that he wished to keep his identity as purchaser a secret and was content to let the rumour that 'the place is intended for a Lunatic Asylum' go undisputed.[20]

From 1862 onwards, buying for the Museum continued at a prodigious rate: some fifteen thousand objects were bought by the Boweses in twelve years. The scope of objects was vast – paintings, sculpture, miniatures, prints, ceramics, glass, metalwork, furniture, clocks and watches, automata, *objets d'art*, tapestries, embroideries, antiquities, geological specimens, architectural woodwork, books and manuscripts.[21] They had originally contemplated world coverage, but eventually reduced their scope to Europe, and every country forming Europe in 1870 is represented in the collections.

Some of the acquisitions must have exasperated successive curators of the Museum, who could be forgiven for wondering what on earth they were to do with them. But the most unlikely objects, if imaginatively treated, can come triumphantly into their own. In an exhibition of lace held at the Museum in 2006, a gilt metal key escutcheon and an iron door-plate were employed to great effect to illustrate the similarity between the patterns used in lace and those used in metal.

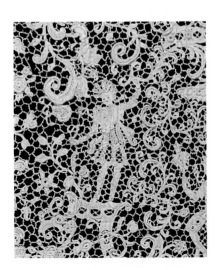

55, 56

The figure at the centre of this late seventeenth-century French doorplate (left) is echoed by the figure in the panel of needle lace (right) made in France in the 1690s.

Buying in bulk, and out of private income, the Boweses could not afford anything expensive. They subscribed to the *Moniteur des Ventes*, which gave information about forthcoming sales, but it would have been impossible to attend them all as many took place outside Paris. Instead, they relied on a small number of dealers who continually deluged them with offers of objects they had purchased with the Boweses in mind. Apart from Gogué, the two main Parisian dealers were A. C. Lamer and Madame Lepautre, and it was 'to a large extent these two who gave The Bowes Museum's collections their distinctive character.'[22]

Lamer's notes, many of them written on flimsy cobalt-blue paper, were frequently dashed off immediately on his return to Paris from a country sale. 'Have just come back from famous sale of Marquis de Villette... magnificent things,' he wrote to Joséphine. He then lists a variety of objects, all of which he assures Madame were 'fiercely fought over at the sale'. The variety of items he offered them over the years is astonishing, ranging from 'a sugar bowl in Marcolini Meissen' to a faïence frog, and from a silver reliquary said to have belonged to Marie-Antoinette to a waffle iron. If the Boweses were in Paris, he would carry his purchases to them at rue de Berlin; if they were out of town, he would visit them wherever they happened to be, 'at Chevreuse or Cernay or even at Rambouillet'.[23]

Lamer's eagerness to please is hardly surprising; although the Boweses were not expending vast sums on any one object, their field of interest was so wide and they bought so much and paid so promptly that they must have been dream clients for any dealer. When Joséphine rejected a little Sèvres cup on the grounds that it was not enamel – as Lamer had assured her – he hastened to exculpate himself. Explaining that he had bought it on the understanding that it *was* enamel from 'a greater connoisseur than myself', he added, 'I can assure you that I had no intention of fooling you. I would never sell one thing as another, still less to you who are so good to me and support me in my small business.'[24] All the bills from Lamer are marked '*payé par papa*' in Joséphine's handwriting ('papa' was her pet name for her husband).

Madame Lepautre was less of an expert than Lamer and her notes are short on detail. Her specialities were porcelain, small paintings and lace, although she once offered Joséphine an iron man-trap. The collection of lace in the Museum was purchased almost exclusively from her.[25]

Every object the dealers submitted was scrutinised by the Boweses before being accepted for the collection. They were often willing to buy against their own personal taste on the dealers' advice, although Joséphine was not always seduced by Lamer's sales talk. She did not, for instance, buy 'a precious fragment' of Voltaire's book on Pope Ganganelli, but wisely did buy a painting by Monticelli. 'Mark my words, Madame,' Lamer wrote, 'the artist is a lad with a great future.'[26] Sometimes she haggled to get the price of an article reduced by a franc or two, but despite her efforts the cost of purchases made from Lamer and Lepautre in the 1860s 'exceeded £3,000' (nearly £130,000 today).[27]

In 1868 the Boweses discovered another art dealer, Rogiers of Ghent, during an extensive ten-week buying trip they made through Germany, Austria, Hungary and Poland, finally arriving in Belgium in late autumn. Rogiers became an important supplier of pictures, tapestries and other works of art. In 1869 he wrote at least twelve letters to the

57

Joséphine collected numerous examples of French faïence (tin-glazed earthenware), an art little appreciated at that time. This charming plate from Nevers, dated 1757, shows a game of Royal tennis in progress.

Boweses offering them a wide selection of items. The following year one consignment he dispatched to Paris contained no fewer than forty-three pictures for their inspection. They bought tapestries from him literally by the metre, regardless of quality or subject matter. Unlike their other purchases, they appear to have bought the majority unseen, disregarding condition in favour of a good price: 'I have been offered', Rogiers wrote in October 1869, 'a tapestry of three square metres in the same state as the one from Bruges but without holes, and dirtier.'[28]

The Bowes Museum's tapestry collection is today one of the largest in Britain. Every well-known centre of manufacture is represented, from early sixteenth-century Flemish and German to seventeenth- and eighteenth-century English, Flemish and French. Important pieces are a fragment from the *Triumph of Time* series woven in Brussels in about 1507 for Philip of Cleves, and two Alsatian panels after Dürer's woodcuts of the *Life of the Virgin*. A magnificent mid-seventeenth century tapestry depicting *Apollo and the Muses*, attributed to the Paris workshop of Raphael de la Planche, was woven for the Grimaldi family of Monaco.[29]

Many of the numerous smaller pieces of tapestry, and an even larger collection of needlework seat covers, form a unique collection of French upholstery textiles of the seventeenth and eighteenth centuries.[30] Joséphine collected almost seven hundred examples, of which more than four hundred remain in the Museum. It is the most important study collection of its kind in Britain. A fine example is a chair seat probably from Beauvais, the first of France's three centres of tapestry weaving to specialise in seat covers. The striking design of peonies would have been vibrant with colour when it was woven in the early eighteenth century.

58
An elaborate Meissen tureen, part of a dinner service made c. 1750 for Count Brühl, director of the porcelain factory near Dresden in Germany. It is moulded with beautiful sprays of flowers and foliage.

Before the mid-nineteenth century, the collection of ceramics was a highly specialised field, limited to a few ardent devotees like the Prince Regent. There were no reference books to guide the unwary until Marryat's *History of Pottery and Porcelain* was published in 1850. One of the first handbooks of ceramic marks, William Chaffers' *Marks and Monograms on Pottery & Porcelain*, did not appear until 1866. In 1862, a '*Special Exhibition of Loans at the South Kensington Museum*' (later the V&A) was visited by nearly nine hundred thousand people in five months, surely an indication of a lively interest in ceramics among the general public.[31]

Although Joséphine was not one of the very first collectors of old ceramics, she did have an exceptionally good eye for quality, combined with a willingness to buy the products of factories which were then little appreciated; these may have had the added advantage in her eyes of being cheap.[32] Unlike many collectors, she did not buy large display pieces but concentrated instead on domestic wares – small-scale, good quality items – giving the collections a special feminine flavour which contrasts with many of the grander museums formed with Government money.

Joséphine was also well served by the two dealers Lamer and Lepautre, who kept up a steady stream of offers of items they thought might be of interest. Lamer's correspondence with Joséphine, held in The Bowes Museum Archive, testifies to the sheer number he offered for selection, while the bills show how many were purchased. Unfortunately, some of these bills give such vague descriptions of the items concerned that it is difficult to link them with the more detailed descriptions of the objects offered. The few that can be identified are usually those with some historical interest, such as two charming plates of 1757 from Nevers which show a game of Royal tennis in progress, bought from Lamer in 1873.

59
This rare teapot, made in 1758, was one of the many Sèvres pieces bought by Joséphine. It is decorated with peacock feathers on the newly created *rose* ground.

Joséphine was known for her fiery temper, and her relationship with Lamer suffered an occasional hiccup. In a letter of 1868 he begs Joséphine to buy from him again for she has 'too much humour and good sense to listen to calumnies... I repeat, I have never spoken of you or Monsieur without the greatest respect...'[33] He then offers Joséphine twelve items from the Carpentier sale, of which she bought three – so peace was clearly restored.

As a result of Joséphine's individual taste and determination, the Museum today owns one of the most comprehensive collections of ceramics in Britain. Examples come from more than a dozen European countries and often represent collecting fields largely unexplored at that date, such as French faïence and Paris porcelain – of which the Museum owns over fifteen hundred items, from all the major centres of production. There is a quantity of Sèvres porcelain, including such rare pieces as a teapot of 1758 decorated with peacock feathers. On their buying trip in 1868 the Boweses visited the porcelain factories at Meissen (near Dresden), Berlin and Nymphenburg (near Munich). From the Meissen factory they purchased a large statue of a monkey and a classical-style vase painted with a view of Dresden.

The Boweses also formed a major collection of pictures. Unable to afford works by famous masters, they bought paintings by artists yet to be recognised, or ones uncharacteristic of the artist, or in poor condition. Many such works have since become valuable and are a credit to their taste or to the prescience of their dealers. For instance, Benjamin Gogué sold them a mysterious *Landscape with Watermill* by the Court painter François Boucher, an artist whose landscapes were not being collected by museums at that date. Today, it is perhaps the finest landscape by Boucher in a British collection.

Boucher is just one of the artists represented in the largest collection of French paintings anywhere in Britain. There are several fine works by important eighteenth-century landscapists such as Vernet, Hubert Robert and Pierre-Henri de Valenciennes. The latter 'is regarded as the originator of key developments in eighteenth- and nineteenth-century French landscape painting... as he was seminal in making landscape accepted as a serious subject' by the French National Academy and the Salon.[34] He was also one of the first to depart from the traditional landscapes of artists like Claude and Poussin – which were composed and painted entirely in the studio – by sketching from nature, or en *plein air*. The Bowes Museum has five landscapes by Valenciennes, one of the largest holdings of the artist's work outside the Louvre.

Four of these landscapes were bought, through Lamer, from an auction in 1865 of the collection of the Vicomte de l'Espine. At the same auction, and again through Lamer, the Boweses bought a pair of paintings by Achille-Etna Michallon, predicted to have become a 'modern Poussin' had his career not been tragically cut short by his early death. Lamer also sold them a dramatic painting by Etienne-Jean Delécluze, *Augustus Rebuking Cinna*. These purchases from Lamer are all valuable examples of Neo-classical art of the early nineteenth century, of which The Bowes Museum has the finest collection in Britain.

The art of portraiture is well represented in the Museum by eighteenth-century masters such as Largillière, Girodet, Gros and Anne Vallayer-Coster (one of several successful women artists in France).

The French collection also includes nineteenth-century works by important artists like Courbet, Boudin, Fantin-Latour and Corot. As an artist herself, Joséphine favoured works by her Salon contemporaries, some of whom – like Baron Gudin and Charles Chaplin – were either friends or acquaintances. Henry James dismissed Chaplin as a painter of 'pink-fingered chiffonné young women... painted with distilled rose leaves and dewdrops',[35] but the artist's paintings of elegant women in an eighteenth-century style clearly appealed to the Boweses as they bought five of his works. Gudin was one of the most distinguished

60
François Boucher's
*Landscape with
Watermill* of 1743 was
bought by the Boweses
on the advice of their
dealer Benjamin Gogué.
A landscape was a rarity
for Boucher, who is
more often associated
with erotic mythological
subjects.

61

*The Harnessing of the Horses of the Sun* by Giovanni Battista Tiepolo is a sketch associated with the fresco he painted in 1731 in the Archinto Palace in Milan. The palace was subsequently destroyed during the Second World War.

seascape artists of his day and in 1865 the Boweses paid the huge sum – for them – of 15,000 francs (£600) for three of his paintings. One, *On the sands near Ostend*, was described by John as 'an atmospheric effect of which the Artist was proud. He presented this picture to Mrs Bowes.'[36] Joséphine's pathological fear of the sea may explain why all six of Gudin's paintings show that element at its most tranquil.

A surprising omission from a collection made by a passionate lover of animals is the work of the famous French artist Rosa Bonheur. But the animal paintings in The Bowes Museum demonstrate a preference for regal, pampered pets – a far cry from the muscular energy and realism of Bonheur's animal paintings.

The numerous portraits of leading French royalists and imperialists, and depictions of some of the tumultuous events which took place during their reigns, demonstrate the Boweses' fascination with the nation's history from 1790 to 1848. There are portraits of Napoléon Bonaparte and members of his family, of Charles X, and a series of paintings of scenes from the Revolution of 1848 by Nicolas Edward Gabé – an event that precipitated John and Joséphine's flight from Paris, to escape the worst of the riots.

The Italian paintings collected by the Boweses provide examples of many schools from the fifteenth to the nineteenth centuries. Some had been bought by John before he met Joséphine, but together they acquired an interesting group of works by seventeenth- and eighteenth-century Neapolitan artists, including a fine oil sketch by Luca Giordano, *The Triumph of Judith*, and two large, vivid paintings of St Peter and St Paul by Francesco Fracanzano. (The latter were sold to them by the dealer Basset, whose daughter was to become indispensable to John as curator of the collection after Joséphine's death.)

62
Joséphine died before the
Impressionists held their first group
exhibition, but her purchase of this
work by Monticelli, *Landscape with
Figures and Goats*, indicates that her
taste would have been sufficiently
avant-garde to appreciate them.

Another oil sketch, *The Harnessing of the Horses of the Sun* by the Venetian artist, Giovanni Battista Tiepolo, may have been a preliminary exploration for the ceiling of the Archinto Palace in Milan. The sketch is all the more important because the ceiling was destroyed in the Second World War.

Visitors to the Museum may wonder why Joséphine bought so many works by contemporary painters yet failed to buy any by the Impressionists. The principal reason for this omission is that she died in 1874, the year of the first Impressionist exhibition and the first time the artists involved became known as a group. Until that date no recognised dealers were promoting their work, nor did it feature regularly in the auctions where Joséphine made many of her purchases; buying pictures direct from the artists was the only way to acquire them.

She did, however, mark Manet's *Olympia* in the catalogue for the 1865 Salon exhibition – nine years before the Impressionist exhibition. Had she bought this highly controversial painting, it would have placed her at the forefront of collectors of her day. In the same year, she gave further evidence of her advanced taste by purchasing *Landscape with Figures and Goats* by Monticelli, who was later to influence both Van Gogh and Cézanne. Possible proof that she was still tempted to buy a work by Manet appears in a sale catalogue for 1868: instead of the usual cross alongside the lot number, which denoted special interest, she had written the price (70 francs) realised by his painting of *Les Fleurs*.

Even a year after Joséphine's death, when the enlightened dealer Durand Ruel organised the second Impressionist exhibition, its violent denunciation by the French press

63
Joséphine met the young French ceramicist, Emile Gallé, at the London International Exhibition of 1871 and immediately recognised the importance of his work. She bought a number of items from him, including this exquisite glass vase.

demonstrated how difficult it was for the artists to gain acceptance. 'It is a frightening spectacle', thundered Albert Wolff of *Le Figaro*, 'of human vanity gone astray to the point of madness.'[37] Henry James, though the author of some of the greatest Modernist novels and still a young man when he was in Paris in 1875, also utterly failed to see the point of this revolutionary style of painting. After visiting the exhibition, he pronounced that 'the effect of it was to make me think better than ever of all the good old rules which decree that beauty is beauty and ugliness ugliness', and that the Impressionists 'abjure virtue altogether, and declare that a subject which has been crudely chosen shall be loosely treated.'[38]

The majority of the furniture now in The Bowes Museum was bought by John and Joséphine from Monbro *fils aîné* for use in their own homes. Since the best examples from the French seventeenth and eighteenth centuries were already too expensive for them, they concentrated on collecting pieces which were 'new'– or relatively so – when they bought them. Though long disregarded by scholars, these pieces are now seen as forming a collection unique in England as an illustration of the opulent style of the Second Empire. Examples such as a pair of ebony cabinets and a piano-cum-harmonium, all bought from Monbro, demonstrate the Boweses' preference for rather showy *boulle* marquetry. Their bed, an elaborately carved and gilded affair, still retains its original curtains and canopy of silk brocade.

The International Exhibition in Paris in 1867 precipitated a frenzy of buying by the Boweses. In all they acquired some two hundred items, many of documentary rather than artistic worth. To judge from the detailed inventory made by John, they bought many of the items principally because they illustrated the daily life and arts and crafts of countries both within Europe and beyond, presumably with the intention of broadening the scope of the Museum. The range of objects is remarkable: a pair of socks from Persia, embroidered slippers from Tunisia, a sugar basin from Turkey, two wooden spoons from Roumania, a fan in the shape of a peacock from India. This frenzied buying is perhaps indicative of a concern that if they continued their hitherto steadier rate of acquisition they would never accumulate enough objects to fill the Museum. It should also be remembered that it *was* a museum the Boweses were creating, not a gallery full of beautiful objects.

The Boweses had also made a number of purchases from the International Exhibition in London in 1862, but on that occasion fewer items of better quality, including a mysterious little Worcester porcelain bust of a veiled woman entitled *The Bride*.

At the London Exhibition of 1871 Joséphine again made many purchases, but almost exclusively of pottery and porcelain. By then her taste had matured, and she bought objects which lack the 'curiosity' approach of many of the purchases she had made at the 1867 Exhibition,[39] including some examples of Salviati glass from Venice and a superb monumental vase from Berlin painted with the figures of Mercury and Hebe.

Her greatest coup, however, was her recognition of the potential of a young French ceramicist, Emile Gallé, who later became famous as the leading maker of Art Nouveau glass. They met at the exhibition and she commissioned a beautiful engraved glass 'cabaret' set from him, one of his first known commissions. Other purchases followed, including an exquisite fluted glass vase engraved with two amorous pigeons in a tree.

Gallé's letters to Joséphine, housed in The Bowes Museum Archive, trace the development of his relationship with her. Within months of the exhibition he was regretting his inability to accept an invitation to visit her at Streatlam, due to pressure of work. A week later he was agreeing with her that the roofs of the Museum 'would benefit from being raised' – evidence that she had such respect for his taste that she had shown him the Museum plans. In the same letter he reveals the main inspiration behind his designs, confiding that 'when I pick a flower, I pick a model and an idea. When I model a new project, I am really dreaming of some unknown flower.'[40] Much of Gallé's later production seems 'encapsulated in this statement, made nearly twenty years before he was creating vases of floral form in the style' of Art Nouveau.[41] In 1872 he presented Joséphine with a faïence jug for the Museum, a gift which confirmed his affection and regard for her.

In 1873 the Boweses bought the Museum's most famous exhibit: the Silver Swan. They almost certainly saw it first at the 1867 International Exhibition in Paris, where it had attracted great attention. Mark Twain gave a marvellous description of it in *The Innocents Abroad:*

> I watched the Silver Swan which had a living grace about his movements and a living intelligence in his eyes – watched him swimming about as comfortably and as unconcernedly as if he had been born in a morass instead of a jeweller's shop – watched him seize a silver fish from under the water and hold up his head and go through all the customary and elaborate motions of swallowing it – but the moment it disappeared down its throat some tattooed South Sea Islanders approached and I yielded to their attractions.[42]

Some of the details of the Swan's swim through history are still disputed – such as its alleged purchase at the Exhibition by either the King of Burma, or Napoléon III for the Prince Imperial, or that it spent a brief period in Spain. However, patient research has revealed that it was probably made by a Belgian, John Joseph Merlin, who styled himself as a 'mathematical instrument maker' and worked for the London jeweller and showman James Cox.[43]

The first written evidence of the Swan occurs in a parliamentary Act of 1773 enabling Cox to 'dispose of his Museum by way of Lottery'. At that date the Swan was surmounted by a 'costly dome of great magnitude, on the top of which is a rising sun, that terminates the whole, and makes it near fifteen feet high' – a truly wondrous sight. There is no record of who won the Swan in Cox's lottery, but in 1834 it appeared in a sale of 'the property of the late Mr Weeks'. Mr Weeks, who owned the Weeks Museum in London, appears to have obtained numerous items from Cox. Either Weeks's son bought the Swan at the sale or it failed to reach its reserve because it was listed as his property when in 1864 it was sold at Christie's for £155 to a certain 'H.E.' – who was almost certainly the London jeweller Harry Emanuel.

65
Made in London around 1773, this spectacular Silver Swan survived a series of vicissitudes, some of them still cloaked in mystery, before appearing at the Paris International Exhibition of 1867. The Boweses bought it in 1873. It has since become the Museum's most famous exhibit.

In 1871, when John Bowes heard from his Paris jeweller Briquet that the Swan was for sale, he asked for more information about its history. Emanuel's version, contained in a letter to Briquet, declared that it had been the subject of a lawsuit and had spent some one hundred years in the Bank of England. When it was finally released, Emanuel claimed that he had bought it for £600, although the evidence of the Christie's sale suggests that he had only paid £155. In 1867 he exhibited it at the Paris Exhibition at a price of 50,000 francs (about £2,000). Oddly enough, Briquet elected to sell the Swan to the Boweses for only 5,000 francs (£200) which according to Bowes was 'the lowest price it seems ever to have fetched.'[44] The fact that Briquet's receipt for the £200, dated March 1873, shows that he also sold Bowes a diamond ring for 20,000 francs on that date may explain why he let the Swan go for so little. The Silver Swan proved to be worth every penny the Boweses paid for it as it has since become the Museum's most famous and best-loved exhibit. In the year 2000 it was adopted as the Museum's logo.

Another delightful automaton in the Museum is a mechanical mouse, bought by Joséphine from a London dealer in 1871. Made of gold with garnet eyes and decorated with seed pearls, the mouse scurries along, stops, changes direction and scurries on again.

Joséphine's ability to transform herself from a clockmaker's daughter into an actress, then an artist, a society hostess and finally a major collector was extraordinary. The *Revue Critique*, although heavily prejudiced in favour of its subscribers, summed her up as follows: 'Mme Bowes has all the distinction and all the charm of a great lady; she has her superior tastes; she loves the arts and she encourages and supports artists. In a word, she is as benevolent as she is appreciative.'[45]

However, the French art critic and novelist Jules Champfleury may have had Joséphine in mind when he ridiculed a hypothetical amateur collector named Desirée Carton in his satirical book on collectors and collecting, *L'Hotel des Commissaires-Priseurs*, published in 1867. The Paris art world must have been aware by that date that the Boweses were buying works of art on a grand scale. It is also significant that Champfleury's lampoon is aimed at a woman – not a sex normally associated with collectors of art.

Champfleury, having discoursed on the passion of collectors for their own subject, and their need to 'possess', describes Desirée Carton (the name itself may be pejorative as it could be translated as 'likes to buy rubbish') as a lady:

> who knows very well that a fine piece of Moustiers with the arms of Mme de Pompadour is worth fifty louis. In order to gain admittance to Mlle Carton's house you must take a piece of Moustiers china; even those invited to her intimate Friday tea-parties must not arrive without some fancy object, even if it is only an egg-cup. In this way Desirée Carton is preparing a fine sale which, unlike the sales of diamonds by her chums at the theatre du Palais-Royal, will lead the public to think that she too has lofty artistic passions. If this fever continues, Paris will be nothing more than a vast bazaar of curiosities.'[46]

His reference to Mlle Carton's 'chums at the theatre' also seems too much of a coincidence... as is the presence in the Museum of a faïence plate adorned with the arms of Mme de Pompadour!

Another possible contender for the target of the lampoon could have been Nélie Jacquemart. Mlle Jacquemart was one of the most successful society portrait painters of the Second Empire. In 1881 she married the rich banker and collector Edouard André, and together they built up a magnificent collection of Italian Old Master paintings, sculpture and works of art. The collection was bequeathed to the Institut de France and now forms the Musée Jacquemart-André in Paris. However, the early date of Champfleury's book, 1867, makes her a less likely target.

While it was clearly Joséphine's taste that governed the selection of objects for the Museum – especially in the fields of ceramics and textiles – and it was she who had the most direct contact with the various dealers, The Bowes Museum would not exist were it not for John Bowes's money. Previous accounts of the founding of the Museum have maintained that Joséphine built up the collection with the proceeds of the sale of the Château du Barry – that it was therefore *her* money. But it was John who had bought the Château, giving it to Joséphine as a wedding present. Joséphine's family was not well off; when her father died in 1852, it was the Boweses who paid the funeral expenses – thanks to John's generosity and highly-developed sense of family duty.

Joséphine herself was perfectly aware of the source of her wealth: in her will, made in 1865, she first provided for her widowed mother and then bequeathed everything else to John. 'This universal bequest', the will declares, 'is thus made by me to Mr Bowes, my husband, as an act of justice and gratitude, all that I possess having come to me from him.'[47]

Although the collection has been added to in the years since Joséphine's death, the majority of items were bought by her and John between 1862 and early 1874 – an extraordinary achievement. Buying as they did at such speed, it is hardly surprising that mistakes were made, opportunities missed, and perhaps too much emphasis placed on 'curiosities', but the Museum as a whole remains as a unique monument to taste in the mid-nineteenth century, and to the dedication and industry of John and Joséphine Bowes.

# CHAPTER 6

❧

# Life in England

The portrait of John Bowes on exhibition in the Museum depicts an affable country gentleman with a twinkle in his eye and dark wavy hair just beginning to show signs of grey. Beside him assorted game spills out of a shooting bag, while at his feet lies a charming little dog of a breed not normally associated with sporting activities. Streatlam Castle is just visible in the top left-hand corner of the picture.

At first glance this is a portrait of the classic country squire, entirely at ease in his three-piece sporting suit, well-worn boots and leather gaiters, his shotgun cradled against his shoulder. Yet the portrait was not only painted in Paris by a French artist, Jacques-Eugène Feyen, but it is said that when Monsignor Witham first saw the portrait he exclaimed, 'Yes, that's my old friend Bowes sure enough, dressed like his own gamekeeper, and surrounded with more game than he shot in his life.'[1]

While it was customary for formal portraits to show sitters accompanied by objects signifying their principal interests – Joséphine is shown with the scripts of her plays on the table beside her – John's wish to be portrayed as a sportsman seems a little incongruous when such pursuits had played very little part in his life since he was a boy growing up at Streatlam. But perhaps he always intended it to hang in one of the rooms at the castle, where it would have looked entirely at home.

This possibility prompts speculation that he and Joséphine may have intended to make Streatlam their home once the Museum was nearing completion. To have supervised the layout of the rooms and the installation of their treasures while they were still living in Paris would have been difficult, despite John's ability to make light of the journey. To add credibility to this supposition, it is known that Joséphine planned to pass her anticipated widowhood in a spacious apartment to be built for that purpose on the top floor of the Museum. As she was fourteen years younger than John, it was natural for her to assume that she would outlive him, and Streatlam would then no longer be available to her because on John's death, ownership of the castle would revert to the Strathmore family, leaving her homeless. But in 1863, when the portrait was painted, Paris was the centre of their lives; Streatlam was where they spent their annual holiday.

Getting Joséphine there was the problem. Because of her fear of the Channel crossing and her frequent bouts of illness, the Boweses were often forced to cancel their journey to England, sometimes at the last minute, and John's complex travel plans had to be rearranged.

It was the long-suffering Ralph Dent, agent for Streatlam and Gibside, who bore the brunt of these annual visits. At least two months before his employers were due to arrive, a deluge of letters would land on his desk containing detailed instructions for the transport not only of Bowes and his wife but also of their personal servants, coachman, groom, four horses, carriage (sometimes two) and dogs.

67
John Bowes, looking every inch the country gentleman, painted in 1863 by Jacques-Eugène Feyen. There is no evidence that Bowes was a keen sportsman, but the countryside, his numerous tenants and the local people of Barnard Castle were very important to him.

The horses and carriage, having made the Channel crossing, travelled first to London, and then by boat to Middlesbrough. From there they went by train to Darlington and then on to Broomielaw, a station a mile from Streatlam Castle (because the railway crossed Bowes's land, the Barnard Castle Railway Company had agreed to build a station at Broomielaw and to allow trains to stop there on request). The Boweses travelled the last mile by open carriage, the servants in the market cart and the luggage – 'there is a good deal of it' – in the long cart.[2]

One year the coachman, already burdened with the responsibility for numerous four-legged and two-legged beings, was entrusted with Joséphine's 'favourite macaw... a remarkably gentle Bird', which she wished to remain at Streatlam.[3] Within weeks of its arrival, John was writing to enquire if 'the Macaw accommodates himself to his new quarters'.[4] In 1865 some hens and a cock were sent over with the servants, as John considered the birds, which came from Cochin in China, 'much better eating than chickens in the North'.[5]

Streatlam Castle itself also required attention before Bowes and his entourage took up residence. A set of bowls was to be procured for the bowling green and Wheatley, the resident handyman, was to whitewash 'the old Wash House', as Mrs Bowes 'may perhaps have to take Sulphur Baths'.[6] Wheatley was also instructed to remove the chandelier in the master bedroom and paint behind it; in addition, he was to lengthen the canopy of their bed and ensure that there was 'a small pleated strip or Valance with fringe attached to the cornice all round so as to hide the rods', while the bed curtains were to be made 'so as to draw all round, or nearly so' and must be drawn by a cord, 'not backwards and forwards *by the hand.*'[7] This is a severely truncated version of Bowes's directions. Alterations to the curtains at the windows were also minutely described. Were they dictated to him by Joséphine? Given his intimate knowledge of everything at Streatlam however, and his obsessive attention to detail, these injunctions may well have originated with Bowes himself.

68
Although resident in France, Bowes lavished endless time and energy on Streatlam. Of the many hundreds of letters in The Bowes Museum Archive, the majority are concerned with the administration of the Castle, seen here in this late nineteenth-century photograph.

The household staff at Streatlam also required some revision. In 1861 Mrs Bainbridge, the housekeeper, was instructed to find a temporary laundry maid to do the bulk of the washing during their visit – Joséphine's lady's maid would wash and iron all her mistress's 'fine Linen such as collars, cuffs, Muslin Drapes, etc.' Apart from the lady's maid, they were bringing with them a woman 'who makes up Mrs Bowes' Dresses'. She was, Bowes assured Dent, 'a very quiet, respectable old Person, but a terrible talker – however, as they will not be able to understand what she says she is not likely to trouble them much with that.'[8] This comment highlights another problem with these visits: neither Joséphine nor any of the French staff could speak much English, so all communication between the resident and incoming servants had to be relayed through John. In 1867 he asked Dent rather desperately if it was possible to have someone at Streatlam who could speak French.

An account by Augustus Hare of a visit he made to Streatlam in September 1861 confirms that Bowes expected his household to be run with military precision. Hare, having survived the first night in 'the ghost-room, looking most grim and weird from its black oak with red hangings, and containing a tall bed with a red canopy', launched into an account of his first day in the house:

> This is the oddest house I ever was in! Everything is arranged for you, from the moment you get up till the moment you go to bed, and you are never allowed to deviate from the rules laid down: I even write this in time stolen from the half-hour for dressing. We are called at eight, and at ten march in to breakfast with the same procession as at dinner, only at this meal 'Madame Bowes' does not appear, for she is then reclining in a bath of coal-black acid, which 'refreshes her system', but leaves her nails black. After breakfast we are all set down to employments appointed for the morning. At twelve Madame appears, having painted the under-lids of her jet-black eyes with belladonna [Joséphine's eyes were, in fact, hazel]. At two the bell rings for luncheon, and we are fetched if not punctual to an instant. At three we are all sent out driving (the coachman having exact orders where to take us) immense drives (twenty-four miles today) in an open barouche and pair. At seven we dine in great splendour, and afterwards we sit in the oak drawing-room and talk about our ancestors![9]

Joséphine had made her first visit to Streatlam in 1858, six years after she and John were married. Before she arrived, Dent had been instructed to find a pony on which she could ride about the estate. It had to be a 'very quiet Poney [sic]... which would carry a very timid Lady without any risk'.[10] A few days later, Joséphine's equestrian needs were reduced to 'a strong quiet donkey' which John thought 'might do, as it would only be to go about the grounds'.[11]

The first pony located by Dent, a chestnut called Lisette, proved to 'have too much spirit, & is too uncertain for Mrs Bowes to ride with comfort'. She would prefer one which she could ride 'without any one walking by the side'.[12] Further thoughts on the subject followed a week later: 'The Poney [sic] has no vice... It has a habit now of stepping back, or making short quick movements, & this like a jolt of a carriage, or even a false step in walking, is very prejudicial to Mrs Bowes at present and I am afraid will be for some time.'[13]

69
Joséphine was very sentimental about animals, surrounding herself with numerous pets ranging from a tame fawn to singing blackbirds. She and John adored the golden labrador Bernardine. The dog's portrait was painted by Antoine Dury.

Joséphine's need to be surrounded by animals caused other headaches for poor Dent. 'I forgot whether I mentioned to you,' John wrote in February 1859, 'that Mrs. Bowes wishes a doe fawn to be tamed for her.'[14] It was to be called Daisy. Obtaining a fawn was not a problem as there were deer in the park at Streatlam, but it would be interesting to know who was given the task of taming it. Daisy's subsequent career can be traced through Bowes's letters; in 1861 she was unwell and Bowes suspected it was because she was being petted too much; in 1865 there were anxious enquiries as to whether she had given birth; two years later Daisy was dead and Dent was instructed to 'look out for another & tame it'.[15]

Dogs, too, come and go through the correspondence. There is a Skye terrier bitch which the Boweses wanted sent to them in Paris. Two dogs of unknown breed and sex, Bisquette and Loo Loo, make a brief appearance. In 1866 Bowes told Dent that Mrs. Bowes was 'very cut up' to hear that Toddy and Pierrot (the latter caught in a rabbit trap) were both dead and wanted to know if their deaths were caused by negligence. Bernardine, the golden labrador lying at Mrs Bowes's feet in the painting by Dury, was such an important feature in their lives that the artist was commissioned to paint her portrait (this picture is on display in the Museum). A French sheepdog which lived in the stables in Paris was 'fretting' at being confined and was to be sent to Streatlam.

In March 1873 Dent's son (Ralph Dent had died in January 1872) received a letter which shows that he had inherited his father's mantle as agent with all its attendant idiosyncrasies: 'Mrs Bowes has a Blackbird which whistles airs in a remarkable way. She is desirous that you should have some quite young male birds taken (better from the nest) say three, or four, & reared in cages. She would then take her Bird to Streatlam, & thinks the others would learn to whistle from him if they were all kept in their cages together.'[16] Six months later, Joséphine had changed her mind: she now wanted the 'two finest Blackbirds' captured at Streatlam to be brought to Paris where they would 'learn to whistle from our Bird here'.[17]

Even the wild birds at Streatlam were not forgotten, the housekeeper receiving instructions that food was to be put out for them. Joséphine was also 'very fond of rooks, & is glad to hear they are collecting in numbers', but hoped they would not 'drive the Jackdaws away from the neighbourhood of the Castle'.[18] Her sentimental attachment to animals and birds utterly failed, however, when it came to rats and mice, which she abhorred.

For one of Joséphine's nervous disposition, noise of any sort had to be kept to a minimum. Their female servants were all required to wear flat shoes about the house so that the click of their heels on the oak floors did not disturb her. Thunderstorms she detested. But it was her fear of the sea which had a fundamental effect on their lives.

An extraordinary story relating to her terror of the sea appeared in the *Sporting Times*, written by a correspondent whose business regularly took him to Dover. He had heard the story from someone who knew Bowes only as the man who had had four Derby winners:

> My informant forgot his name at the moment, but said he was called by the packet sailors and pier men 'Lord Samphire'... I asked the reason, and was told that his wife (a French Countess) was so awfully nervous at crossing the Channel that she would not do so unless there were two boats crossing at the same time and that Mr Bowes had to charter a special boat which must be the *Samphire* to go when his wife could make up her mind to cross. This hestitation often lasted for many days, even a week or so, steam being got up on calm mornings in case the boat was wanted, and if the passage was made the lady insisted that the captain and another man each took her arm, generally walking the deck the whole time. I believe the passage alone cost Mr Bowes sixty guineas...[19]

70
Joséphine's fear of the sea often obliged the Boweses to postpone or cancel a visit to England. While waiting for calm weather, Joséphine often painted. Her *Squally Weather, A Sketch near Boulogne-sur-Mer* was called 'a portrait of your enemy' by her friends.

Even this elaborate and costly machination would often not tempt Joséphine to commit herself to the deep, yet despite the frequency with which John's plans collapsed about him – he had to cancel their visit five years running, from 1865 to 1869 – his letters never show the slightest sign of impatience or irritation with his wife.

The only letter from Joséphine to John which has survived was written from the Hôtel Meurice in Boulogne in early September 1867, when John had once again been obliged to go to England without her:

> My darling daddikins,
> Ah! what a time it seems – and it is only two days – that I have missed having you with me.
> The hotel would not be too bad, but there are hordes of mice and I can't sleep at night.
> Yesterday the weather was dreadful – very cold with rain. I went for a warm sea-water bath. As for painting the mussel rocks, it is really too far, especially with the heavy tides.
> I have written to old Mrs Budd – and to that man about Cernay, I assure you. Today I'm playing at being an old notary just as you do... I am sending you all the letters that came this morning from Paris...
> Daddy, postman goes at four o'clock today.
> Behave yourself. Think of poor little Puss who loves you so tenderly, and come back soon – very soon – if you can finish the business about the servants. I would rather be in Paris where everything around me reminds me of you. In this room here there's nothing that knows you.
> Goodbye my dear and best beloved daddy. A million kisses.

It is signed 'Joséphine Bowes' and dated 8 or 9 Sept 1867. On the letter, Bowes has written 'Puss – answered le 10 Sept...'[20]

This letter gives the impression of a very different Joséphine from the astute and somewhat imperious collector, or the charming hostess and lady of fashion. Instead, it reveals a vulnerable, needy little woman, utterly dependent on the husband whom she worships and adores. It is also a testament to the strength of their marriage, which by 1867 had lasted for fifteen years.

For John, this devotion must have compensated in full for the strains Joséphine's dependency and frail health imposed on their lives. All the patience, stoicism and selflessness he had at his command were required to keep his many commitments running smoothly. From time to time Gibside, Streatlam, the collieries or the stables at Malton made his presence in England essential and he would have to leave Joséphine either in Paris or marooned in some hotel on the French coast. And judging by her letter, she did not make his abandonment of her easy. Even in Paris their lives were hardly peaceful, as the process of building up the collection was relentless. So too were the constant changes of staff at rue de Berlin. It is no wonder that, despite John's calm exterior and ability to shoulder so many responsibilities, he once confessed to Dent that he suffered from shortness of breath, especially at night, and sometimes had to sit up in bed for an hour or more. 'I attribute [this] to nervousness.'[21]

71
William Hutt played an important part in John Bowes's life: he was a devoted stepfather (having married John's mother in 1831), adviser, confidant and loyal friend. His interests included the cultivation of rare orchids and collecting exotic birds.

Apart from Joséphine's fear of the sea, rats, mice, cold draughts and thunderstorms, she was also prey to constant bouts of illness which included neuralgia and violent pains in the pit of her stomach. Her most persistent problems, however, were rheumatic ailments and chest infections. The former were treated by warm sea-water baths or the sulphur baths that, according to Augustus Hare, turned her finger-nails black. These sulphur baths, or 'Barèges' baths as her Paris doctor called them, were made up of a solution of potassium sulphide to which sulphuric acid was sometimes added. (The Barèges bath was often used to cure diseases of the skin, and might have been used to treat a woman suffering from the side effects of venereal disease.) But in 1861, while Joséphine was taking sea-water baths in a hotel in Boulogne, Bowes told Dent that although she was a little better, 'it is a surgical case requiring a constant, & I am afraid long treatment – which however will not prevent her travelling'.[22] Frustratingly, he does not explain what surgery she had required.

In 1864 she was ill for two months with 'bilious fever & jaundice, two attacks one immediately after the other.' John told Dent, '& [these with] constant confinement to bed have reduced her very much in strength & spirits & I have been obliged to be constantly with her & have thus neglected many things'.[23] This illness subsequently proved to be caused by gallstones, and recurred two years later.

While Bowes's letters reveal a slow but inexorable decline in Joséphine's health over the years, when he first took her to Streatlam in 1858 she was fit enough to undertake all the various excursions that had been meticulously planned for her. These included a prolonged visit to Gibside to stay with John's mother, the Countess of Strathmore, and her husband William Hutt.

John's relations with his mother are difficult to assess. If several letters from Hutt are sufficient evidence, it would appear that John was a poor correspondent. 'Her Ladyship

72
Turner's watercolour of c.1817 shows Gibside, John's second property in County Durham, set among the wooded hills of the River Derwent. The house, barely visible at the centre of the picture, was occupied by John's mother and stepfather.

thinks you are forgetting her,' Hutt wrote to John. 'It would please her if you wrote and told her about the [race] horses.'[24] Or: 'Her Ladyship has been counting the weeks since we had any tidings of you.'[25] Nor did she feel that he visited her often enough. Her pleas for him to do so are contained in letters not from her but from Hutt, on her behalf. In 1844, quoting Lady Strathmore, Hutt wrote: 'Tell Bowes that I hope he will come here as soon as he possibly can, for I am sure it will do him a great deal of good to be out of that dusthole, London.'[26] On another occasion, Hutt expressed his wife's regret that John has postponed his visit, then adds: 'Her Ladyship has been coaxing some auriculas into bloom to exhibit them to you & now they must waste their sweetness on the desert air!'[27] – a remark surely intended to inspire guilt in the errant son.

Christmas was the time when Lady Strathmore particularly missed her son's presence. In November 1850, possibly in the hope of deflecting his mother's importuning for him to celebrate Christmas at Gibside, he had sent her lavish presents from Paris. But it was Hutt who writes to thank John for these gifts. The dress had been 'much approved' and the slippers 'charmed Her Ladyship. *They fit exactly*'.[28] Despite these peace offerings, Lady Strathmore persisted: 'As your coming over will be so near Christmas time,' Hutt wrote in early December, 'I hope you will make up your mind to spend Christmas here. Her Ladyship often laments that you have not spent Christmas with her *for many years.*'[29]

After 1846 Bowes's apparent reluctance to visit his mother may be explained by his wish to spend all his time with Joséphine, whose liaison with her son was probably unknown to Lady Strathmore until shortly before their marriage. (There is no evidence that the Countess met her future daughter-in-law before June 1852, barely two months before Joséphine and John were married in Paris.)

The year 1852 was a frantic one for John Bowes, who dashed to and fro across the Channel as if it were the River Tees. But in November, while he was briefly at Barnard Castle to fulfill his duties with the Militia, Lady Strathmore pounced, this time writing to him herself. After enquiring about his Militia duties, and informing him that 'some more Pineapples' would be sent to him in a few days, she added: 'I hope and trust that you will come to Gibside before you go to Paris. I shall be very much *disappointed if you do not.*'[30] John's letter diary for 1852 reveals that he did not yield to this pressure, but it does show that, despite his frenzied schedule, he had already spent time at Gibside in February, July

73
The building of the Palladian Chapel at Gibside was begun by John's great-grandfather and completed by his father. The vault was a temporary resting place for the coffins of John and Joséphine before they were moved to the church on the edge of The Bowes Museum Park.

and again in October, leaving there only two weeks before he received this fresh appeal from his mother.

In April 1860, *en route* from Gibside to London, Lady Strathmore caught a chill which rapidly developed into a serious illness. On 4 May Hutt wrote to John in Paris informing him that she was unwell, but this was followed next day by a telegram: 'Come as soon as you can, I fear she is sinking.'[31] A few hours later it was all over, and Hutt telegraphed, 'She has ceased to live.'[32] John joined Hutt in London and arrangements were made for Lady Strathmore's body to be taken to Gibside and buried in the vault under the Chapel where the body of her first husband had lain for forty years.

A letter of condolence from John's old friend the Rev Arthur Pearson expresses the general view held of Lady Strathmore: 'I never knew her to say an angry or an unkind word – no wonder then that she was loved by all who knew her, and most, by those who knew her best.'[33] During the difficult years between the Earl's death – when she was Countess of Strathmore in little more than name – and her marriage to Hutt, she had maintained her dignity in spite of her equivocal situation. Her marriage gave her a new life with fresh interests and established her as the bonafide châtelaine of Gibside. When Parliament was sitting she accompanied her husband to London, entering into the social life of an MP's wife, although her reference to London being a 'dusthole' indicates that she remained a country girl at heart.

Her reluctance to put pen to paper had extended to some areas of the administration of her household; instead, these were left to Hutt to deal with. Thus his letters to Dent, while attending to more weighty matters concerning the estate, included orders for hams, pigs, cheeses and elderflower water. 'Her Ladyship says if you send the linen off this week as it did not come last, she wishes you would put up in the parcel a Barnard Castle Ginger-bread cake.'[34]

There is no record that Lady Strathmore ever visited John and Joséphine in Paris. She may well have shared her daughter-in-law's fear of the sea, or perhaps she was daunted by the sheer foreignness of Joséphine and her world. The two women came from such utterly different backgrounds. Joséphine, with her French habits and mannerisms, her sentimentalised view of country life and her inability to speak English, must have represented something of a challenge to Lady Strathmore. But the two women did have one major factor in common: they had both been first the mistress and then the wife of a man of rank and fortune.

Although Hutt's marriage to Lady Strathmore had undoubtedly gained him access to John Bowes's wealth and influence, he was a man of some substance in his own right. An MP for forty-two years, in 1860 he was appointed vice-president of the Board of Trade and a Privy Councillor, and in 1865 he was made a Knight Commander. He was also involved in the annexation of New Zealand to Great Britain, and a commissioner for the foundation of South Australia. His interests included the cultivation of rare orchids and collecting exotic birds, which were kept on the lake at Gibside.

To John Bowes, he was not only a wise counsellor on business affairs but a careful custodian of Gibside, trusted confidant and staunch friend. He and John had become partners in the Marley Hill Coal Company, formed in 1840, and since Hutt had little surplus wealth, he was 'carried' by his wife and stepson, a generous gesture he never forgot. The following letter, written by Hutt to John in 1867, may refer to this financial assistance: 'Nothing will ever make me unmindful of the kindness and forbearance you have shown me in regard to these debts.'[35]

The only recorded hiatus in the relationship between the two men was precipitated by Hutt's announcement to John in February 1861 that he was to remarry. In a previous letter Hutt had explained that John's cousin Susan Davidson – with whom he had been 'on terms of the greatest friendly intimacy' – had shown signs of wanting 'a closer relationship than friends'. Hutt had extricated himself from the situation by confessing that he had another lady in mind.[36] John's reaction to the news of Hutt's engagement has not survived, but judging from Hutt's reply, it had clearly been unfavourable:

> I cannot conceal from you, my dear Bowes, that the manner in which you have received the confidence I made to you has given me much pain, and that it seems to me not in accordance with your usual consideration and kindness... I feel that you have treated the matter as one of ordinary haste and loose avowal... and do not admit my perplexities.
>
> ...Your and Madame's kindness... would have been particularly grateful to me.[37]

John's reply was immediate and obviously contrite as Hutt wrote by return:

> ...The tone of your letter of the 20th weighed heavily on my spirits, and perhaps I had partly misunderstood it. I am somewhat relieved by that which I have just received... I have no right to complain of your expression of repugnance to the abruptness of my engagement, for I have had, God knows, that feeling myself...[38]

John's reaction is perhaps understandable considering that less than nine months had elapsed between Lady Strathmore's death and Hutt's engagement. Although the exact form of his reproof to Hutt is unknown, it had been strong enough to cause his stepfather considerable distress. It is also one of the very few instances in John's voluminous correspondence of him allowing his emotions to overcome his usual courtesy and

74, 75, 76

The bows and arrows of John Bowes's arms (left) are
flanked by the white mountain and crown of the arms
(centre) of the Countess of Montalbo, created for Joséphine
in 1868 by the Republic of San Marino. A design for a stone
carving (right) shows their entwined initials.

reserve. Hutt himself had once commented 'I know you to be a very *prudent* person' –
but for once John's prudence had deserted him.[39]

Four months after this awkwardness between them, the two men now reconciled, Hutt
married Fanny Anne Hughes, daughter of Sir Francis Stanhope and widow of Colonel
James Hughes. Unlike her predecessor she was a keen letter-writer and traveller and, as
Hutt had prophesied, appears to have become 'an amiable and warm-hearted friend' to
Joséphine.[40] Fanny wrote frequently to Joséphine in excellent French, her letters revealing
a shared sentimental passion for dogs. Hutt, too, wrote to Joséphine, his letters full of
warmth and genuine affection.

In 1868 Joséphine became the Countess of Montalbo, a title created for her by the
Republic of San Marino. This title can only have been 'bought' for her by John, and
his reasons for doing so are baffling. Was it at Joséphine's request? Or was it John's
instigation from a desire for her to have a crest and coat of arms to match his own?
As John himself was the most unpretentious of men, it is tempting to assume that it
was Joséphine who entertained *illusions de grandeur*. John evidently felt uncomfortable
about it, as he pretended to his old friend Henry Morgan Vane that it had been 'obtained'
for her by her parents when she 'was a little girl'[41] – a statement manifestly untrue as
she did not become Countess of Montalbo until two years after her mother's death (her
father had died in 1852).

John's wish to protect Joséphine, to surround her with love and comfort, runs like a
thread through the correspondence. Sometimes his over-protectiveness seems a little
excessive. 'Whether from those I know well or those I know little I am not in the habit of
suffering anything in the nature of an insult...' he wrote angrily to someone who had been
a guest in their box at the Paris Opéra and who had allegedly commented indiscreetly
on a remark of Joséphine's about a flirtation between two of their acquaintances.

77
John Scott, affectionately known as 'The Wizard of the North', trained all of Bowes's most famous horses at his stables at Whitewall near Malton in Yorkshire. Scott's brother Bill was one of Bowes's principal jockeys.

'An offence offered to my wife I consider in a stronger light than one offered to myself... If anything insulting was intended I think you will not doubt that [had I heard it] I should have immediately requested you to leave the Box.'[42]

As someone who had carried the taint of illegitimacy throughout his life, it is not surprising that John was hypersensitive to any insult, real or imagined, offered either to himself or to Joséphine – whose career as a vaudeville actress must have been common knowledge. 'No public women whatever are admitted into good French company,' declared the anonymous author of *Life in Paris before the War and during the Siege*. 'Once "upon the boards"... no matter how irreproachable their character may be, they can never be received by women of character and condition, except in their professional capacity.'[43] Nor would respectable society readily receive a woman who had made the transition from mistress to wife. This attitude was even more marked in England where a 'fallen' woman would face almost certain social ostracism were she to marry her lover.

Although writing about society at the end of the nineteenth century, Marcel Proust explains in *Swann's Way*, the first volume of his *Remembrance of Things Past*, that 'middle-class people in those days took what was almost a Hindu view of society, which they held to consist of sharply defined castes, so that everyone at his birth found himself called to that station in life which his parents already occupied, and nothing, except the chance of a brilliant career or of a "good" marriage, could extract you from that station or admit you to a superior caste.'[44]

78

Bowes's horse Cotherstone, painted by John Frederick Herring junior, which won the Derby in 1843. In the same year the horse also won the 2000 Guineas and narrowly missed winning the St Leger.

Joséphine's 'good' marriage to John Bowes had enabled her to free herself from the stigma of a life 'upon the boards' and become not only accepted by respectable society but a successful society hostess – a tribute, surely, to her own force of character and to John's vigilant protection. The spirit of the times was also in her favour; during the Second Empire the distinction between women of dubious social standing and those from the upper classes became increasingly blurred until it was difficult to tell them apart. 'Never has the low world of gallantry reflected high society as it does now...' grumbled the Goncourts in their *Journal* for 1 January 1857. 'Today [the prostitute] dictates behaviour, she bespatters opinion; she eats marrons glacés in her theatre box, next to your wife.'[45] Indeed, in terms of dress, it was often the *demi-mondaines* who 'generally displayed in their clothing a simplicity and sobriety of taste which gave them... a sufficient air of distinction and bearing to deceive even the keenest physiognomists as to their social status.'[46]

John's vigilance is also apparent in his administration of Streatlam. No detail, however small, escaped his notice. The orange trees which had been shipped back to England when Château du Barry was sold were a constant source of concern. As they were unused to the English climate, he reminded Dent that they must be taken indoors before the first frost. Each year there were anxious enquiries as to whether they had flowered yet. And had the Pinetum suffered from the severe winter? One year he was annoyed that the gardener had moved a peach tree without consulting him. He even altered the quantity of groceries ordered from London by the housekeeper, and instructed her to stop rewinding the clocks when he and Mrs Bowes were not in residence. The butler was ordered to leave good oil in the lamps when they were not being trimmed or used.[47] This last injunction reveals a frugality at odds with the generosity he displayed in so many areas of his life.

For John Bowes, with his myriad responsibilies, to have concerned himself with such minutiae was extraordinary. That he was able to do so was due in part to the loyalty, ability and industry of men like Ralph Dent (and later his son Ralph John Dent) and Thomas Wheldon, who was succeeded by his nephew by marriage, John Dickonson Holmes.

79
A romantic view of Barnard Baliol's Castle, which gave Barnard Castle its name, painted by Thomas Creswick in c.1860. The castle figures in Walter Scott's poem *Rokeby*.

John Bowes's preoccupation with detail was evident in everything he undertook. In 1852, the year in which he crossed the English Channel eighteen times, he was in Durham in early March to attend the various ceremonies connected with his appointment as High Sheriff. His correspondence reveals his determination to ensure that his own outfit was correct in every particular. As he told Holmes, he had rejected the idea of attiring himself 'in the uniform of Lieut Col of the Durham Militia, but as in this costume one has a regulation sword, and altogether what old Davidson would have called, "a more ferocious appearance", the Judges might mistake one for the Executioner'. Instead, he opted for Full Dress as he felt 'it would be more respectful to their *Ludships'* to appear with a *chapeau à bras* and without a sword. The coach was to be painted yellow 'with a drab lining' and emblazoned with his arms and crest.[48]

Bowes and his entourage clearly impressed the reporter from the *Durham Chronicle*:

The LIVERIES of the High Sheriff are this year of an unusually elegant and costly description, consisting of a full dress coat of white cloth edged with gold lace and gold aiguillettes. The waistcoat is of crimson cloth edged with gold lace, and the breeches of crimson plush with a gold band [this was, in fact, the Bowes livery]... The tout ensemble has a very handsome and imposing appearance.[49]

Another area of John's crowded life which took up much of his attention was the racing stables at Whitewall, near Malton. That he found the time to pursue this interest is evidence of a love for horses probably inherited from his father, and of his determination to breed the perfect racehorse. In furthering this ambition he was fortunate to have John Scott as his trainer. Scott came to be regarded as one of the best in the country, earning for himself the title of 'Wizard of the North'. He trained all Bowes's most famous horses: Mündig, which won the Derby in 1835, Cotherstone, which won both the Two Thousand Guineas and the Derby in 1843, Daniel O'Rourke, winner of the 1852 Derby, and West Australian, which in 1853 won the Triple Crown (the Derby, the Two Thousand Guineas and the St Leger), the first horse ever to do so. These remarkable results were obtained from a comparatively small stud and with horses all of Bowes's own breeding.

Contrary to the widely held belief that John Bowes seldom watched his horses race, his letters indicate that in his youth he made frequent visits to Doncaster, York, Newmarket and Goodwood and, according to William Hutt, never missed a Derby. But after 1847 his life in Paris and his many commitments made it increasingly difficult for him to find the time to attend race meetings.

A story about the jockey George Fordham, who rode for Bowes for almost twenty years, perpetuated the myth that he was an uninterested owner. Fordham was approached by an old gentleman at a race meeting who asked his opinion of the horse he was about to ride, and Fordham suggested he should ask the owner. 'I *am* the owner; let me introduce myself – I am Mr Bowes,' came the reply.[50]

On another occasion, Bowes was watching his horse Epirus run in the St Leger of 1837. Suddenly there was consternation among the spectators in the Jockey Club Stand; there had been an accident on the course. Bowes, who was watching the race through a telescope, was asked if he could see what had happened. 'Without a trace of emotion, and without removing his eye from the telescope, he announced that "Epirus has fallen into the ditch. Bill Scott [Bowes's jockey] is lying prostrate and unable to move. I think he is killed." '[51] (He had, in fact, broken his collar bone.)

John Bowes was the most private of men, preferring to keep his own counsel and to come and go as he pleased. His obituary in *The Times* quoted 'one of his oldest friends' as describing him as a shy and reticent man with 'the peculiar faculty of being able to conceal from his interlocutor all evidences whether he liked him or not.'[52]

It has often been suggested that this reserve and wish for anonymity stemmed from his illegitimacy, that his bastardy cast a long shadow, inhibiting him from entering fully into society. Yet surely a man who had joined the Catch and Glee Club in his youth, was a member of no fewer than five clubs in England and two of the most exclusive clubs in Paris, could not be accused of a want of conviviality. And his correspondence reveals that he was on friendly terms with numerous members of the aristocracy, from the Duke of Cleveland to Lord Arran and from the Marquis of Londonderry to the Earl of Derby (Lord Derby, whose grandfather had founded the two racing Classics, the Oaks and the Derby, once invited Bowes to stay with him at Knowsley Hall in Lancashire for the 'Liverpool Races').

There is, however, one inescapable fact about John Bowes: he does not feature in the autobiographies, journals or memoirs of any of the leading figures of his day – apart from the journals of Thackeray and Macready – even of those who were known to be members of his many clubs. This silence may not be significant, but it is curious. That he earned a living as an industrial entrepreneur rather than passing his time in a state of genteel idleness may also have militated against his full acceptance into English society.

His marriage, too, possibly added to any sense of displacement he may have felt. Had he been able to marry a conventional English girl of good family, the *beau monde* would have found it easier to forget the circumstances of his birth. But Joséphine was too exotic a mixture of imponderables for English society to find her anything but perplexing.

At Streatlam she would have been accorded the courtesy due her as John Bowes's wife, but she must have remained something of an enigma to the county set – a circumstance exacerbated by her inability to speak English. That she should seriously have intended to live alone in the Museum at Barnard Castle after John's death is a baffling thought. Either she was very courageous, or she had deluded herself into believing that she would be accepted by local society. There is evidence, however, that she already had a reputation as a generous benefactress in the area. *La Revue Critique* declared that she had 'a name justly respected and revered, for she always interested herself in aspects of the moral and material well-being of the town of Barnard Castle.'[53] The word 'moral' in this otherwise complimentary statement perhaps implies that she was just a little inclined to interfere in local affairs.

Despite his permanent residence in Paris, there was never any doubt about John's love for Streatlam or his commitment to County Durham. His membership of the Militia, his year as High Sherriff, his fifteen years as MP for South Durham and his frequent donations to good causes, all attest to his involvement in the county. His affection for the local people, especially those who had worked for him for many years, is evident from the frequency with which he quotes them in his correspondence. 'Nobody works on the place, and everything is going into a state of *captivity*'[54], or '"The tottle of the whole" as Joe Hume would say, is considerable.'[55]

His commitment to his home town of Barnard Castle, and to the county as a whole, could not have been more generously or magnificently expressed than by his building of the Museum.

# CHAPTER 7

❦

# The Collection in Peril

In 1869 the Boweses took a decisive step towards the building of their Museum by laying the foundation stone. On 27 November Joséphine used a silver trowel to manipulate the stone and said to John: 'I lay the bottom stone, and you, Mr Bowes, will lay the top stone.'[1] The only other people present were Ralph Dent, J. E. Watson the architect, and Joseph Kyle, a Newcastle builder; Watson and Kyle were to interpret the original design for the Museum, which had been drawn up by the French architect Jules Pellechet.

Deciding where to site the museum had presented little difficulty. Today's visitor will be struck by the way the building stands on high ground, set well back from the road into Barnard Castle, its great windows looking out towards the River Tees and the open country beyond. The architecture, too, is arresting. Although there was a rumour current in 1869 that it was to be an exact replica of the Louvre, a reporter on the *Teesdale Mercury* was better informed when he declared it to have been 'designed in the French Renaissance style of architecture, very elaborate and ornate in character, portions and details of which are taken from the Tuileries in Paris, the Hotel de Ville, Havre; and other public buildings in France.'[2]

The Boweses, having completed discussions with J. E. Watson and instigated several alterations to Pellechet's design, left Streatlam for Dover in early December. During their customary wait for the sea to be calm enough for Joséphine, they heard that Paris was in the grip of a smallpox epidemic. Leaving Joséphine at Dover, John made a brief trip alone to Paris to check that all was well at rue de Berlin and to consult with Carpentier, Joséphine's colourman, about entering her picture for the 1870 Salon. Their house had been left in the care of the housekeeper, Hortense Chevrier, whose husband Robert had been concièrge at the Variétés during Bowes's tenure of the theatre.

News in early March that the epidemic was abating encouraged John and Joséphine to hope they would soon be able to return to France. But something far more sinister was to prevent them from seeing their Paris home for another eighteen months – the outbreak of war between France and Prussia.

In February Spain had offered her vacant throne to the Hohenzollern Prince Leopold, a cousin of King William I of Prussia, and he had accepted it. France reacted so violently to the prospect of a German monarch on the Spanish throne, fearing it would upset the balance of power in Europe, that Leopold withdrew his candidature. But France rashly insisted on a guarantee that the offer would never be renewed. Bismarck, who saw a war with France as a means of achieving his great ambition of unifying the German states, further inflamed the French by skilfully sharpening the tone of a telegram from William – the famous Ems telegram – to make it appear that William had insulted them, and released it to the world's press. 'It will have the effect of a red flag on the Gallic bull,' Bismarck announced with relish to General von Moltke.[3]

80
Following France's humiliating defeat by the Prussians in the war of 1870, a revolutionary government tried to turn Paris into a self-governing Commune. This detail of a lithograph shows the centre of the city burning during the vicious fighting that broke out between the insurgents and the forces of the national government.

81
Napoléon III at the height of his power. This copy by Jules de Vignon after Winterhalter was painted in 1867, three years before the outbreak of the Franco-Prussian War which led to the Emperor's capture and subsequent exile.

He had judged the situation correctly: on 15 July 1870, France declared war on Prussia. In Paris, the news was greeted with joy verging on hysteria. Mobs sang the banned 'Marseillaise' and surged through the streets shouting '*A Berlin!*' Napoléon, suffering agonies from a stone as big as a pigeon's egg in his bladder, left for the front to take command of his armies. 'Thus by a tragic combination of ill-luck, stupidity and ignorance France blundered into war with the greatest military power that Europe had yet seen, in a bad cause, with her army unready and without allies.'[4]

Six weeks later it was all over; on 1 September the French forces were defeated at Sedan and Napoléon taken prisoner. Goncourt recounted the mood in the capital when news of the disaster reached Paris: 'Who can describe the consternation written on every face, the sound of aimless steps pacing the streets at random, the anxious conversations of shopkeepers and concièrges on their doorsteps... Then there is the menacing roar of the crowd, in which stupefaction has begun to give place to anger.'[5]

The Second Empire came to an abrupt end and France was declared a republic. Empress Eugénie fled from the Tuileries and was smuggled out of France and into England by her American dentist. The Prussian armies marched on Paris. 'The whole of Paris became suddenly transformed into one vast drill-ground, and the clang of arms resounded through the city day and night,' wrote Albert Vandam.[6] By 20 September, the Prussians had surrounded the capital and the Siege of Paris had begun.

The Boweses watched these events unfold with mounting concern. To risk returning to Paris under such circumstances would be madness. Even the British Ambassador Lord Lyons and almost his entire staff had left the capital, a move castigated by Robert Peel in the House of Commons as 'an ungenerous and unmanly flight'.[7] One of the few members of the diplomatic corps to remain was the American Minister Mr Washburne, whose presence in Paris was to prove invaluable to the Boweses.

In mid August the Boweses had received assurances from Gogué that the collection, housed in the Temporary Gallery at rue Blomet, was safe: 'Your beloved pictures are perfectly all right here; they are waiting for you to come and see them... I repeat, rely on me.'[8] But news from rue de Berlin was worrying: Hortense, the housekeeper, was seriously ill with a tumour and being nursed by her husband and her sister-in-law, Eléonore Chevrier.

The Boweses were not the only ones to fear for the safety of their treasures. Most of the contents of the Louvre were moved to Brittany, with the exception of the *Venus de Milo* which was hidden in a secret cellar at the Préfecture. In August, when the war was at its height, the reclusive, incredibly mean 4th Marquess of Hertford (he once boasted, 'When I die I shall at least have the consolation of knowing that I have never rendered anyone a service'[9]) breathed his last at Bagatelle, his villa outside Paris, leaving his entire collection to his illegitimate son Richard Wallace. With the Prussians at the gates of Paris, Wallace

82
Following Napoléon's capture by the Prussians at the battle of Sedan, the Emperor met with Chancellor Bismarck at a weaver's cottage at Donchery to discuss the terms of the French capitulation.

83
As the siege tightened, famine set in. Parisians were reduced to eating anything they could find. This drawing by French cartoonist Cham, entitled *The Queue for Rat's Meat*, satirises the desperate quest for food.

hurriedly moved the contents of Bagatelle to his father's house at rue Lafitte, where the pictures were laid flat on the floor and covered with thick planks. Accurately predicting a bombardment of the city, he ordered layers of earth to be spread over the roof of the house to deaden the effect of falling shells.[10]

As the siege tightened its grip on Paris, communications began to break down. Although Eléonore Chevrier and Gogué continued to write to the Boweses, over a period of four months none of Gogué's letters and only two of Eléonore's reached Streatlam.

Inside Paris, conditions rapidly deteriorated. The city contained well over two million people, and they needed to be fed. By December the herds of cattle and sheep had been eaten that in September had filled the Bois de Boulogne. 'People are talking only of what they eat, what they can eat, and what there is to eat...' Goncourt noted. 'Hunger begins and famine is on the horizon.'[11] For those who could afford it, food could still be obtained. 'I had a slice of spaniel the other day,' wrote Henry Labouchere, correspondent for the *London Daily News*. A week later he reported a man who was fattening up a large cat which he planned to eat on Christmas Day, 'surrounded with mice, like sausages'.[12] At John Bowes's old haunt, the Jockey Club, they were serving such delicacies as *salmis de rats* and rat pie.[13]

84
With Paris under siege, the Boweses became
desperate for news of their precious collection.
In September 1870 a balloon post was at last
established. Here, the resistance leader Gambetta
escapes from Paris to raise a provincial army.

Even the animals in the zoo had been slaughtered, all except the lions and tigers which were too dangerous to kill. The last to go were the monkeys. In the opinion of Thomas Bowles, 'These were kept alive from a vague and Darwinian notion that they are our relatives, or at least the relatives of some of the members of the Government.'[14] On 31 December Goncourt described visiting Roos's, the English butcher's shop, and seeing 'all sorts of weird remains. On the wall, hung in a place of honour, was the skinned trunk of young Pollux, the elephant at the Zoo; and in the midst of nameless meats and unusual horns, a boy was offering some camel's kidneys for sale.'[15] Meanwhile Bismarck, living in splendour at the Prussian army's headquarters at Versailles, was tucking into turtle soup, wild boar's head and sauerkraut boiled in champagne.

Increasingly anxious about their house and the collection, the Boweses cast about for some means of contacting Gogué and the Chevriers. John's old friend Kinglake suggested a possible route through Madame du Quaire, an acquaintance of his who seemed able to get letters through the Prussian lines into Paris. John immediately sent two messages: one to his banker Edward Blount, asking him to provide the Chevriers with what money they needed, and one to Hortense Chevrier, pleading for news. 'Write by balloon post,' he pleaded, 'and tell Gogué to write too.'[16] (A regular balloon post linking the besieged city with the outside world had been established in late September: 'Altogether some

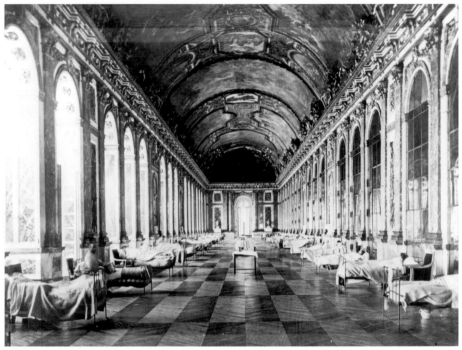

85
Having defeated the French on the battlefield,
the Prussians established their headquarters at
Versailles and laid siege to Paris. In the Palace, the
Hall of Mirrors was converted into a hospital.

sixty-five manned balloons left Paris during the Siege. They carried one hundred and sixty-four passengers, three hundred and eighty-one pigeons, five dogs and nearly eleven tonnes of despatches, including approximately two and a half million letters, and only two balloonists died.'[17])

The Boweses were so desperate for news that when John saw an advertisement in *The Times* maintaining that 'Anxious enquirers can obtain reliable INFORMATION respecting FRIENDS in PARIS...', he asked his friend Henry Vane, who was in London, to visit the address given in the advertisement. When it proved to be the home of a clairvoyant, John abandoned this particular line of communication.[18]

But Vane had two further suggestions: the parents of Mr Henry, a young man who worked in Vane's office, regularly sent letters to their cousin in Paris through Mr Washburne, the American Minister. Bowes immediately sent a letter to Mr Henry's father to forward to the cousin, asking him to visit both the Chevriers and Gogué. Secondly, Vane advised Bowes to put an advertisement in *The Times* himself, intended for Mrs Anne Schleicher, an American friend of the Boweses'; apparently one of Washburne's attachés was in the habit of perusing the advertisements.

86
No sooner had the war ended than Paris descended into the chaos of the Commune. Barricades went up all over the city and Frenchman turned on Frenchman, as recorded by Manet's shocking sketch.

Both stratagems worked: word reached Mrs Schleicher who promptly called at rue de Berlin and on 23 January wrote a long letter to Joséphine which was sent by diplomatic bag, reaching Streatlam a week later. While it contained reassuring news about the house, it confirmed that Hortense was dangerously ill. Chevrier, however, had managed to persuade the authorities that although the house was ostensibly vacant, it was too full of valuable works of art to be used to lodge people fleeing from the bombardment of southern Paris and St-Denis. The dog Palette was safe and well but had to be carefully watched 'to prevent him being stolen to make *mutton* chops of'.[19] But there was nothing in the letter to alleviate the Boweses' fears for the collection in the Temporary Gallery, situated in the area hardest hit by the bombardment.

Mr Henry's cousin also responded when he received the message from Bowes, checking both rue de Berlin and the Temporary Gallery. His subsequent letter to Mr. Henry confirmed that all was well at the Gallery, although a Prussian shell had burst in the garden. However, by the time this welcome news reached Streatlam, the Boweses had already heard from Gogué – the letter prompted by the message he had received through Kinglake's lady friend – that their beloved pictures were safe.[20]

87
The Commune ended in a week of street fighting
in which thousands of Parisians were killed. On the
nights of 24 and 25 May 1871 the centre of Paris
was engulfed by fire and the Tuileries Palace burnt
to the ground.

On 28 January 1871 the French government accepted an armistice and the fighting
ceased. 'In a newspaper giving the news of the capitulation,' Goncourt noted sadly in
his journal on 30 January, 'I read the news of King William's enthronement as Emperor
of Germany at Versailles, in the Hall of Mirrors, under the nose of the stone Louis XIV in
the courtyard outside. That really marks the end of the greatness of France.'[21] Forced to
agree to savage peace terms – the loss of Alsace, part of Lorraine and an indemnity of
£200 million – France suffered further ignominy when on I March German troops made a
triumphal entry into Paris, marching in glittering splendour through the Arc de Triomphe
and along the Champs-Élysées.

The Boweses' relief that their collection had survived the siege intact was shattered
when they received a letter from Eléonore Chevrier with the news that both Hortense
and Gogué were dead.[22] Hortense's death had been expected, but Gogué's came as
a complete shock. They had only just heard from him – a sad letter revealing personal
anxieties of which they had known nothing. His brother had died the previous year, deeply
in debt, and in paying off his creditors Gogué had himself become desperately short of
money. Enclosed with the letter was a statement showing that the Boweses owed him

some 7,000 francs for all the various sums he had paid out on their behalf during their absence.[23] The sum was immediately paid, but too late to reach Gogué before his death. His sister accepted the payment on his behalf and also took charge of the Temporary Gallery in rue Blomet until the Boweses could return to Paris. Now that the war was over, prospects for this seemed promising. But there were further horrors to come.

To the citizens of Paris, physically and psychologically undermined by the long siege, the National Assembly's acceptance of Prussia's draconian peace terms was a bitter disillusionment. Determined to turn Paris into a self-governing Commune, they voted into power a range of republicans, socialists and anarchists. One of the Commune's main supports was the National Guard, whose numbers had been increased to some 300,000 men. On 18 March Adolphe Thiers, leader of the government, ordered the national forces to remove some four hundred cannons from the National Guard. The attempt was a dismal failure and Thiers and the government fled to Versailles, leaving Paris in the control of the Commune.

On 2 April the second siege of Paris began, but this time the besiegers were the forces of the national government – the *Versaillais*. 'Thank God, civil war has broken out!'[24] exclaimed Goncourt on that day, echoing the view of the majority of Parisians who loathed the Commune and longed for the 'forces of order' to return to the city.

On 21 April Eléonore Chevrier wrote to assure the Boweses that all was well at both rue de Berlin and rue Blomet, but added:

> ...Since the 1st of the month they have been fighting incessantly. You cannot imagine what Paris looks like, most of the Shops are shut there is hardly anyone in the streets, Barricades and guns in nearly every neighbourhood, the theatres except two or three are closed, no work anywhere and frightful poverty...[25]

On 21 May the *Versaillais* entered Paris through the unguarded Porte de Saint-Cloud. In what became known as *la semaine sanglante* the French fought each other, street by street, barricade by barricade, with savage intensity. The Tuileries, symbol of French monarchy, was burnt to the ground and the Palais Royal, the Palais de Justice and the Préfecture of Police were set alight. By the night of the 25th, the centre of Paris was on fire.

*The Times's* correspondent, writing on 29 May, was appalled by the vengeful manner in which the *Versaillais* had been 'shooting, bayonetting, ripping up prisoners, women, and children during the last six days'. Two days later he declared: 'The French are filling up the darkest page in the book of their own or the world's history.' And on 1 June: 'Human nature shrinks in horror from the deeds that have been done in Paris.'[26] With the surrender of the last of the Communards, a shocked city began to bury its dead. Up to twenty-five thousand had been killed in a few days, more than during the year-long Reign of Terror which had followed the Revolution.

With the defeat of the Commune, Eléonore Chevrier evidently felt it safe to give the Boweses an account of what she and her brother had gone through. Her letter of 2 June describes Communards being marched off to Versailles to be shot, and the bodies of the dead which seemed to be everywhere. What had terrified her most 'were the fires, the sky was so black with smoke and then red as fire that you had to think the fire was quite close to the house'.[27] However, all was well at rue de Berlin, apart from what she called 'a terrible disaster' which proved to be severe flooding of the drawing-room and irreparable damage to Joséphine's marquetry table, caused by a hurricane that had torn a hole in the roof. Given what Paris had suffered – the British Embassy had sustained six direct hits – it seemed the Boweses' property had escaped remarkably lightly.

The *Venus de Milo* had also survived, emerging from her secret hiding place in the smouldering remains of the Préfecture, saved apparently by a burst water-pipe. 'As she was removed from her "coffin",' wrote Théophile Gautier, 'everybody leaned forward avidly to contemplate her. She still smiled, lying there so softly... this vague and tender smile, her lips slightly apart as if all the better to breathe in life...'[28]

One of the heroes of the traumatic events in Paris was Richard Wallace. His father's death in August 1870 had made him a multi-millionaire at the age of fifty-two, and following the defeat of the French at Sedan he began to pour money into numerous good causes. That winter a British Charitable Fund was established to distribute relief to the English in Paris, with Wallace as its Chairman and Edward Blount (Bowes's banker, and acting British Consul) as one of his principal helpers. Wallace was so shocked by what he saw during the siege and the Commune that he decided to move back to England and take the bulk of his collection with him. Before leaving Paris, he presented fifty drinking fountains to the city. Nicknamed *wallaces*, some of the fountains survive in Paris today; one can also be seen outside Hertford House, home of the Wallace Collection in London.[29]

It is tempting to speculate how John and Joséphine would have fared had they remained in Paris throughout this period. To John, with his strong sense of public duty – and as a resident in Paris for many years – joining Wallace and Blount in their charitable activities would have seemed a natural course to take. To Joséphine, hypersensitive and nervous to a degree, the shelling of the city and the carnage of the Commune would have been deeply distressing. Whether it would have been preferable to being stranded in England while her home and the collection were under continual threat, is debatable. But there is no doubt that the anxiety caused by their lack of news from Paris fatally damaged her already precarious health.

The Boweses finally returned to Paris in October 1871 after an absence of two years and three months. John's first letter to Dent after their arrival makes no mention of how they found things at rue de Berlin but adds a P.S. to say that 'nothing of importance connected with the Museum has suffered in any way – but the Temporary Picture Gallery had a miraculous escape for besides the Shells which fell in the Garden, a large Washing Establishment which stands against one end of it wall to wall was *shelled* to pieces by the Germans.'[30]

CHAPTER 8

✌

# The Legacy Realised

In January 1871, while the Boweses were still in England, the Museum was given wide publicity in architectural circles by the appearance in *The Builder* of an article entitled 'Mrs Bowes's Mansion and Galleries at Barnard Castle, Durham', accompanied by a full-page engraving from J. E. Watson's drawing of the building and a plan of the ground floor.[1] The Boweses sent copies of the journal to various friends, including William Hutt, Alexander Kinglake and Emile Gallé.

'I like it exceedingly & so does Lady Hutt,' was Hutt's response. 'I was fearful that it might be in the Tudor or Gothic style which are so much the rage just now in England... The Italian Renaissance is a beautiful creation [the Hutts had just spent several months in Italy] and it is in proper harmony with the artistic sentiment of this museum.'[2] Kinglake also gave the design of the Museum his enthusiastic endorsement – 'what a majestic palace it will be!' – but added a caveat about the roofs – 'I have an idea that for that kind of architecture great loftiness is essential...' – and blamed a lack of it for the failure of the design of the Duke of Buccleuch's house in London.[3]

Kinglake's concern about the roofs was evidently shared by Joséphine. 'I am entirely of your opinion, Madame,' Emile Gallé wrote in September 1871. 'The roofs, in particular those above the entrance pavilions, will certainly gain by being elevated (either by capping or by adding a gallery), and this modification will without doubt add even more to the grandeur of the whole.'[4] This advice from a man whose artistic taste she respected possibly tipped the balance for Joséphine, as the architect Pellechet was instructed to raise the height of the roofs to the level they are today.

MRS. BOWES'S MANSION AND MUSEUM, BARNARD CASTLE, DURHAM.——Mr. J. E. Watson, Architect.

89

In January 1871 *The Builder* magazine published an article, accompanied by this drawing, of the proposed appearance of The Bowes Museum. The article excited great interest in architectural circles and among the Boweses' friends.

88

A view through one of the galleries at The Bowes Museum reveals how closely the pictures were packed together on the walls when this photograph was taken c. 1900.

123

Joséphine's will and codicil of July 1871 appointed her Trustees and bequeathed to them the Park and Museum, for the benefit of the public. In the sort of detail so loved by John, she gave instructions for everything from the opening hours to staff appointments, and from conservation of the collection to fire precautions – the heating of the Museum was to be effected by stoves and kitchen ranges as she had a horror of gas. The codicil ends:

> And I request and adjure the inhabitants of Barnard Castle with a common accord to aid the Committee as far as possible in guarding their Museum the contents of which it has taken so much of my time and trouble to collect and bring together and their Park.[5]

This is stern stuff, and a little hard on John, whose time *and* money had also been spent assembling the collection. But the wording may have been his, not Joséphine's, as he always insisted 'that the idea, and project of the Museum and Park originated entirely with her...'[6] It is typical of his generous nature to have wanted her considerable contribution to the genesis and realisation of the Museum to be recorded for posterity. Joséphine was never to see her creation completed: when they left England in late 1871, the outside walls of the building were only a few feet in height.

When they returned to Paris they were however happily unaware of what the future held, although Joséphine's health was precarious. John was also unwell, complaining to Dent of 'a slight attack... in my left arm and leg' which the doctors considered '*nervous*, & not rheumatic'; but it had been bad enough to prevent him from going upstairs for a while.[7]

They must have been surprised to find Paris not the ruin they expected. The omnibuses and *fiacres* were back on the streets, the theatres had reopened and the boulevards were again thronged with people. Henry James, in Paris during 1875 and 1876, was amazed by 'the elasticity of France. Beaten and humiliated on a scale without precedent, despoiled, dishonoured, bled to death financially – all this but yesterday – Paris is today in outward aspect as radiant, as prosperous, as instinct with her own peculiar genius as if her sky had never known a cloud.'[8]

In October 1871 the sudden demise of Bowes's trainer John Scott heralded a series of deaths, all equally unexpected: Joséphine's brother-in-law died in November and her sister two months later. On 19 January 1872 Ralph Dent died after a short illness; for more than thirty years he had faithfully and efficiently administered John Bowes's estates. 'I have lost in him an old, valued and valuable Friend,' Bowes wrote to Ralph John Dent, Dent's son, when he heard the news.[9] Bowes wanted to attend the funeral but explained that Mrs Bowes was in such a nervous state from 'the number of losses she & I have sustained by death that I cannot safely leave her here alone.'[10]

Ralph John Dent, who knew the estate well, stepped into his father's shoes. A few weeks later he had to write to Bowes to inform him of the tragic death of Isaac Walker, the Streatlam stud groom for nearly forty-four years. Walking home in the dark, Walker had lost his footing and plunged over the edge of the track and 'must have slipped straight away into the water'.[11]

Over the next two years John's letters reveal a steady decline in the quality of life at rue de Berlin. Throughout 1872 and 1873 he was beset by problems with the household staff (of the one hundred and thirty-four letters for 1872 in the Museum archives, the majority are devoted to the hiring and firing of staff). In urgent need of a new butler, he instructed Dent to locate one in England. 'He must understand that tho' [this is] a quiet place it is one where he would have a great deal to do...' Moreover, he must do things 'in a very quiet, & stylish manner... and exactly according to our directions, & habits.'[12]

The butler selected by Dent was unsatisfactory, so Bowes took up the search in France. His appointment of a man he thought suitable not only illustrates the unexpected pitfalls to be encountered by a householder, but throws light on the mood in France in the period immediately following the war. Although the man when interviewed for the job had insisted he was Belgian, Bowes now suspected he was German. If this proved to be the case, 'the hatred of them is still so great in France, that if it got out it might create disagreements in the French part of the Household, though of course to Mrs Bowes, & me it is a matter of indifference.'[13]

The new footman, whose procurement from England had also entailed numerous letters to Dent, was found to have 'many personal defects'. John's description conjures up a man of alarming appearance: 'He has only the sight of one eye, he wears a wig, has very large feet, & hands, and seems to have some defects in his speech, & appears altogether an unhealthy subject.'[14]

There were also problems with a groom at Streatlam who had proved to be an evil-tempered, even dangerous individual. Bowes's letter to Dent is a good instance of his charitable nature: 'I really only had kept him on because he appeared steady and regular, and I thought his personal appearance, which is his misfortune, and not his fault, would prevent him from getting a place elsewhere.'[15]

Another concern for the Boweses was the slow progress of the Museum. This was caused not by lack of money – the coal trade was flourishing as never before in John's lifetime[16] – but by a shortage of men to work the stone at Dunhouse Quarry. Until the building had a roof the crates despatched from Paris had to be stored at Streatlam, the large ones in the entrance hall and the smaller ones in the dining-room. By September 1872 there were more than eighty cases at the Castle, effectively reducing it to a storehouse. Bowes's letters are full of concerns about their safe arrival, particularly about that handsome faïence jug presented by Emile Gallé to Joséphine for the Museum in 1872 (it was intact, and can be seen in the Museum today).

The real drain on John's spirits, however, was the state of Joséphine's health. In June 1872 she had been laid up by a swollen foot and ankle caused by 'exerting herself too much in attending to the Packing for the Museum,'[17] a task that both she and John resumed immediately on their return to Paris. This relatively minor indisposition was succeeded by far more serious ailments – prolonged bouts of asthma and bronchitis. However, as Bowes told Dent, they had arranged 'large dinner Parties, & later on a large Dancing Party, or two',[18] and Joséphine had prepared herself for these occasions by spending 11,184 francs on dresses from Worth.[19]

In February 1873 Bowes wrote a letter for Dent to pass on to the *Teesdale Mercury*. It explained Mrs Bowes's anxiety during the war and the Commune and continued: 'The loss by death during that period and subsequently of Relatives and many attached Friends, and Dependants has seriously affected her naturally nervous and highly sensitive

90

In 1872 the young glass maker, Emile Gallé presented this jug to Joséphine in recognition of her generous patronage. His letters to Joséphine reveal his affection and respect for her. The figure depicted is King Stanislas, responsible for the beautification of Gallé's home town of Nancy, France.

temperament.' Bowes added that Mrs Bowes was now on a 'strengthening regimen' which 'will doubtless before long restore her to her usual health'.[20]

But a letter to Dent in March reveals that Joséphine had been in bed for a month and had lost her appetite. In September she was again ill with 'Rheumatic Bronchitis' which by October had eased sufficiently for her to continue with the packing of the porcelain, although she was still troubled by 'a kind of asthmatic oppression, a difficulty in breathing which affects her at nights, & weakens her much from want of proper sleep.'[21] She had been further distressed by the sudden death of their cook from cholera. They were unable to have the body removed or even put into a coffin until the authorities gave their consent, so it had remained in the house much longer 'than was under the circumstances advisable.'

From now on Bowes's letters to Dent almost invariably contain the sad refrain 'Mrs Bowes, I am sorry to say, still continues very ill...' Bowes was in constant touch with William Hutt, whose sympathy and understanding must have been a great solace to him in the months leading up to Joséphine's death. Hutt also supplied practical help: in January 1874 he sent John a dozen Whitbread's Extra London stout as a stimulant to Joséphine's appetite. The bottles were followed by a barrel, which required 'a few hours quiet to be fit for use'.[22] Hutt also suggested chloral for sleeplessness and encouraged John to get a good nurse for Joséphine.

91

Joséphine's death in 1874 is remembered a year later by this card which mourns her early demise and prays that the 'day will come when we shall all, as dear friends, be reunited in Heaven'.

Only one event could possibly have brought any cheer to the Boweses during those dark months at rue de Berlin: with some of the roof timbers at last in place on the Museum, on 23 January the French and English flags were flown above the building amid loud cheers from the seventy workmen.[23] Dent told Bowes that he was sure Mrs Bowes 'would be pleased to see the progress the Museum has made, it is now a very prominent object in the landscape & is the first thing which catches the eye in looking at B[arnar]d Castle from the east, west or south.'[24]

On 26 January Hutt was pleased to hear that Joséphine was 'in better spirits about herself and had taken some nourishment',[25] but five days later he was disappointed to hear bad news of her again. The letters and telegrams immediately before and after her death on 9 February are missing.

Joséphine's death came as a great shock to everyone except to those, like Hutt and John's cousin Susan Davidson, who were in close touch with John in the last months of her life. She had been ill so often, but had so often recovered that it was assumed she would do so again. She was only forty-eight.

William Hutt and E. Y. Western, Joséphine's solicitor, went immediately to Paris. The funeral took place on 17 February at the Église de la Sainte-Trinité, the church Joséphine habitually attended. It was hung inside and out with mourning draperies, and on the façade the arms of Bowes were flanked by those of Montalbo. The solemnity and sadness of the occasion were intensified by the music of the grand organ, the Mass sung by an augmented choir, the funeral marches of Beethoven and Chopin, the Kyrie Eleison and Cherubini's Requiem.[26]

Letters of condolence flooded in from every quarter. Bowes's reply (written on a very small sheet of paper with a black border a centimetre wide) to one from his friend Richard Bowser expressed with great clarity what Joséphine had meant to him:

Without exaggeration I can assure you that the heaviness of the affliction which has fallen on me is such that I alone can appreciate it, and I have the firm conviction that I shall never be able entirely to surmount it. My wife and I have lived especially of late years, so much together and separated from the rest of the world and occupied with the same pursuits and objects that her loss coming so suddenly is doubly severe and leaves me very lonely and wretched.[27]

His lifelong friend Alexander Kinglake was quick to respond to the news, his letter exhibiting a deep understanding of John's character and containing wise advice on how to find the strength to keep going.

Knowing the immensity of the loss you are sustaining, & the depths of your seemingly calm, yet really devoted nature, I dare not hope that this terrible grief will pass away, but rather that the time may come when in a sense you may give expression to it by carrying out the purpose upon which your dear wife had so earnestly set her heart. She had a sustained enthusiasm which enabled her to look beyond the grave, & for your sake I like to think of this, because it seems to me that your desire to fulfil her wishes must give an interest to your life.[28]

While Bowes's ability to hide his emotions was an asset in most areas of his life, with Joséphine he had given free rein to his 'really devoted nature'. He had loved her profoundly, protected and pampered her, and nursed her through her frequent illnesses. His wealth had enabled her to indulge her many talents, as actress, artist, society hostess, patron, connoisseur and collector. His devotion had been returned in full by Joséphine. Henry Morgan Vane's letter of condolence recalled the many times he and his wife had witnessed 'the unusual devotion & admiraton which Mrs Bowes unintentionally manifested towards you & the return of your love & attachment for her...'[29]

There are further instances of the affection she inspired in others. Monsignor Thomas Witham of Lartington told Bowes, 'I even felt an attachment to Her, from the first moment I saw Her.'[30] And the young Emile Gallé (he was only twenty-four when he first met Joséphine at the London Exhibition in 1871) expressed his regret, with Gallic effusiveness, 'for the loss of this generous spirit that could find so quickly the way to one's heart, this high appreciation of the beautiful, this exquisite delicacy of taste, this lively love of art, which made of Madame Bowes an enlightened patron, beloved by artists.'[31]

William Hutt's wife Fanny, who appeared to have enjoyed a warm friendship with Joséphine – aided possibly by her ability to speak and write good French – wrote that she had been told that Joséphine's 'quickness in detecting a curious picture or hidden curiosity was like instinct' and that 'Her mind seemed to have no limit, for whatever she wished to comprehend she mastered.'[32]

Although her health and fear of the sea had prohibited Joséphine from making frequent visits to England, she had taken a close interest in everything at Streatlam. Probably the only areas of John's life in which she had not become involved were the collieries and the racing stables, both of them outside her scope of understanding. Otherwise, they had shared everything. The Museum project had brought out the best in both: Joséphine possessed what Kinglake described as a 'sustained enthusiasm which enabled her to look beyond the grave', while John had the administrative abilities and flair for minute attention to detail required to make it all happen. He had been content to remain in her shadow, even to the extent of allowing her to take the credit for the Museum's conception and creation.

Despite her *petit bourgeois* upbringing, Joséphine held remarkably liberal views. Her solicitor E. Y. Western, having counselled John to 'take comfort from a trust in the Divine Governor of all things', continued: 'You mentioned that Mrs Bowes while disbelieving the nonsense taught by the Roman Catholic Church, adhered sincerely to all that she considered true in it. That would include all those things which I firmly believe myself & which I am sure would be a comfort to you.'[33]

John once declared that Joséphine was 'the kindest person in the world' and many of the letters of sympathy he received confirm that this kindness was extended to numerous deserving causes in and around Barnard Castle. In the two years the Boweses had spent at Streatlam during the exile imposed on them by the Franco-Prussian War, Joséphine had become a familiar figure in the locality.

The Streatlam tenants assembled at the Castle and signed a letter of sympathy to Bowes. One paragraph in particular expresses the affection and respect they felt for their landlord: 'Having lived many of us on your Estate for a number of years – in some cases over fifty years – we beg to assure you that an event which concerns you so deeply, is a source of sorrow to us all.'[34]

In April Bowes responded to an enquiry about his health from his solicitor John Dickonson Holmes by saying that he was well but still troubled by a swollen foot and ankle. 'I cannot give so favourable a report of myself in other respects', he continued. 'Shakespeare was right when he said, "Who can minister to a mind diseased?"'[35] Bowes was misquoting from *Macbeth* (Act V, Scene iii), but if Macbeth's plea to the doctor to cure Lady Macbeth's madness is read in full, his reason for remembering it becomes immediately apparent:

Canst thou not minister to a mind diseas'd,

Raze out the written troubles of the brain,

And with some sweet oblivious antidote

Cleanse the stuff'd bosom of that perilous stuff

Which weighs upon the heart?

In the same letter Bowes confessed to Holmes that although he had begun the process of identifying, recording and packing the Museum exhibits for despatch to Streatlam, 'it is now to me a most dreary and laborious occupation.'[36] In their haste to build up the collection, the Bowes had kept few records of their purchases, relying instead on Joséphine's ability to remember where, when and from whom the various objects had been bought. 'Mrs Bowes used always to say to our Friends here,' he wrote to Dent, 'that she shuddered when she thought of the trouble, anxiety, & labour she would leave to me if she should die before the Museum was completed... Nobody but I can appreciate the loss entailed on the Institution by her premature death.'[37]

William Hutt was concerned about John's low spirits and kept urging him to 'leave the melancholy labour' and go away somewhere. He could 'resume the museum when more in condition to face the trial'.[38] Bowes took his advice, and in the autumn spent several weeks in Italy, returning to Paris in November.

By the time he arrived in London on his way to Streatlam for Christmas, the attack of gout which had delayed his departure from Paris had become so serious that he was confined to bed in the British Hotel in Jermyn Street, where he was to remain for more than five months. During this long period of enforced inactivity he continued to administer his affairs, although in the early months he was obliged to accept E. Y. Western's offer to act as his amanuensis. Although he had some friends in London, such as Henry Morgan Vane, those months of inactivity while incarcerated in an impersonal hotel must have been profoundly lonely and depressing, coming so soon after Joséphine's death.

Bowes at last reached Streatlam in March 1875. It was the first time he had been there for almost four years, and there had been many changes. One that affected him personally was the departure of the Hutts from Gibside for their new home on the Isle of Wight. On his retirement from Parliament Hutt had bought Appley Towers, the house which had once belonged to his father and where Hutt himself had been born and brought up. The contents of Gibside had been auctioned and the house let to a new tenant. Although the correspondence between the two men never faltered, the void left by his old friend must have added to Bowes's sense of isolation.

The changes in the appearance of the Museum were considerable. When the Boweses left Streatlam in May 1871, the outer walls were only a few feet high. Now the roof was nearing completion and the rate of progress on the rest of the building had accelerated. However, costs were mounting and Bowes, now faced with declining revenue from the collieries, was pressing Watson the architect to proceed more slowly.

Lack of funds had also obliged Bowes to halt the construction of the chapel in the Museum Park, begun in April 1875. It had been Joséphine's wish that she should be buried there, but instead it was arranged for her body to be brought back from Paris, where it had lain in the crypt of the Église Sainte-Trinité since the funeral, and interred in the vault of the Chapel at Gibside. The coffin left Sainte-Trinité on 15 June 1875 accompanied, according to *La Revue Critique* – which always took a close interest in its subscribers – by 'an immense crowd representing the most distinguished persons'.[39] Bowes did not attend his wife's body to Gibside as it was feared the journey would aggravate the swelling in his leg and ankle.

In search of a cure, Bowes decided to take the mineral baths at Salies in the Basses-Pyrénées. In his absence the collection would be looked after by Amélie Basset, daughter of his old dealer friend who had died the previous year. Miss Basset was to become indispensable to Bowes, supervising the cleaning and repairing of the paintings in the Temporary Gallery and organising their dispatch to England. Bowes later demonstrated his gratitude by leaving her a generous annuity in his will.

Bowes was accompanied to Salies by his valet, Joseph Smith, and a lady friend, Alphonsine de Saint-Amand, Comtesse de Courten. He had known the countess since she was twelve years old and was on friendly terms with her mother and stepfather,

92
John bought very few items for the Museum after Joséphine's death, but on a trip through Italy in 1875, accompanied by the countess, he bought a richly-ornamented sedan chair.

Hippolyte Lucas, a curator of the Bibliothèque de l'Arsenal. Lucas had been theatre critic for *Le Siècle* and Bowes 'had known him well for upwards of thirty years'.[40]

The countess had made an unfortunate marriage to a man whose conduct was so cruel that she was granted a separation. Their only child had died at the age of eight. It may have been partly out of kindness that Bowes invited her to be his companion on the trip. A woman of forty recovering from a failed marriage and the loss of her child, while an object of sympathy, would none the less find herself in a state of limbo, obliged to remain on the fringes of society. But to travel with an eminently respectable family friend twenty-four years her senior would not have sullied her reputation. She was an intelligent and agreeable companion and ensured that Bowes treated the holiday as a rest cure. When he returned from the tour, which had taken them as far as Florence, his general health had improved but his leg was still a cause for concern.

The following year the trip to Salies was repeated, again with the countess as companion. From Salies the couple journeyed to Italy, travelling as far south as Naples. On his return to Paris fourteen weeks later Bowes spent only a short time at rue de Berlin before leaving for Streatlam on 26 December 1876.

93
In 1878 John Bowes inherited from his cousin Susan Davidson her collection of pottery and porcelain. It included this fine Chelsea plate with botanical decoration (which was originally purchased by Mary Eleanor Bowes) and nearly all the Oriental porcelain in the Museum today.

By now the shell of the Museum was completed. A photograph taken in the spring of 1876 shows the building in all its vastness and splendour. The pavilions at either end had been roofed, leaving only the central pavilion still open to the skies. E. Y. Western, who had seen it in the autumn of 1876, declared it to be 'exceedingly handsome and grand'.

Before leaving England again, Bowes visited his cousin Susan Davidson at Ridley Hall. Her health had been failing for some time and shortly after his visit she died, in June 1877. After her death a letter dated 1859 was found in her writing desk. 'My dearest Bowes,' she had written, 'You have ever been the one of my male relations for whom I have had the truest regard and affection. I have therefore the more gratification in giving you what I value the most.'[41] What she valued most were her beloved house, her husband's superb library of rare books, and her not inconsiderable collection of pottery and porcelain. Nearly all the Oriental porcelain now in the Museum comes from her, Bowes having given his cousin's magnificent bequest to the Museum in its entirety.

Soon after his return to Paris Bowes wrote a surprising letter to Lord Strathmore (Claude, the 13th Earl, who had succeeded to the title on the death of his brother in 1865), to inform him that he was about to be married again. 'Of course at my age it would be simply ridiculous were I married to a very young Person, and my own character would have prevented me from uniting myself to a Person whose acquaintance I had only just made. I have known the Lady in question and her Family since she was about 12 years of age.' The letter continues with details about the countess's parents and her superior mental qualifications. It concludes, 'I say nothing of her personal appearance but enclose

94
Alphonsine de Saint-Amand, Comtesse de Courten, the daughter of old friends of John Bowes. She was a sophisticated and cultured woman, with many contacts in the world of the arts, but her marriage to John was a disaster.

two photographs taken about a month ago and which are a good likeness tho' the smile in one of them is not natural to her, and may have been assumed at the instigation of the photographer.'[42]

The only photograph of the countess in The Bowes Museum Archive (which may be a duplicate of one of those sent to Lord Strathmore) shows her wearing a hat like a wedding cake and leaning her ample bosom on a piece of furniture. The smile on her face may well be the one alluded to by Bowes.

Accustomed as he had been to female company of the most intimate kind, it may have been loneliness that precipitated Bowes into the marriage. Having known the countess and her family for so long, and having spent several months travelling with her, he must have felt confident that she would make a sympathetic and congenial companion in his last years. Highly cultured, and with many contacts in the art world, she also had the perfect credentials to become his partner in the Museum project – or Bowes certainly thought so. 'If when the time comes for arranging the interior of the Museum,' he told Holmes 'and she is induced to assist therein, the Barney Cassell People will have no cause to regret my marriage as she has a thorough knowledge of these matters and great taste and judgement in arrangement...'[43] (it is touching that he should have minded so much about the approval of the people of Barnard Castle).

Once Alphonsine's divorce had been finalised she and John were married, in London on 18 August 1877 at St James's Church, Piccadilly. Those present included the countess's mother and stepfather, Lord Strathmore, and Bowes's particular friends Kinglake and Henry Morgan Vane. Hutt was too unwell to be there. Twenty-seven guests sat down to the wedding breakfast in the Alexandra Hotel, and in Barnard Castle there were celebrations and fireworks at the Museum.[44] A honeymoon of two weeks at the most fashionable hotel in Trouville was followed by a seven weeks' tour through Switzerland, Italy and Austria.

95
Although undated, this photograph shows John Bowes near the end of his life. By then his health was failing, the Museum project had become an expensive burden and his marriage was on the rocks.

Leaving his wife in Paris, Bowes arrived in England in December 1877 to find the windows of the Museum glazed, the roof completed, a deep trench excavated for the terrace wall in front of the Museum, and all the cases transferred from Streatlam. The French *parqueteurs* had laid many of the floors, but the stoves to heat the building had yet to be installed and several of the picture galleries were undecorated. Still short of funds, Bowes confided to Holmes that had he known the Museum 'would have been so heavy a pull on my purse as it has been, I never would have undertaken it on such a scale'.[45] Nevertheless, he refused to compromise on any of the elements of the original design.

By the end of 1880, all the pictures at the Temporary Gallery had been catalogued and despatched to Barnard Castle. The Museum's first Curator, Robert Harley, had been appointed and took up residence in the palatial apartments which were to have been Joséphine's home when John died.

The Museum building was nearing completion, although plumbers, glaziers and painters were still at work. The massive iron entrance doors, which had been made in Paris for far less than it would have cost to manufacture them locally, had been installed. The two lodges which guard the main entrance to the Museum were under construction, and the monkey-puzzle tree (*araucaria*) which the Boweses had planted in 1871 was flourishing. (It is still there today, now twenty metres high. John Bowes seldom did anything without a reason, so he may have planted it there because he knew that the *araucaria* is the nearest living example of the trees of the Carboniferous Period – which gave rise to our main coal deposits – and it was principally the revenue from his collieries that had built the Museum.)

Another drain on Bowes's finances were the alterations he was making to Streatlam Castle. These included new stables, a pinetum, an Orangery built of stone to replace the dilapidated wooden one, and an armorial ceiling to be installed in the dining room. The ceiling had required detailed research and much correspondence with the College of Heralds and the heraldic artist who painted it (the ceiling is now in the Museum).

A photograph of John Bowes, which though undated was probably taken in the last few years of his life, shows him seated at a small table on the terrace at Streatlam. His black hat is pulled down over his eyes and one hand is resting on the stick which by then had become a permanent fixture. His shoulders droop and he gazes into the distance with an air of resigned melancholy. Gone is the good-humoured benevolence of the portrait by Feyen painted in 1863. Instead, the photograph portrays a man who is tired of life.

His weariness had many causes, not least his health. In 1878 he had suffered what he described to Vane as 'an attack of something like congestion of the brain', and was advised by his doctor 'not to read or write for some time'.[46] A year later he was again troubled by his leg and experienced difficulty in walking.

At the end of 1879 Hippolyte Lucas, his friend and Alphonsine's stepfather, died. This was followed by the sudden death of his solicitor and friend John Dickonson Holmes. William Hutt and Richard Bowser both followed in 1882, leaving voids which it was impossible to fill. Almost his only old friends left alive were Kinglake and Vane.

It was also becoming apparent that the new Mrs Bowes wanted nothing to do with John's life at Streatlam, nor did she have any intention of exercising her 'great taste and judgement in arrangement' on his Museum. In 1879 she made her first visit to England since the wedding, but after a fortnight's holiday in Scotland she returned alone to Paris. (she *had* expressed a desire to go to Streatlam, but in view of the alterations being carried out Bowes had vetoed the idea). This was to become the pattern of their marriage: John made frequent, sometimes lengthy, visits to England to supervise progress on the Museum and the alterations to Streatlam while Alphonsine remained at rue de Berlin. On the three occasions that she accompanied him, she returned to France with almost indecent haste, pleading the inclemency of the weather.

But the weather, surely, was not the root of the problem. Alphonsine was a sophisticated woman, a Parisienne to her fingertips, and she must have felt suffocated by the provincial atmosphere of Barnard Castle. In Paris, however, the doors to fashionable society had been reopened by her marriage to Bowes, and his wealth had enabled her to make the most of her new status. Now mistress of a large house in an elegant neighbourhood, she could entertain in some style. The allegation that she held brilliant salons is difficult to prove as The Bowes Museum Archive contains very few invoices of the kind which make it possible to reconstruct social activities of this nature. But John's letter informing Lord Strathmore of his forthcoming marriage to the countess had stressed the fact that she was a 'very superior Person', used to mixing 'with the highest intellectual society', and there is no reason to suppose that she did not continue to do so once married to Bowes.

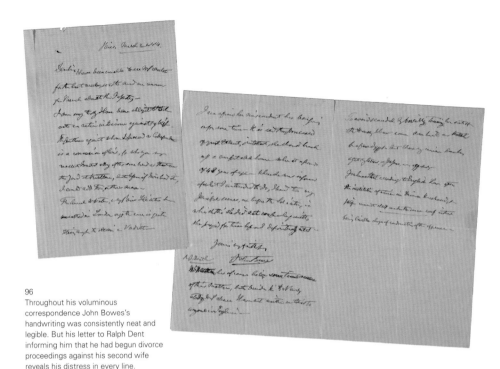

96
Throughout his voluminous correspondence John Bowes's handwriting was consistently neat and legible. But his letter to Ralph Dent informing him that he had begun divorce proceedings against his second wife reveals his distress in every line.

However, possible evidence of her cultural activities comes from an unlikely source: the memoirs of Louis Andrieux, Prefect of Police in Paris from 1879 to 1881. One such recollection is an account of how Léon Gambetta (then Président de la Chambre), acting on information that Bowes was in possession of paintings belonging to the Louvre, in late 1879 or early 1880 ordered a search of rue de Berlin. Bowes himself was in England, but Alphonsine did not hesitate to express her extreme annoyance at the unexpected invasion. Her reaction was enough to convince the authorities of the absurdity of their investigation, and it was dropped.[47] A paragraph in Andrieux's account supplies a glimpse of life at rue de Berlin: 'Mr Bowes, who has lived in Paris for many years, has made use of his great wealth to buy works of art. All Parisian society has been able to admire them at his receptions, where Mme Bowes, an attractive Parisienne, presided with much wit and charm.'[48]

In early 1884 Bowes began divorce proceedings against Alphonsine. His letter to Dent explains all:

...I am sorry to say I have been obliged to take out an action in divorce against my wife. The gentleman against whom I proceed as co-defendant is a cousin of hers [Monsieur Millet]... but I fear if I wished it, I could add two or three more... I am afraid her misconduct has been going on for some time... When she was informed of what I intended to do, I had two very painful scenes [and] she prayed for time before I definitely acted.[49]

Bowes was in such distress when he wrote this letter that it is barely legible. To establish Alphonsine's guilt he had been obliged to employ someone to spy on her. He had also been forced to question his valet Joseph Smith, who revealed that he had seen Alphonsine and Millet 'together in an indelicate and indecent attitude' at rue de Berlin, and 'about a fortnight later in the act of adultery'.[50] The discovery of what had been going on under his own roof and the indignity of having his private life exposed to servants and lawyers must have been mortifying to a man of his retiring habits and upright character.

Alphonsine's plea for time may have been prompted by her intention to throw herself on the mercy of Lord Strathmore. Between early March and late May 1884 she wrote him four long, rambling, sometimes almost hysterical letters in which she begged him to use his 'undoubted influence' on her husband to stop the divorce, and laid the blame for the lawsuit on the lawyers who 'will make a lot of money out of it';[51] on Bowes's valet, who was 'at the root of this sad conspiracy';[52] on the English servants who hated her; and on Bowes's 'feeble state of mind'[53] which allowed others to manipulate him. Most startling of all her accusations was that Bowes's decision to leave her 'was obviously due to the revenge and jealousy of other women', that one woman in particular (whom she did not name) 'persisted in trying to become his mistress,'[54] and that once Bowes was divorced, she would marry him.[55]

Lord Strathmore certainly replied to at least one of these letters and apparently offered to write to Bowes. But he also took steps to establish John Bowes's side of the story by asking his son Ernest, who was in Paris, to visit him. Ernest did so and was 'received in the most friendly manner by the old gentleman'. During their long conversation, Bowes confessed that 'if he had only known all about her goings on previous to his marriage to her that he now knew, he should never have married her'. Ernest hoped that if his father had replied to Alphonsine, his letters had been 'couched in careful terms' as she 'would not hesitate to produce any letters which could possibly serve her *in any way*'.[56]

Two months later Lord Strathmore received another letter from his son, this time from The Hague. Ernest had had a letter from 'one of his colleagues at the Embassy at Paris' which he copied verbatim for his father. The colleague had met Mr Treitt, the Legal Adviser to the Embassy, who had received a visit from Alphonsine during which she had claimed that Bowes visited Amélie Basset 'every day of his life from 4 to 6.30 and may well be in collusion and concubinage with her'. In Mr Treitt's view, 'Mrs Bowes would find it easy to prove B's intimacy with Basset & so stop the divorce, which, if successful, presents the danger of his marrying Mme Basset'.[57] This, of course, was the crux of the matter for the Strathmores: if Bowes became free to remarry, his wife might produce a child who would stand to inherit his vast estates and possessions, which would otherwise revert to the Strathmore family when he died.

The idea that Bowes, now seventy-three and a sick man, should have entered into a liaison with any woman, let alone Amélie Basset, is surely preposterous. Miss Basset was largely responsible for the packing and dispatching of the collection to England – an arrangement which must have been known to Alphonsine. Yet despite the gathering eividence of Alphonsine's dubious character, it seems Bowes had his doubts about divorcing her – 'for what good', he had asked Ernest, 'could a divorce be to me at my time of life', a sentiment he repeated on at least one other occasion.

Alphonsine's last letter to Lord Strathmore indicates that no help was forthcoming from that quarter. However, she had other tricks up her sleeve. Although Bowes's lawyers were confident that the evidence against Alphonsine was enough to obtain a divorce, her lawyers succeeded in having the first hearing postponed. They were probably aware that in May Bowes had suffered what sounds like a slight stroke – notwithstanding his doctor's assurance that it was merely a *parésie* or general relaxation of the muscles – and might be too ill to continue with the divorce proceedings.

There followed two more adjournments, each one engineered by Alphonsine's lawyers. When the case was at last heard, in March 1885, it was sabotaged by the judge insisting on the witnesses being present, rather than having their written evidence read out in court – as had previously been agreed. Also, Joseph's evidence was thrown into doubt by Millet, the co-respondent, asserting that at the time of the alleged adultery he had been suffering from angina pectoris and had been forbidden excitement of any kind – an assertion that was backed by his doctors. Sick at heart and in body, Bowes decided to 'let the divorce drop' and, although convinced of Alphonsine's guilt, agreed to a compromise.

Alphonsine's terms for the compromise were so outrageous it is impossible not to conclude that she had married John Bowes for his money. Taking advantage of his age, failing health and loneliness, she had lulled him into marriage. He had paid a high price, both emotionally and financially, for his gullibility and faulty judgement. And there were yet more problems to come.

97
The Entrance Hall of
The Bowes Museum,
photographed c. 1910.
The staircase, pillars
and balcony are made
of pink polished granite,
the mosaic floor of white
Hopton Wood stone and
black Belgian marble.

98
The Museum's massive iron entrance doors – each one weighing between four and five tons – were made in Paris, then transported by steamboat to London and from there by train to Barnard Castle.

In August, before leaving Paris for Streatlam, Bowes told Dent that he would have to return to Paris in the autumn 'to see about the removal of Mrs B's furniture & things [from rue de Berlin], about which there will I daresay be some difficulties, as she claims a lot of things besides what belongs to herself...' (the removal of Alphonsine's furniture was only temporary, as the house would belong to her when Bowes died). The 'things' included some jewellery which Alphonsine had been ordered by the judge to return to John but she did 'not appear anxious to obey the order...'[58]

When Bowes arrived at Streatlam, he found the Museum nearing completion. The hanging of pictures and the arrangement of exhibits were progressing, although some of the collection had yet to leave Paris. But any pleasure he may have taken in the magnificent building must have been marred by his state of health: not only was his leg troubling him but he was suffering from asthma and an illness of a dropsical nature. Alphonsine's conduct and the frustrations of the divorce proceedings had also taken their toll. As he warned Lord Strathmore, who was due to visit Streatlam with his wife in September, 'I am not a very lively body at any time, especially just now.'[59] The visit had to be cancelled and Bowes retired to bed. He died on 9 October 1885, aged seventy-four.

The funeral took place a week later. John Bowes's body, enclosed in a plain wooden coffin, was carried in a hearse drawn by four black horses from Streatlam to the station at Barnard Castle. It was followed by fourteen mourning coaches and was met *en route* by a large crowd which had walked through driving rain from the town. A special train took the coffin to Rowlands Gill, the nearest station to Gibside. The funeral was held in the Gibside Chapel, filled to overflowing with mourners. The coffin was laid close to Joséphine's in the Bowes family vault. The last – and the largest – of many wreaths to be placed on the coffin was sent from Alphonsine.

It was a sad end to a life which for so much of its course had run smoothly. But Joséphine's death was a blow from which John never fully recovered. In his rudderless state, he had made the fatal error of marrying Alphonsine. Her treachery, the unsavoury nature of the divorce proceedings and his declining health all combined to hasten him to his grave.

On his death, Bowes's affairs were found to be 'in a state of considerable complication and embarrassment'.[60] He was owed an enormous sum of money by Mr Palmer, one of the partners in the Marley Hill Coal Company (later renamed John Bowes Esq. & Partners), and all his other legacies had to be paid before the bequest to the Museum. Thus the trustees 'found themselves possessed of a palatial building containing a very valuable collection of works of art' but with no money either to complete or to maintain it.[61]

The Museum was to exist in a state of limbo for seven years, maintained by a skeleton staff and financed partly by the trustees and partly by loans. Owen Scott, who had been appointed as Curator in 1884 following Harley's death, continued to arrange the exhibits in the galleries.

The Museum finally threw open its great iron doors to the public in 1892. In his opening speech, delivered to a crowd of some four thousand citizens including the Earl of Strathmore and dignitaries of Barnard Castle, Sir Joseph Pease, MP, declared: 'I consider that today we have opened to the public a priceless boon... a great centre of education for this district... leading peoples' minds from those things that are gross and grovelling to those which are higher and which raise men's minds...'[62] Bold words to match a bold venture. That neither of its creators was alive to see their great project realised was a tragic outcome to all their endeavours.

Streatlam Castle, together with its five hundred acres of deer park, gardens, farms and smallholdings, was sold by the Strathmores in 1922. Five years later the Castle was broken up and sold piecemeal, and the resultant ruin was razed to the ground in 1959. Today nothing remains beyond a lone arched gateway and the stable block. At Gibside, although the outer walls of the house still stand, the roof has gone and its mullioned windows gaze blankly towards the Long Walk. The Chapel, however, has not only survived but in 1965 was restored to its Palladian beauty by the National Trust. In 1928 the coffins of John and Joséphine were removed from the vault and reinterred in the graveyard of the church on the edge of The Bowes Museum Park.

After all the time, care and affection lavished by John Bowes on his two great houses, it is profoundly regrettable that they should have both suffered such a dismal fate. But the Museum, standing proudly on its grassy eminence overlooking the River Tees, is a magnificent and lasting tribute to its founders who laboured so diligently to create it.

# Epilogue

There is a photograph in The Bowes Museum Archive, taken around the spring of 1876, that shows the vast building under construction. The complex architectural arrangement of rafters spanning a dozen individual roofs are in place, but have yet to be covered by slates and leadwork. A solitary figure can be seen standing atop the huge central dome that dominates the skyline for miles around. If he was to face south, the unidentified man could take in panoramic views of North Yorkshire, with the River Tees providing the boundary between Yorkshire and County Durham.

Back on the ground, on what would become the Terrace in front of the Museum, nestles the builder's compound – by today's standards a quaint little hamlet – that sheltered the community of tradesmen for the many years it took for the Museum to reach completion.

At the time this photograph was taken John Bowes was in mourning, having recently buried his beloved Joséphine at the relatively tender age of forty-eight. Joséphine, fourteen years younger than John, had naturally assumed she would outlive her husband, and had eyed the suite of rooms along the third floor of the west wing as a home for herself after her husband's death. That was not to be, but a succession of curators and their families enjoyed the views from this spacious apartment until the 1950s. Since that time this area has been developed into offices for the growing number of staff who work at the Museum.

Since it opened in 1892, the Museum's history has been colourful, eventful and, at times, difficult. Financial issues have been a relatively constant factor for a serious museum with an important collection, one that would perhaps have been better suited to a location in a major urban conurbation rather than in the relative remoteness of Upper Teesdale.

As the end of the twentieth century approached, the long-term future of The Bowes Museum became precarious, evidenced by the large number of buckets strategically placed at various points along the upper floors of the building to collect water from the badly leaking roof. For years it was frequently a daily ritual for those staff, whose office was closest to the bucket, to empty it and replace it in order to await the next downpour. As the twentieth century closed, this state of affairs symbolised the Museum's recent history.

In 1998 the Bowes had been threatened with closure over the winter due to insufficient funds, a situation avoided when the Friends of the Museum stepped in. In 1999, the Department of Culture, Media and Sport (DCMS) commissioned a report to examine what could be done to deal with a building placed high on English Heritage's 'Buildings at Risk Register'. The late Sir Richard Foster was the author of the report which sought to review the structure, funding, governance and management of The Bowes Museum. The Foster Report recommended the establishment of an Independent Charitable Trust to allow the Museum greater freedom to access funding and to respond to opportunities

99
This beautiful Chelsea pot-pourri vase is from The Lady Ludlow Collection of English Porcelain, which was presented to the Museum by the Art Fund in 2004. This gift greatly enhanced the Museum's existing collection of European decorative arts.

100
This remarkable photograph, taken in early 1876, shows the main structure of The Bowes Museum nearing completion, with only the windows and great dome still open to the skies. Just visible on the central dome is a minute figure.

such as business and tourism initiatives, thus making it a more dynamic and flexible organisation. The Report also recommended the preparation of a detailed business and development plan, the recruitment of a director and management team, the investigation of possible partnerships with national museums, the commencement of a programme of capital works for the building, and the introduction of an attractive public programme.

In 2000, with the consent of the Charity Commission, the DCMS and RE:source the Council for Museums, Archives and Libraries (now MLA), Durham County Council handed over responsibility for the Museum to a new Independent Charitable Trust which became accountable for the collections, building, assets, personnel and management of the Museum. This trust has become incorporated as a company limited by guarantee and as a registered charity. Durham County Council remain a key partner, providing significant core funding for the Museum.

Whilst the 1990s had seen The Bowes Museum experience some difficult moments, it also enjoyed recognition of its importance when in 1997 it was designated by RE:source and English Heritage as a museum with an outstanding collection. This status acknowledged that The Bowes Museum is of *international* significance for the quality and diversity of its collections, and of *exceptional* significance in terms of:

- The visual impact of the building and setting
- An art museum in the French tradition
- The unity of the Collections, Museum and Park
- The relatively unaltered nature of the building
- A major bequest to the public

Following this seal of approval and recommendations of the Foster Report, on 1 August 2000 the new Independent Charitable Trust took over the day-to-day responsibility of The Bowes Museum. Chaired by the Viscount Eccles (to December 2007), and currently by Lord Foster of Bishop Auckland, a Board of fifteen Trustees provide a broad range of financial, managerial and cultural skills.

The first decade of the twenty-first century has been an exciting one for The Bowes Museum, culminating in a period of intensive and extensive refurbishment and, most importantly, the repair of the complicated roof space. Thankfully, The Bowes Museum's collections should be safe from the elements for many decades to come.

In 2003, two years after the Trust had been formed and the Museum had adapted to its change of governance, a book entitled *The Great Smaller Museums of Europe* was published. Its author, James Stourton, identified a tier of museums below that of the élite of, say, the Louvre in Paris, the Alte Pinakothek in Munich or the National Gallery in London, but which were nonetheless major collections. So, while Austria was represented by the Academy of Fine Arts in Vienna, and Spain by the Salvador Dali Theatre Museum in Figuerás, the majority of entries were located in France, Italy and the United Kingdom. Stourton identified seven institutions in Britain, amongst them The Bowes Museum. The grouping makes for interesting comparison since it suggests The Bowes Museum's peer group on British soil to be the Ashmolean Museum, Oxford, the Fitzwilliam Museum, Cambridge and, in London, the Dulwich Picture Gallery, Sir John Soane's Museum, the Wallace Collection and the Courtauld Institute of Art. Look at this list again; four major collections in the capital, the great world-class university collections of Oxford and Cambridge – situated near London – and The Bowes Museum in the market town of Barnard Castle, population six thousand (almost) in the northern county of Durham.

At the time Stourton's book was published The Bowes Museum had yet to embark on the process of major capital works. The thirty-six buckets placed at strategic points along the third floor of the Museum reflected the scale of what lay ahead if it was to reposition itself as one of Europe's great museums. Certainly, at that moment, it felt as if we were many leagues away from the 'peer' group Stourton had suggested. However, in 2002, the year before Stourton's book was published, The Bowes Museum staged a major exhibition, *The Road to Impressionism: Joséphine Bowes and Painting in Nineteenth Century France*, which explored the developments in French painting leading to Impressionism, a movement that followed the first exhibition of Impressionist painters in Paris in 1874 – the year of Joséphine's death – and changed the face of the art world for ever. The exhibition was a great success, and a version of it travelled to London to show at the Wallace Collection.

More ambitious exhibitions followed: *Boudin, Monet and the Sea Painters of Normandy* (2004); *Cotman: Watercolours of Durham and Yorkshire* (2005); *J.M.W. Turner: Tours of Durham and Richmondshire* (2006); *Émile Gallé and the Origins of Art Nouveau* (2006). For many of these the Museum was able to attract loans from major museums in this country and abroad, testament to a growing confidence in its ability to meet exacting standards from lenders. In 2004 the first exhibition in partnership with a national museum was staged: *Toulouse-Lautrec and the Art of the French Poster* was proposed by The Bowes Museum and produced with assistance from the Victoria and Albert Museum, using their collections. There followed two more high profile exhibitions: *Sudan: Ancient Treasures* from the British Museum in 2005, while in 2006, The Bowes Museum was one of four regional venues which hosted the National Gallery's triumphant tour of Raphael's masterpiece, *The Madonna of the Pinks*. The philosophy behind these exhibitions was, and continues to be, to bring key works to the region whenever possible, thereby providing a base for audiences to see shows of equal stature to those in the capital.

The effect of these exhibitions was to raise confidence, improve our profile and increase audiences. By 2006 a plan was in place that would see the Museum progress from being a building at risk to being one of the iconic nineteenth-century buildings in the North of England, with galleries and amenities appropriate to the twenty-first century.

As with exhibitions, so with acquisitions. The twenty-first century has seen the Museum acquire some important works which have added a unique dimension to its collecting policy and its ability to interpret the collections. Works by some more avant-garde artists of the late nineteenth century – such as Paul-César Helleu, Théodore Deck, Lucien Lévy-Dhurmer and Jacques Gruber – have been purchased in what might be seen as a bold move to anticipate the tastes of John and Joséphine Bowes had Joséphine's premature death not ended their collecting activities on the cusp of one of the most sensational movements in art history. In the last decade the Museum has also been the fortunate recipient of two major collections, one of eighteenth-century English porcelain and another of historic lace, both of which have undoubtedly enhanced its existing collections of European decorative arts. And it has also been able, due to the generosity of its Friends organisation and to its ability to attract funding from the MLA/V & A Purchase Grant Fund and The Art Fund, to respond to opportunities to acquire items at auction, or as the result of an export stop licence. Thus, in late 2009 the Museum was engaged in a campaign, together with the V & A and the Fashion Museum in Bath, to raise a substantial sum of money to acquire a collection of dresses from the 1920s and 1930s designed by the French couturier Madeleine Vionnet. The Bowes Museum acquired three of these dresses in time for display, in the early months of 2010, in its ground-breaking new Fashion and Textile Gallery.

The years from 2006 to 2010 have seen the Museum engaged in almost constant redevelopment which has completely transformed parts of the Museum interior and made it a more rewarding experience for visitors and staff alike. As well as revitalising visitor facilities and refurbishing galleries, there have been improvements to Museum stores and the fabric of the building, thereby safeguarding the collections and ensuring that the Museum is 'fit for purpose' in the twenty-first century. A vindication of our decision to undertake such an ambitious programme of work has been recognised by the 2010 Award for Building Conservation from the Royal Institution of Chartered Surveyors.

The most dramatic transformation has taken place within the central dome of the building. Here, three floors of modern, well-equipped storage space for the Museum's major collections of fine art, historic books and archive resources have been surmounted by a beautifully appointed reading room from which can be seen magnificent views of North Yorkshire, Barnard Castle and the surrounding hills. This space creates a wonderful asset for the Museum, one that allows for wider physical and intellectual access to its collections, as well as holding the key to its ambitions for the future: developing its potential as a major research institution with links to universities, libraries and galleries – regionally, nationally and internationally – thus connecting both its collections and its library and archive with the highest standards of research and collections knowledge.

Quite by chance, the recent building redevelopments have offered all of us involved with The Bowes Museum an opportunity to reconnect to its past. In December 2009 eighteen-year-old Joe Kipling of Barnard Castle, working for the local stonemasons Coverdales, was drilling through a wall in the Museum's entrance hall to create an

101
The Bowes Museum owns one of the most significant collections of textiles in Britain. Among the exhibits on display in the Fashion and Textile Gallery, opened in 2010, are tapestries, the Blackborne Collection of lace, and a dress collection which covers the late 18th century to the 1960s.

archway into what has become our new shop. As he was breaking through he happened upon a chimney flue where he spotted something quite unexpected. It was a brown beer bottle, in perfect condition. As he picked the bottle out of the rubble he noticed something strange; inside was a folded piece of paper. He passed the bottle to our conservation team who managed to extract the piece of paper without breaking the bottle. Unfolding the paper the conservators quickly realised that Joe had stumbled upon a small time capsule that had been inserted into the chimney flue in the vague hope that one day it would be rediscovered. The letter was dated 14 April 1906 and its author was the second curator of The Bowes Museum, Owen Stanley Scott. And so, in December 2009, one hundred and three years after it was written, the letter's contents could be read as follows:

This flue, which with two others on the north side of this Hall, six in the Picture Gallery, and Eight in the Sculpture Gallery, was formerly connected to stoves for heating the Museum, was blocked up on Easter Eve, April 14th 1906, the Stoves having been superseded by a Hot Water Heating Apparatus.

I wonder if this flue will ever be reopened! If it should be, and this bottle should still survive, the finder may be interested to find this brief record, which I now deposit. I, the writer, am the second Curator of the Museum, and have held the appointment for nearly twenty-two years. I am nearly fifty-four years of age – a Churchman & Conservative, and a Past Master of the Barnard Lodge of Freemasons, no.1230.

Owen Stanley Scott

When I absorbed the letter's contents I was reminded of a curious fact. Scott was Curator of The Bowes Museum when it opened its doors to the public in 1892 – John Bowes had appointed him just before he died in 1884 – and so was responsible for curating the first displays in the Museum. Among the exhibits was the collection of Spanish paintings mostly purchased by the Boweses at the sale of the Conde de Quinto's collection by his widow in 1862. At that time the National Gallery in London had twenty Spanish paintings and the National Gallery in Scotland just three, while The Bowes Museum owned seventy-six. Thus, from the end of the nineteenth century to the beginning of the twentieth, the place to study Spanish painting in Britain was in a small market town in County Durham. Today the National Galleries of England and Scotland both have many more Spanish pictures and the balance has shifted in their favour.

Scott's letter made me wonder what he would have made of Stourton's peer group. I suspect that he would have been relatively unperturbed to find that The Bowes Museum was being compared with the Wallace Collection, the Ashmolean or the Courtauld. Indeed, it would probably have appeared a more natural grouping to him than it seemed to me over a century later. But for John and Joséphine Bowes, neither of whom lived to see their magnificent building completed, the knowledge that their Museum was now recognised as one of the great museums of Europe would be both astonishing and gratifying.

Adrian Jenkins, 2010
Director, The Bowes Museum

102
The view from The John Eccles Reading Room, which was created by the major redevelopment of the Museum carried out from 2006 to 2010.

# Notes

The quotes from the Strathmore Estate Archives are reproduced by the permission of Durham County Record Office and Lord Strathmore.

## Abbreviations

| | |
|---|---|
| AB | Alphonsine Bowes |
| DCRO | Durham County Record Office |
| JB | John Bowes |
| JDH | John Dickonson Holmes |
| RD | Ralph Dent |
| RJD | Ralph John Dent |
| TBMA | The Bowes Museum Archive |
| TW | Thomas Wheldon |
| WH | William Hutt |

## Prologue

[1] Robert Surtees, *History of Durham*, 1820, Vol. II, p. 254

## Chapter 1: John Bowes: Early Years at Streatlam

[1] Enquiry by the Lords' Committee of Privilege, Minutes of Evidence, 5 April 1821
[2] Margaret Wills and Howard Coutts, 'The Bowes Family of Streatlam Castle and Gibside and Its Collections', in *Metropolitan Museum Journal*, The Metropolitan Museum of Art, 1998, p. 237
[3] Ibid, p. 239 (or British Library, Add. MS 40748, Bowes MS, pp. 103-4)
[4] Jessé Foot, *Lives of Andrew Robinson Bowes and the Countess of Strathmore*, London, 1810, p. 27
[5] Wills and Coutts, art. cit., p. 240
[6] Mary Eleanor Bowes, *The Confessions of the Countess of Strathmore, written by herself, Carefully copied from the original lodged in Doctor's Commons*, London, 1793, p. 5
[7] TBMA: 9th Earl of Strathmore to the Countess, n.d.
[8] Wendy Moore, *Wedlock*, London 2009, p.88
[9] J. V. Wilkinson, 'John Bowes and Mrs. Joséphine Benoîte Bowes: With Special Reference to their Connection with France', (unpublished thesis), 1961, p. 12
[10] William Howitt, *Visits to Remarkable Places*, London 1888, pp. 351-2
[11] *The Auckland Chronicle*, 1881
[12] Charles Hardy, *John Bowes and the Bowes Museum*, Bishop Auckland, Co. Durham, 1978, p.19
[13] *The Auckland Chronicle*, 1881
[14] TBMA: 10th Earl of Strathmore to JB, 26 November 1817
[15] TBMA: 10th Earl of Strathmore to JB, 16 August 1819
[16] TBMA: 10th Earl of Strathmore to JB, 27 January 1820
[17] Augustus Hare, *The Story of my Life*, 1896, Vol. II, p. 179
[18] Henry de Gelsey, 'Famous Breeders of the Past, No. 1', in *The British Racehorse*, 1955
[19] TBMA: JB to TW, 25 August 1833
[20] Hare, op. cit., p. 179
[21] *Darlington & Stockton Times*, 17 November 1885
[22] *Fraser's Magazine*, March 1837, p. 382: Anon., 'Going to the theatre'.
[23] TBMA: R. Dobson to Robert Surtees, 19 January 1828
[24] Charles Hollis, *Eton: A History*, London 1960, pp. 201-2
[25] Ibid., p. 197
[26] DCRO: D/St/C1/10/75, C. Yonge to Lady Strathmore, 2 December 1827
[27] A. W. Kinglake, *Eothen*, London 1982, p. 162
[28] Gordon Ray, *Thackeray: The Uses of Adversity*, Oxford 1955, Vol. I, p. 116
[29] Bowes bought this painting believing it to be by David Teniers.
[30] TBMA: JB to TW, 8 January 1832

31  Hardy, op. cit., p. 37
32  Ibid., p. 256
33  Ibid., p, 38
34  Hare, op. cit., p.180
35  Hardy, op. cit., p. 36
36  TBMA: JB to TW, 5 November 1833
37  TBMA: JB to TW, 25 July 1833
38  TBMA: George Silvertop to TW, 12 October 1833
39  TBMA: JB to TW, 5 August 1833
40  TBMA: JB to TW, 19 May 1842
41  *Memoirs of Sir Edward Blount*, (ed.) Stuart J. Reid, London 1902, p. 41
42  TBMA: JB to TW, 25 September 1841
43  Blount, *Memoirs*, p. 41
44  Francis Trollope, *Paris and the Parisians*, London 1835, p. 230
45  *The Letters and Private Papers of William Makepeace Thackeray*, collected and edited by Gordon N. Ray, London 1945, Vol. I, p. 232
46  Ray, *Uses of Adversity*, Vol. I, p. 128
47  *Thackeray Letters*, ed. Ray, Vol. I, p. 277
48  *Fraser's Magazine*, 'Notes on the North What-d'ye-Callem Election. Being the Personal Narrative of Napoleon Putnam Wiggins, of Passimaquoddy', Vol. 24, pp. 352-8, London, 1841
49  Ray, *Uses of Adversity*, Vol. I, p. 339
50  *Durham Chronicle*, 2 July 1841
51  TBMA: JB to TW, 16 August 1834

## Chapter 2: Le Théâtre des Variétés

1   William Makepeace Thackeray, *The Paris Sketch Book*, Cologne, Germany 2000, p. 56
2   Gordon N. Ray, *Thackeray: Uses of Adversity*, London 1955, p. 170
3   Joanna Richardson, *La Vie Parisienne 1852-1870*, London 1971, p. 109
4   Philip Mansell, *Paris Between Empires 1814-1852*, London 2001, p. 158
5   TBMA: JB to TW, 2 March 1842
6   Albert Vandam, *An Englishman in Paris: Notes and Recollections*, London 1893, p. 38
7   Robert L. Jacobs and Geoffrey Skelton (ed. and trs.), *Wagner Writes from Paris*, London, 1973, pp. 22-3
8   Mansell, op. cit., p. 366
9   *Newcastle Daily Chronicle*, 12 October 1855
10  DCRO: D/St/C1/16/545: script of *The Old Maid of Barbrous Love, a Comedy in Two Acts*, by John Bowes
11  Donald Roy (ed.) *Romantic and Revolutionary Theatre, 1789-1860*, Cambridge 2003, p. 262
12  F. W. J. Hemmings, *Culture and Society in France 1789-1848*, Leicester 1987, p. 195
13  J. V. Wilkinson, 'John Bowes and Mrs. Joséphine Benoîte Bowes: With Special Reference to their Connection with France', (unpublished thesis), 1961, p. 86
14  William Toynbee (ed.), *The Diaries of William Charles Macready 1833-1851*, London 1912, Vol. II, p. 278 and p.490
15  Ibid., p. 490
16  E. Texier, *Tableau de Paris*, Paris 1852, p. 112
17  Robert Baldick (ed. and trs.), *Pages from the Goncourt Journal*, London 1980, p. 129
18  TBMA: JB to TW, 13 July 1847
19  Charles Hardy, *John Bowes and the Bowes Museum*, 1978, p. 83
20  Ibid., p. 83
21  David Hillery, *The Théâtre des Variétés in 1852*, Durham 1996, p. 48
22  Ibid., p. 47

23  Hugues-Marie-Desiré Bouffé, *Mes Souvenirs 1800-1880*, Paris 1880, p. 263
24  Macready, *Diaries*, Toynbee, Vol. II, p. 282
25  TBMA: JB to TW, 11 April 1846
26  Jacobs and Skelton, op. cit., p. 23
27  TBMA: JB to TW, 29 July 1847
28  Richardson, op. cit., p. 127
29  Hardy, op. cit., p. 84
30  Wilkinson, op. cit., p. 161
31  Hardy, op. cit., p. 84
32  Wilkinson, op. cit., p. 170
33  Baldick, op. cit., p. 78
34  Emile Zola, *Nana*, Oxford 1998, p. 121
35  Ibid., p. 125
36  Ibid., p. 2
37  Ibid., p. 27
38  Octave Uzanne, *Fashion in Paris. The Various Phases of Feminine Taste and Aesthetics from 1797 to 1897*, London 1898, p. 174
39  Zola, op. cit., p. 10
40  Baldick, op. cit., p. 88
41  Roger Boutet de Monvel, *Les Variétés 1850-1870*, Paris 1905, p. 8
42  P. Guedella, *The Hundred Years*, London 1936, p. 54
43  Gerald Carson, *The Dentist and the Empress*, Boston 1983, p. 8
44  Ibid., p. 9
45  TBMA: JB to RD, 3 March 1848.
46  Wilkinson, op. cit., p. 178
47  Hardy, op. cit., p. 88
48  Ibid., p. 87
49  Arthur Moss and Evalyn Marvel, *The Legend of the Latin Quarter: Henry Murger and the Birth of Bohemia*, New York 1946 , p. 125
50  Sarah Kane, 'Turning Bibelots into Museum Pieces: Joséphine Coffin-Chevallier and the Creation of The Bowes Museum, Barnard Castle', in *Journal of Design History*, Vol. IX, No.1, 1996
51  TBMA: Personnel of the Théâtre des Variétés to JB, 26 May 1855

## Chapter 3: Life in Paris

1   The painting was retouched in 1861 by Eugène Feyen, the artist who painted the portrait of John Bowes
2   Sarah Medlam, The Bowes Museum
3   TBMA: JB to TW, 11 October 1848
4   G. E. Haussmann, *Mémoires du Baron Haussmann: grands travaux de Paris*, Paris [1979], pp. 54-5
5   C. Hibbert (ed.), *Captain Gronow: His Reminiscences of Regency and Victorian Life 1810-1860*, London 1991, p. 289
6   Robert Baldick (ed. and trs.), *Pages from the Goncourt Journal*, London 1980, p. 73
7   Sir Herbert Maxwell (ed.), *The Creevey Papers*, London 1903, Vol. II, p. 204
8   Elisabeth Vigée-Le Brun, *Memoirs*, London 1989, p. 293
9   Mark Girouard, *Life in the French Country House*, London 2000, p. 237
10  Philip Mansell, *Paris Between Empires*, London 2003, pp. 160-1
11  Charles Hardy, *John Bowes and the Bowes Museum*, Bishop Auckland, Co. Durham 1978, p. 111
12  Henry de Gelsey, 'Famous Breeders of the Past, No. 1', in *The British Racehorse*, 1955
13  A. D. Vandam, *An Englishman in Paris*, London 1893, p. 313.
14  Académie Goncourt, *The Colour of Paris*, 1925 , p. 140

[15] Joanna Richardson, *La Vie Parisienne 1852-1870*, London 1971, pp. 235, 237
[16] Ibid., p. 190
[17] D. Seward, *Eugénie: The Empress and her Empire*, London 2004, p. 53
[18] The bills from Briquet and Monbro are in either The Bowes Museum Archive or the Durham County Record Office
[19] Hardy, op. cit., p. 123
[20] TBMA: A. Kinglake to JB, 26 January 1855
[21] TBMA: JB to RD, 8 August 1867
[22] TBMA: JB to RJD, 7 October 1875
[23] This information was given to Elizabeth Conran by the granddaughter of a housemaid who had worked for the Boweses
[24] TBMA: JB to RD, 18 June 1869
[25] TBMA: JB to RJD, 23 December 1873
[26] TBMA: JB to RJD, 17 November 1872
[27] TBMA: JB to RD, 21 December 1866 and 13 February 1867
[28] TBMA: JB to JDH, 2 March 1865
[29] *Darlington & Stockton Times*, 17 October 1885
[30] *La Revue Critique*, December 1868-January 1869
[31] Richardson, op. cit., p. 152
[32] Ibid., pp. 63-4
[33] Henry James, *Parisian Sketches: Letters to the New York Tribune 1875-1876*, ed. with intro. by Leon Edel and Ilse Dusoir Lind, London 1958, p. 191
[34] TBMA: invoice dated 15 June 1864
[35] Richardson, op. cit., p. 111
[36] Ibid., p. 108
[37] Alistair Horne, *The Fall of Paris: the Siege and the Commune*, London 1965, pp. 4-6
[38] Baldick, p. 149
[39] Alistair Horne, *Seven Ages of Paris*, London, 2002, p. 281, but estimates for the number of visitors to the Exhibition vary from 6 million to 11 milliion
[40] Richardson, op. cit., p. 152
[41] S. C. Burchell, *Upstart Empire: Paris during the brilliant years of Louis Napoléon*, London 1971, pp. 132-134
[42] Richardson, op. cit., p. 273
[43] Pierre de la Gorce, *Histoire du Second Empire*, Paris 1894-1905, Vol. V, p.151

## Chapter 4: Joséphine and the Paris Salon

[1] Griselda Pollock, *Mary Cassatt: Painter of Modern Women*, London, 1998, p. 76.
[2] W. M. Thackeray, *The Paris Sketch Book*, Cologne, Germany 2000, pp. 55-6
[3] Arthur Moss and Evalyn Marvel, *The Legend of the Latin Quarter: Henry Murger and the Birth of Bohemia*, New York 1946, p. 125
[4] Gordon N. Ray, *Thackeray: The Uses of Adversity*, London 1955, Vol. I, pp.170-1
[5] Frances Borzello, *A World of Our Own*, London 2000, p. 133
[6] Germaine Greer, *The Obstacle Race*, London 2001, p. 319
[7] Linda Nochlin and Ann Sutherland Harris, *Women Painters: 1550-1950*, Los Angeles County Museum 1976 p. 185
[8] Howard Coutts, *The Road to Impressionism: Joséphine Bowes and Painting in Ninteenth Century France*, The Bowes Museum 2002, p. 26
[9] Borzello, op. cit., p. 121
[10] Jacques Lethève (trs. by Hilary E. Paddon), *Daily Life of French Artists in the Nineteenth Century*, London 1972, p. 101
[11] Borzello, op. cit., p. 155

12  TBMA: JB to RD, 16 September 1865
13  TBMA: JB to RD, 26 September 1865
14  Andrew Lambirth, 'Birth of the Seaside', *The Spectator*, 4 August 2007
15  Coutts, op. cit., p. 14
16  Lethève, op. cit., p. 11
17  Borzello, op. cit., pp. 132-3
18  Lethève, op. cit., p. 113
19  Ibid., p.116
20  Pollock, op. cit., p. 80
21  Lethève, op. cit., p. 120
22  Emile Zola, *The Masterpiece*, London 1950, p. 308
23  *La Revue Critique*, December 1868-January 1869
24  Coutts, op. cit., p. 68
25  Ibid., p. 110
26  Lethève, op. cit., p. 143
27  Ibid., p. 144
28  Ibid., p. 139
29  TBMA: JB to RD, 25 August 1865
30 & 31  Notes by Elizabeth Conran to accompany an exhibition of Joséphine Bowes's paintings, held at The Bowes Museum in 1992
32  Elizabeth Conran et al., *The Bowes Museum* (Scala), 1992, p. 9

## Chapter 5: Assembling the Collection

1  Howard Coutts, 'Cosmopolitan Collectors', *The Antique Collector*, April 1992, pp. 68-73
2  Brandon Taylor, *Art for the Nation: Exhibitions and the London public 1747-2001*, Manchester 1999, p. 71
3  Giles Waterfield in catalogue for the exhibition *In Celebration: The Art of the Country House*, p. 13
4  James Stourton, *Great Smaller Museums of Europe*, London 2003, p. 244
5  Christopher Hibbert, *The Grand Tour*, New York 1969, p. 238
6  The painting is now in the Strathmore family home at Glamis Castle, Scotland. It later proved to be a version of Franz Snyders's *Fruit Market*, the original of which is in the Hermitage, St Petersburg
7  Elizabeth Conran et al., *The Bowes Museum*, Short Guide, n.d. [1985] p. 7
8  Elizabeth Conran et al., *The Bowes Museum* (Scala), 1992, p. 18
9  This theory was suggested by Elizabeth Conran and first aired by Jane Martineau in the catalogue for the exhibition *Art Treasures of England: The Regional Collections*, held at the Royal Academy in 1998, Cat. No: 273, p. 332
10  Elizabeth Conran et al., *The Bowes Museum*, (Scala), 1992, p. 18
11  Eric Young, *Catalogue of Spanish Paintings in the Bowes Museum*, Second Edition (Revised) 1988, introduction by Elizabeth Conran, translations by John Swift, p. 2
12  TBMA: Gogué to JB, 16 June 1862
13  Young, 1988, p. 7
14  TBMA: Gogué to JB, July 1862
15  TBMA: Gogué to JB, 10 July 1862
16  TBMA: Gogué to JB, 25 July 1862
17  TBMA: Gogué to JB, 7 September 1862
18  TBMA: Gogué to JB, late October, 1862
19  TBMA: Gogué to JB, late October, 1862
20  Charles Hardy, *John Bowes and the Bowes Museum*, Bishop Auckland, County Durham 1978, p. 143
21  Ibid., p. 142

22  Howard Coutts, 'Joséphine Bowes and the Craze for Collecting Ceramics in the 19th century', catalogue to the *International Ceramics Fair*, London June 1992, pp. 16-23
23  TBMA: Lamer to JB and Joséphine, n.d.
24  TBMA: Lamer to Joséphine, n.d. but probably 1867
25  In 1970 The Bowes Museum was gifted The Blackborne Collection containing hundreds of examples of lace
26  TBMA: Lamer to Joséphine, n.d. but probably 1867
27  Hardy, op. cit., p. 154
28  TBMA: Rogiers to Joséphine, 12 October 1869
29  Conran et al., *The Bowes Museum*, Short Guide, n.d. [1985], p. 20
30  Ibid., p. 20
31  Coutts, art. cit., handbook to the *International Ceramics Fair*, 1992, pp. 16-23
32  Ibid.
33  TBMA: Lamer to Joséphine, 12 May 1866
34  Howard Coutts, *The Road to Impressionism: Joséphine Bowes and Painting in Nineteenth Century France*, The Bowes Museum 2002, p. 91
35  Griselda Pollock, *Mary Cassatt: Painter of Modern Women*, London 1998, p. 78
36  Hardy, op. cit., p. 159
37  Henry James, *Parisian Sketches: Letters to the New York Tribune 1875-1876*, ed. with intro. by Leon Edel and Ilse Dusoir Lind, London 1958, p. 248, f/n no. 2
38  Ibid., p. 131
39  Howard Coutts and Sarah Medlam, 'John and Joséphine Bowes' Purchases from the International Exhibitions of 1862, 1867 and 1871', *Journal of the Decorative Arts Society, 1850 to the present*, 1992, pp. 50-61
40  TBMA: Emile Gallé to Joséphine Bowes, 18 September 1871
41  Howard Coutts, *Emile Gallé and the Origins of Art Nouveau*, The Bowes Museum 2006, p. 9
42  Hardy, op. cit., p. 183
43  The most recent, detailed and extensive research on the history of the Silver Swan comes from Sarah Kane, 'The silver swan: The biography of a curiosity', *Things*, No. 5, Winter 1996-7, pp. 39-57
44  TBMA: JB to RD, 21 July 1878
45  *La Revue Critique*, December 1868-January 1869
46  Jules Champfleury, *L'Hôtel des Commissaires-Priseurs*, Paris 1867, p. 4; translation by Margaret Harley, volunteer archivist at The Bowes Museum
47  Talk given by Charles Hardy to the Friends of The Bowes Museum, 1973

## Chapter 6: Life in England

1   Charles Hardy, *John Bowes and the Bowes Museum*, Bishop Auckland, Co. Durham 1978, p. 33
2   TBMA: JB to RD, 1 August 1861
3   TBMA: JB to RD, 21 May 1861
4   TBMA: JB to RD, 1 June 1861
5   TBMA: JB to RD, 11 June 1865
6   TBMA: JB to RD, 30 June 1865
7   TBMA: JB to RD, 10 May 1861
8   TBMA: JB to RD, 10 May 1861
9   Augustus Hare, *Story of My Life*, 1896, Vol.II, pp. 274-5
10  TBMA: JB to RD, 12 May 1858
11  TBMA: JB to RD, 16 May 1858
12  TBMA: JB to RD, 26 November 1861
13  TBMA: JB to RD, 3 December 1861
14  TBMA: JB to RD, 7 February 1859

15  TBMA: JB to RD, 15 December 1867
16  TBMA: JB to RJD, 28 March 1873
17  TBMA: JB to RJD, 21 December 1873
18  TBMA: JB to RJD, 12 May 1872
19  Hardy, op. cit., p. 150
20  TBMA: Joséphine Bowes to JB, 8 or 9 September 1867
21  TBMA: JB to RD, 8 November 1866
22  TBMA: JB to RD, 1 June 1861
23  TBMA: JB to JDH, 31 May 1864
24  Hardy, op. cit., pp. 132-3
25  DCRO: D/St/C5/114/86, WH to JB, 27 December 1855
26  DCRO: D/St/C5/54/74, WH to JB, 10 August 1844
27  DCRO: D/St/C5/46/46, WH to JB, 4 April 1843. The latter part of this quotation is an adaptation of a line from Thomas Gray's *Elegy Written in a Country Churchyard*
28  DCRO: D/St.C5/88/88b, WH to JB, 19 November 1850
29  DCRO: D/St/C5/88/92, WH to JB, 4 December 1850.
30  DCRO: D/St/C5/095/086, Lady (Mary) Strathmore to JB, 15 November 1852
31  DCRO: D/St/C5/137/32b, WH to JB, 9 April 1860
32  DCRO: D/St/C5/137/32c, WH to JB, 9 April 1860
33  DCRO: D/St/C5/137/38, Rev. Arthur Pearson to JB, 9 May 1860
34  TBMA: WH to JB, 29 August 1837
35  DCRO: D/St/C5/215/16, WH to JB, 8 May 1867
36  DCRO: D/St/C5/143/9, WH to JB, 16 February 1861
37  DCRO: D/St/C5/143/11, WH to JB, 21 February 1861
38  DCRO: D/St/C5/143/12, WH to JB, 24 February 1861
39  DCRO: D/St/C5/29/30, WH to JB, 15 July 1840
40  DCRO: D/St/C5/143/10, WH to JB, 18 February 1861
41  Hardy, op. cit., p. 156
42  Ibid., p. 137
43  Joanna Richardson, *La Vie Parisienne 1852-1870*, London 1971, p. 67
44  Marcel Proust, *Remembrance of Things Past, Vol. I, Swann's Way*, trs. by C. K. Scott Moncrieff, London 1966, p. 18
45  Richardson, op. cit., p. 72
46  Sarah Kane, 'Turning Bibelots into Museum Pieces: Joséphine Coffin-Chevallier and the Creation of The Bowes Museum, Barnard Castle', in *Journal of Design History*, Vol. 9 No. 1, 1996
47  TBMA: JB to RD, 17 October 1870
48  TBMA: JB to JDH, 19 January, 1852
49  Hardy, op. cit., p. 95
50  Ibid., pp. 245-6
51  Elizabeth Conran, *John Bowes, Mystery Man of the British Turf*, 1985, p. 7
52  Hardy, op. cit., p. 254
53  J. V. Wilkinson, 'John Bowes and Mrs. Joséphine Benoîte Bowes: With Special Reference to their Connection with France', (unpublished thesis), 1961, p. 247
54  Hardy, op. cit., p. 255
55  Ibid., p. 256

## Chapter 7: The Collection in Peril

1  Charles Hardy, *John Bowes and the Bowes Museum*, Bishop Auckland, County Durham, 1978, p. 162
2  Ibid., p. 161

[3] *Time-Life History of the World: The Colonial Overlords*, Time-Life Books, London 1990, p. 54

[4] Michael Howard, *The Franco-Prussian War*, London 1961, p. 57

[5] Edmond de Goncourt, *Pages from the Goncourt Journal*, ed., trs., and intro. by Robert Baldick, London 1980, p. 188

[6] A. D. Vandam, *An Englishman in Paris*, London 1893, p. 417

[7] Cynthia Gladwyn, *The Paris Embassy*, London 1976, p. 117

[8] TBMA: Gogué to John and Joséphine Bowes, 11 August 1870

[9] Alistair Horne, *The Fall of Paris: The Siege and the Commune 1870-1*, London, 1965, p. 167

[10] Donald Mallett, *The Greatest Collector*, London 1979, p. 119

[11] Horne, op. cit., p. 176

[12] Ibid., p. 178

[13] Ibid., p. 179

[14] Alistair Horne, *Seven Ages of Paris*, London 2002, p. 296

[15] Goncourt, *Journal*, p. 199

[16] TBMA: JB to H. Chevrier, 31 December 1870

[17] Horne, op. cit., p. 291

[18] Hardy, op. cit., p. 169

[19] TBMA: Mrs. Schleicher to Joséphine, 23 January 1871

[20] TBMA: Gogué to Joséphine, 2 February 1871

[21] Goncourt, *Journal*, p. 202

[22] TBMA: E. Chevrier to Joséphine, 8 March 1871

[23] Hardy, op. cit., p. 172

[24] Goncourt, *Journal*, p. 204

[25] TBMA: E. Chevrier to Joséphine, 21 April 1871

[26] Horne, *The Fall of Paris*, p. 417

[27] TBMA: E. Chevrier to Joséphine, 23 April 1871

[28] Horne, op. cit., p. 421

[29] Peter Hughes, *The Founders of the Wallace Collection*, London 2006, p. 41

[30] TBMA: RD to JB, 31 October 1871

## Chapter 8: The Legacy Realised

[1] Charles Hardy, *John Bowes and the Bowes Museum*, Bishop Auckland, Co. Durham, 1978, pp. 177-8

[2] TBMA: WH to JB, 21 February 1871

[3] TBMA: A. W. Kinglake to JB, 21 February 1871

[4] TBMA: Emile Gallé to Joséphine, 18 September 1871

[5] Hardy, op. cit., pp. 179-180

[6] TBMA: JB to RJD, 5 October 1874

[7] TBMA: JB to RD, 19 November 1871

[8] Henry James, *Parisian Sketches: Letters to the New York Tribune 1875-1876*, ed. with intro, by Leon Edel and Ilse Dusoir Lind, London 1958, p.40

[9] TBMA: JB to RJD, 20 January 1872

[10] TBMA: JB to RJD, 21 January 1872

[11] TBMA: RJD to JB, 15 March 1872

[12] TBMA: JB to RJD, 18 August 1872

[13] TBMA: JB to RJD, 22 November 1872

[14] TBMA: JB to RJD, 5 January 1873

[15] TBMA: JB to RD, 31 October 1871

[16] Hardy, op. cit., p.185

[17] TBMA: JB to RJD, 28 June 1872

18 TBMA: JB to RJD, 18 August 1872
19 TBMA: invoice from Worth and Bobergh, 1 June 1872
20 TBMA: JB to RJD, 17 February 1873
21 TBMA: JB to RJD, 5 October 1873
22 DCRO: D/St/C5/358/2, WH to JB, 7 January 1874
23 DCRO: D/St/C5/343/1, JDH to JB, 27 January 1874
24 DCRO: D/St/C5/384/5a, RJD to JB, 29 January 1874
25 DCRO: D/St/C5/358/7, WH to JB, 26 January 1874
26 Hardy, op. cit., pp. 188-9
27 TBMA: JB to Richard Bowser, 11 March 1874
28 DCRO: D/St/C5/357/1, A. W. Kinglake to JB, 13 February 1874
29 DCRO: D/St/C55/375/3, Henry Morgan Vane to JB, 10 February 1874
30 DCRO: D/St/C5/365/3, Rev. Thomas Witham to JB, 27 March 1874
31 TBMA: Emile Gallé to JB, 10 March 1874
32 DCRO: D/St/C5/370/2, Fanny Hutt to JB, 24 March 1874
33 DCRO: D/St/C5/353/2, E. Y. Western to JB, 15 February 1874
34 Hardy, op. cit., pp. 189-90
35 TBMA: JB to JDH, 7 April 1874
36 TBMA: JB to JDH, 7 April 1874
37 TBMA: JB to RJD, 26 July 1874
38 DCRO: D/St/C5/358/31, WH to JB, 29 September 1874
39 J. V. Wilkinson, 'John Bowes and Mrs Joséphine Benoîte Bowes: With Special Reference to their Connection with France', (unpublished thesis), 1961, p. 289
40 TBMA: JB to Henry Morgan Vane, 29 November 1878
41 Hardy, op. cit., p. 205
42 DCRO: D/St/C1/18/2, JB to Lord Strathmore, 31 July 1877
43 TBMA: JB to JDH, 11 August 1877
44 Hardy, op. cit., pp. 208-9
45 TBMA: JB to JDH, 15 February 1879
46 TBMA: JB to Vane, 10 November 1878
47 Hardy, op. cit., pp. 216-8
48 Wilkinson, op. cit., pp. 299-300
49 TBMA: JB to RJD, 2 March 1884
50 TBMA: JB to RJD, 22 March 1885
51 DCRO: D/St/C1/18/5(3), AB to Lord Strathmore, n.d.
52 DCRO: D/St/C1/18/5(4), AB to Lord Strathmore, 1 March 1884
53 DCRO: D/St/C1/18/5(1), AB to Lord Strathmore, 6 April 1884
54 DCRO: D/St/C1/18/5(4), AB to Lord Strathmore, 1 March 1884
55 DCRO: D/St/C1/18/5(1), AB to Lord Strathmore, 6 April, 1884
56 DCRO: D/St/C/1/18/5(7), Ernest Bowes-Lyon to Lord Strathmore, 21 March 1884
57 DCRO: D/St/C1/18/5, Ernest Bowes-Lyon to Lord Strathmore, 8 May 1884
58 TBMA: JB to RJD, 16 June 1885
59 Hardy, op. cit., p. 239
60 Ibid., p. 262
61 Ibid., p. 262
62 Ibid., p. 266

# Bibliography

## Manuscript Sources

The Bowes Museum Archive
Strathmore Estate Archives, Durham County Record Office

## Printed Sources

Académie Goncourt, *The Colour of Paris*, Paris 1925

Arnold, Ralph, *The Unhappy Countess*, London 1957

Baldick, Robert (ed. and trs.) *Pages from the Goncourt Journal*, London 1980

Boime, Albert, *The Academy and French Painting in the Nineteenth Century*, London 1971

Borzello, Frances, *A World of Our Own*, London 2000

Bouffé, Hugues-Marie-Desiré, *Mes Souvenirs 1800-1880*, Paris 1880

Boutet de Monvel, Roger, *Les Anglais à Paris 1800-1850*, London 1911

Bowes, Mary Eleanor, *Confessions of the Countess of Strathmore, written by herself, Carefully copied from the original lodged in Doctor's Commons*, London 1793

Burchell, S. C., *Upstart Empire: Paris during the Brilliant Years of Louis Napoléon*, London, 1971

Carson, Gerald, *The Dentist and the Empress*, Boston 1983

Champfleury, Jules, *L'Hôtel des Commissaires-Priseurs*, Paris 1867

Chapman, J. M. and Brian, *The Life and Times of Baron Haussmann*, London 1957

*The Creevey Papers*, (ed.) Sir Robert Maxwell, London 1903

Dickens, Charles, *The Uncommercial Traveller*, London 1862

Du Maurier, George, *Trilby*, London 1895

Foot, Jessé, *The Lives of Andrew Robinson Bowes, Esq., and the Countess of Strathmore, written from Thirty-Three Years Professional Attendance, from Letters and other Well Authenticated Documents*, London 1812

*Galignani's New Paris Guide*, Paris 1842

Girouard, Mark, *Life in the French Country House*, London 2000

Gladwyn, Cynthia, *The Paris Embassy*, London 1976

Gorce, Pierre de la, *Histoire du Second Empire*, Paris 1894-1905

Greer, Germaine, *The Obstacle Race*, London 2001

Guedella, Philip, *The Hundred Years*, London 1936

Hare, Augustus, *The Story of My Life*, London 1896

Hardy, Charles, *John Bowes and the Bowes Museum*, Bishop Auckland, Co. Durham 1978

Hemmings, F. W. J., *Culture and Society in France 1789-1848*, Leicester 1987

Hibbert, Christopher (ed.), *Captain Gronow: His Reminiscences of Regency and Victorian Life 1810-1860*, London 1991

—, *The Grand Tour*, New York 1969

Hillery, David, *Théâtre des Variétés*, Co. Durham 1996

Hollis, Christopher, *Eton: A History*, London 1960

Horne, Alistair, *The Fall of Paris: The Siege and the Commune 1870-1*, London 1965

—, *Seven Ages of Paris*, London 2002

Howard, Michael, *The Franco-Prussian War*, London 1961

James, Henry, *Parisian Sketches: Letters to the New York Tribune 1875-1876*, ed. with intro by Edel, Leon and Dusoir Lind, Ilse, New York, 1957

Jordan, David P., *Transforming Paris: The Life and Labours of Baron Haussmann*, London c.1995

Kinglake, J. W., *Eothen*, London 1982

Lethéve, Jacques, (trans. by Hilary E. Paddon) *Daily Life of French Artists in the Nineteenth Century*, London 1972

McConnell, James (ed.), *Treasures of Eton*, London 1976

Mainardi, Patricia, *Art and Politics of the Second Empire: the Universal Expositions of 1855 and 1867*, New Haven 1987

Mallett, Donald, *The Greatest Collector: Lord Hertford and the Founding of the Wallace Collection*, London 1979

Mansel, Philip, *Paris Between Empires 1814-1852*, London 2003

Marly, Diana de, *Worth: Father of Haute Couture*, London 1980

*Memoirs of Sir Edward Blount*, (ed.) Stuart J. Reid, London 1902

Moore, Wendy, *Wedlock*, London, 2009

Moss, Arthur and Marvel, Evalyn, *The Legend of the Latin Quarter: Henry Murger and the Birth of Bohemia*, New York 1946

Murger, Henry, *The Bohemians of the Latin Quarter: Scènes de la Vie de Bohème*, London 1888

Norman, Geraldine, *Nineteenth-Century Painters and Painting: a Dictionary*, London 1977

Philadelphia Museum of Art, *The Second Empire: Art in France under Napoleon III*, Philadelphia 1978

Picard, Liza, *Victorian London: The Life of a City 1840-1870*, London 2005

Pollock, Griselda, *Mary Cassatt: Painter of Modern Women*, London 1998
Proust, Marcel, *Remembrance of Things Pas*t, Vol. I, *Swann's Way*, (trs.) C. K. Scott-Moncrieff, London 1922
Ray, Gordon N., *Thackeray: The Uses of Adversity 1811-1846*, London 1955
Ray, Gordon N. (ed.), *Letters and Private Papers of William Makepeace Thackeray*, Oxford 1945
Richardson, Joanna, *La Vie Parisienne 1852-1870*, London 1971
Rounding, Virginia, *Grandes Horizontales*, London 2003.
Roy, Donald (ed.), *Romantic and Revolutionary Theatre 1789-1860*, Cambridge 2003
Saunders, Edith, *The Age of Worth*, London 1955
Seward, Desmond, *Eugénie: The Empress and her Empire*, Stroud 2004
Sitwell, S., *La Vie Parisienne: A Tribute to Offenbach*, London 1937
Stourton, James, *Great Smaller Museums of Europe*, London 2003
Taylor, Brandon, *Art for the Nation: Exhibitions and the London public 1747-2001*, Manchester 1999
Thackeray, William Makepeace, *Etchings by the late William Makepeace Thackeray while at Cambridge, illustrative of university life*, 1878
—, *The Paris Sketch Book*, Cologne, Germany 2000
*Time-Life History of the World: The Colonial Overlords*, London 1990
Toynbee, William (ed.), *The Diaries of William Charles Macready 1833-1851*, London 1912
Trollope, Frances, *Paris and the Parisians in 1835*, London 1835
Uzanne, Octave, *Fashion in Paris: The Various Phases of Feminine Taste and Aesthetics from 1797 to 1897*, London 1898
Vandam, Albert, *An Englishman in Paris: Notes and Recollections*, London 1893
Vigée-Le Brun, Elisabeth, *The Memoirs of Elisabeth Vigée-Le Brun*, (trs. Siân Evans), London 1989
Wagner, Richard, *Wagner Writes from Paris*, (eds) Jacobs, Robert and Skelton, Geoffrey, London 1973
Washburne, E. B., *Recollections of a Minister to France, 1869-77*, London 1877
Wilkinson, James V., 'John Bowes and Mrs. Joséphine Benoîte Bowes: With Special Reference to their Connection with France', (unpublished thesis), 1961
Wills, Margaret, *Gibside and the Bowes Family*, Newcastle upon Tyne 1995
Yriarte, Charles, *Cercles de Paris 1828-1864*, Paris 1864
Zola, Emile, *Nana*, Oxford 1998
—, *The Masterpiece*, Paris 1928

## Articles

Anon, 'Going to the Theatre', *Fraser's Magazine*, March 1837
Coutts, Howard, 'The Bowes Museum, Barnard Castle: a French museum in the English Countryside', *Antiques and Art*, February 2008
—, 'Cosmopolitan Collectors', *The Antique Collector*, April 1992
—, 'Joséphine Bowes and the Craze for Collecting Ceramics in the 19th century', *The International Ceramics Fair* [Handbook], London 1992
Coutts, Howard and Medlam, Sarah, 'John and Joséphine Bowes' Purchases from the International Exhibitions of 1862, 1867 and 1871', *Decorative Arts Society [Journal] 1850 to the present*, 1992
Coutts, Howard and Wills, Margaret, 'The Bowes Family of Streatlam Castle and Gibside and Its Collections', *Metropolitan Museum Journal*, The Metropolitan Museum of Art, New York 1998
Gelsey, Henry de, 'British Horse Breeders of the Past No. 1', *The British Race Horse*, July 1955
Kane, Sarah, 'The silver swan: The biography of a curiosity', *Things*, No. 5, Winter 1996-7
—, 'Turning Bibelots into Museum Pieces: Joséphine Coffin-Chevallier and the Creation of the Bowes Museum, Barnard Castle', *Journal of Design History*, Vol. 10, No. 1, 1996
Lambirth, Andrew, 'Birth of the Seaside', *The Spectator*, 4 August 2007
Thackeray, William Makepeace, 'Notes on the North What-d'ye-Callem Election. Being the Personal Narrative of Napoleon Putnam Wiggins, of Passimaquoddy, *Fraser's Magazine*, Vol. 24, 1841

## Catalogues and Booklets

Conran, Elizabeth et al., *The Bowes Museum*, The Bowes Museum (Scala), 1992
—, *The Bowes Museum*, The Bowes Museum, Short Guide, n.d.
Conran, Elizabeth, *John Bowes, Mystery Man of the British Turf*, The Bowes Museum, 1985
Coutts, Howard, *Emile Gallé and the Origins of Art Nouveau*, The Bowes Museum, 2006
—, *The Road to Impressionism: Joséphine Bowes and Painting in Nineteenth-Century France*, The Bowes Museum, 2002
Hughes, Peter, *The Founders of the Wallace Collection*, London 2006
Hearn, Karen, Upstone, Robert and Waterfield, Giles, *In Celebration: The Art of the Country House*, Tate Gallery, London 1998
Young, Eric, *Catalogue of Spanish Paintings in the Bowes Museum*, Second Edition (Revised) 1988, intro. by Elizabeth Conran, trans. by John Swift

# Index

Page numbers in *italic* refer to an illustration
Individual paintings appear under both title
and artist.

## A

About, Edmund 65
Academy of Fine Arts, Vienna 145
Alcott, Louisa May 64
Alte Pinakothek, Munich 145
André, Edouard 90
Andrieux, André, 136
Anglomania in France 25, 47, 55, 56
Appley Towers, Isle of Wight 130
Art Fund 142, 146
art in France 59, 60, 61
art dealers 66, 79
Art Nouveau 87-88, 145
Ashmolean Museum, Oxford 145, 148
*Auckland Chronicle* 11, 12
*Augustus rebuking Cinna* 83

## B

Backer, Jacob de 74
Bainbridge, Mrs 95
Balzac, Honoré de 66
Barbizon School 61
'Barèges' bath 99
Barnard Castle, Co. Durham 2-3, *2*, 15, 18, 73,
74, 78, 93, 100, *106*, 108, 111, 123, 124, 127,
129, 133, 134, 135, 139, 140, 145, 146
Barnard Castle Railway Company 94
*Barricade at Porte St Denis 39*
Barry, Jeanne, Comtesse du 36, 46
Bashkirtseff, Marie 60
Basset, A 84, 130
Basset, Amélie 84, 130, 137
*Beach Scene at Low Tide 64*
Berlin Royal Gallery (*now* Alte Nationalgalerie,
Berlin) 73
Bernardine 2, 38, 43, 96, *96*
Bernhardt, Sarah 55
Bismarck, Count Otto von 56, 111, *113*, 115
Blackborne Collection *147*
Blount, Sir Edward 20, 115, 120
*Boar Hunt 72*

Bonheur, Rosa 62, 84
Boucher, François 2, 82, 83
Boudin, Eugène 63, *64*, 83, 145
Bouffé, Hugues-Marie-Desiré 27, 29, *29*, 37
*Boulevard Haussmann in the Snow 44*
Bowes, Adam 7
Bowes, Alphonsine (*formerly* Saint-Amand,
Alphonsine de, Comtesse de Courten) 130-131,
132-134, *133*, 135-140
Bowes, Andrew Robinson Stoney 8-10, *9*, 22
Bowes, Elizabeth (*née* Blakiston) 7
Bowes, George 4, 7, 8, 11, 72
Bowes, John  portraits of, 2-3, *6, 15, 24, 92,*
93, 134, 135; appearance, 2-3, 13, 15, 25, 93,
135; attachment to Streatlam, 3, 12, 108; as
racehorse owner, 4, 18, 19, 25, 45, 104, 106-
107; birth, 7, 12; illegitimacy, 7, 12, 13, 14, 16,
22, 25, 71, 104, 107-108; family background,
7-11; education, 12, 15-17; sporting interests,
12, 15, 93; father dies, 12; father's will
contested, 13; character, 13, 16, 18, 20, 22,
28, 30, 33, 36-37, 48, 94, 95, 98, 102, 103,
105-106, 107, 120, 124, 125, 128, 134, 137;
as colliery owner, 13, 18, 33, 45, 98, 128, 135;
attitude to employees, 13, 19, 40, 129; passion
for theatre, 15, 20, 26 33; goes on 'Grand Tour',
16, 72; political ideals, 17; religious beliefs,
17; parliamentary career, 17-18, 21-22, 32, 45,
108; comes of age, 18; mother remarries, 18;
relations with Hutt, 18, 102-103, 126; finances,
18-19, 28, 38, 39-40, 90, 102, 125, 130, 134
135, 140; health, 19-20, 98, 124, 129, 130,
134, 135, 138, 139, 140; lack of children, 20,
51, 71; first visits Paris, 20, 25; and life at
Streatlam, 21-22, 93-98, 105; and life in Paris,
25, 32-33, 48, 52, 54, 55, 125; and Théâtre des
Variétés, 27-28, 29, 35-36, 37-38, 39-40, 56;
meets Joséphine, 31; and love for Joséphine,
32, 33, 103-104, 128, 143; takes up residence
in Paris, 32; flees Paris after revolution, 36, 39;
and Château du Barry, 40, 45, 46, 47-48, 50,
51-52, 73, 74; as letter writer, 44-45, 53, 93,
94, 98, 102, 136, 137; as High Sheriff, 45, 106,
108; marries Joséphine, 45; buys rue de Berlin,
51; and servants, 51, 93-95, 105, 124-125;
and the Museum project, 71, 73, 77-78, 108,
111, 123-124, 125, 127, 128-130, 132, 133,
134, 139, 140; as young collector, 71-73, 84;
assembling the Museum collection, 73-90, 98,

129, 131; buys land for Museum, 78; relations with mother, 99-101; mother dies, 101; and fears for the collection, 113-120; Joséphine dies, 127; Joséphine's funeral, 127; friendship with Alphonsine, 130-131; legacy from Susan Davidson, 132; marries Alphonsine, 132-133; attempts to divorce Alphonsine, 136-139; death, 139; funeral, 139

Bowes, Joséphine (*née* Benoîte Coffin-Chevallier) portraits of, 2-3, *30*, 32, *42*, 43, *58*; appearance, 2, 32, 43, 95; lack of children, 20, 51, 71; meets John, 31; birth and background, 31; as actress, 33, 37, 38, 39, 59, 89, 104, 105, 128; as animal lover, 38, 84, 94, 96-97; character, 43, 67, 82, 89, 97, 98, 102, 105, 108, 120, 125-126, 128-129; and Château du Barry, 43, 46, 47-48, 50, 51-52, 73, 74; marries John, 45; as artist, 45, 59, 60-63, 65, 66-68, 89, 111, 128; and life in Paris, 48, 52-54, 56, 125; and fashion, 48, 50; as society hostess, 50-51, 52-54, 59, 89, 98, 105, 125, 128; and servants, 51, 93-95; health, 51, 68, 93, 94, 95, 98, 99, 124, 125-127, 128; as collector, 53-54, 59, 66-67, 71, 79-80, 81, 82, 85, 86, 87, 89-90, 128; exhibited at Salon, 59, 66, 67, 68; and fear of sea, 63, 84, 93, 97-98, 97, 101, 111, 128; and the Museum project, 71, 73, 77-78, 87, 111, 123-124, 127, 128-130; assembling the Museum collection, 73-90, 98, 129; will, 90, 124; and life at Streatlam, 93-97, 99, 108; letter to John, 98; and love for John, 98, 28; and Lady Strathmore, 101-102; created Countess of Montalbo, *103*, 103; fears for the collection, 113-120; death, 127; funeral, 127; religious beliefs, 129

Bowes, Mary 9, 14

Bowes, Mary (*second wife of* George Bowes) 72

Bowes, Mary Eleanor (*see* Strathmore, Countess of)

Bowes Museum, The 2-3, 4, 20, 66, 67, 71, 74, 77-78, 79, 83, 83, 84, 87, 90, 108, 111, *122*, *123*, 123, 124, 125, 127, 128-129, 130, 132, 133, 134, 135, 138, 139, *139*, 140, 143-148, *144*, *147*, *148*

Bowes Museum Archive, The 33, 61, 81, 94, 135, 143, 146

Bowes Museum Park, The 78, 101, 124, 130, 140, 144

Bowes, Sir William 7

Bowes, William Johnstone 9

Bowes-Lyon, The Hon. Ernest 137

Bowles, Thomas 115

Bowser, Richard 127-128, 135

Briquet 50, 89

Brodie, Sir Benjamin 19

Broomielaw Station 94

Brown, Mather *10*, 11

*Builder, The 123*, 123

**C**

Caillebotte, Gustave *44*

*Candide* 37

Carpentier *63*, 67, 82, 111

Catch and Glee Club 107

ceramics 78, 79, 81-82, 87, 146
Berlin 82, 87
Chelsea *132*, *142*
faïence 2, 79, *80*, 82, 88, 90, 125, *126*
Meissen 79, *81*, 82
Moustiers *89*, 90
Nevers *80*, 81
Nymphenburg 82
Oriental 132
Sèvres 79, 82, *82*
Worcester 87

Cernay-la-Ville 62-63, 79

Cézanne, Paul 85

Chaffer, William 81

Cham *114*

Champfleury, Jules 89-90

Champney, Benjamin 59

Chaplin, Charles 60, *60*, 83

Charity Commission, The 144

Château du Barry, Louveciennes (or Luciennes) 36, 40, 43, *45*, *46*, 45-52, *50*, 53, 73, 74, 90, 105

*Château du Barry at Louveciennes 45*, 47

Chesterfield, Lord 7

Chevrier, Eléonore 113, 114, 115, 116, 118, 119-120

Chevrier, Hortense 111, 113, 115, 116, 117, 118

Chevrier, Robert 111, 113, 115, 116, 117

Claude, Lorrain 67, 83

Claudin, Gustave 56
Coffin-Chevallier, Joséphine Benoîte (see Bowes, Joséphine)
Coffin-Chevallier, Mme 36
Cole, Charles Augustus 54
collieries 9, 13, 18, 33, 98, 128, 135
Commune of Paris (see Paris)
Compiègne 48
Conran, Elizabeth 75
Corot, Jean-Baptist-Camille 64, 83
Cotherstone 105, 107
Cotman, John Sell 145
Council for Museums, Archives and Libraries (now MLA) 144
Courbet, Gustave 61, 61, 68, 83
Cox, James 88
Creevey, Thomas 46
Creswick, Thomas 106
Crimean War 40, 51
crinoline 49
Crucifixion 17, 72
Cybele Beseeching Saturn to Spare her Child 74

D

Daniel O'Rourke 45, 107
Darjou, Victor 29
Darlington & Stockton Times 14
Daubigny, Charles-François 62
David, Jacques-Louis 66
Davidson, John 12
Davidson, Susan (née Jessup) 12, 13, 102, 127, 132
Deck, Théodore 146
Déjazet, Virginie 27, 33, 37
Déjeuner sur l'Herbe 64
Delacroix, Eugène 61, 62
Delaval, Lord 11
Delécluze, Etienne-Jean 83
Delorme, Joséphine (see Bowes, Joséphine)
Dent, Ralph 36, 44-45, 51, 53, 62, 67, 93-96, 99, 101, 105, 111, 120, 124
Dent, Ralph John 96, 105, 124, 125, 126, 127, 136, 139

Department of Culture, Media and Sport 144
Derby, The 4, 18, 19, 25, 45, 48, 97, 105, 107
Derby, Earl of 107
Desanges, Louis William 30, 32
Dickens, Charles 14, 27, 47
Dixon, Mrs 53
Dobson, Richard 13, 15
Don Juan Antonio Meléndez Valdés 77
Doré, Gustave 14
Downman, John 9
Dunhouse Quarry 125
Durand-Ruel 65, 66, 85
Dürer, Albrecht 80
Durham Chronicle 22, 37, 106
Durham County Council 144
Durham County Record Office 17, 26, 30, 33
Durham Militia 100, 106, 108
Dury, Antoine 32, 42, 96, 96

E

Eccles, Viscount 144
El Greco 74, 75, 75, 76-77
Elizabeth, The Queen Mother 13
Emanuel, Harry 88-89
en plein air 61, 63, 83
Engleheart, J. C. D. 8
English Heritage 143
Epirus 107
Ernestine, Mlle 30, 31
Espine, Vicomte de l' 83
Eton School 7, 15, 16
Eugénie, Empress 48, 49, 56, 63, 112

F

Fantin-Latour, Henri 65, 83
Fashion Museum, Bath 146
Fashion and Textile Gallery, The Bowes Museum 146, 147
Feyen, Jacques-Eugéne 92, 93
Fiennes, Charles Matharel de 33, 37, 38
Fitzwilliam Museum, Cambridge 145
Flore et Zéphyr 38
Foot, Jessé 9, 22,
Fordham, George 107

Forest of Fontainebleau 61
Foster, Lord 144
Foster, Sir Richard 143
Foster Report 143-144
*Foyer of the Variétés 37*
Fracanzano, Francesco 84
Fragonard, Jean Honoré 67
Franco-Prussian War 56, 112-118, 119, 125, 129
Fraser, James 22
*Fraser's Magazine* 21
Frederick, Duke of York 11
French National Academy *62*, 83
Friends of The Bowes Museum 13, 143
furniture 43, 73, 78, 86
    *boulle* 2, *43*
    Monbro *fils aîné* 47, 48, 51, *52, 53*, 73, 86

# G

Gabé, Nicholas Edward *39*, 84
*Galignani's Messenger* 37
Gallé, Emile 2, *86*, 87-88, 123, 125, *126*, 128, 145
Gambetta, Léon *115*, 136
Gautier, Théophile 55, 66, 120
Gelsey, Baron Henry de 13, 48
Gibside 4, 7, 9, 10, 11, 18, 33, 72, 73, 93, 98, 99, *100, 101*, 101, 130, 139, 140
Giordano, Luca 84
*Girl in a Pink Dress Sitting at a Table with a Dog 60*
Girodet, Anne-Louis 83
Glamis Castle 7, 10, 13
glass 78
    Emile Gallé (*see* also Gallé, Emile) *86*, 87-88, 145
    Salviati 2, 87
*Globe, The* 37
Gogué, Benjamin 74-77, 82, 113, 114, 115, 116. 117, 118-119
Goncourt, Edmond and Jules 27, 32, 33, 35, 36, 44, 49, 56, 105, 112, 114, 115, 118, 119
Goodenough, Rev William 12, 17
Gorce, Pierre de la 56
Gossaert, Jan, circle of 74

Goya, Francisco de 74, 75, *76*, 77
Grand Tour 71, 72
Gray, George 8-9
Grey, Lord 17
Gronow, Captain Rees 44
Gros, Baron Antoine-Jean 83
Gruber, Jacques 146
Gudin, Baron Jean-Antoine-Théodore 83-84
Guedella, Philip 36
Guys, Constantin *37*

# H

Hardy, Charles 47
Hare, Augustus 13, 18, 95, 99
Harley, Robert 134, 140
*Harnessing of the Horses of the Sun 84*, 85
Haussmann, Baron Georges-Eugène 43
Hearne, Thomas *2*
Helleu, Paul-César 146
Henry, Mr 116, 117
Herring, John Frederick junior *105*
Herring, John Frederick senior 18, *19*
Hertford, 3rd Marquess of 25, 71
Hertford, 4th Marquess of 40, 71, 72, 113
Holmes, John Dickonson 53, 78, 105, 106, 129, 134, 135
Hotel Meurice, Boulogne 98
Hughes, Colonel James 103
Hugo, Victor 31, 34, 55
Hutt, Lady Fanny (*née* Hughes) 102-103, 123, 128
Hutt, William 11, 18, 20, 47, 48, *99*, 99-103, 107, 123, *126*, 127, 128, 130, 133, 135

# I

Impressionists 85-86, 145
Independent Charitable Trust, The Bowes Museum 144
Ingres, Jean-Dominique *62*, 66
*Interior of a Prison 76*, 77

# J

Jackson, John *6, 15*, 15
Jacquemart, Nélie 90

James, Henry 55, 83, 86, 124
Jessup, Anna Maria 12
Jessup, Henry 12
Jessup, Susan (*see* Davidson)
John Eccles Reading Room, The 146, 148
Jopling, Louise 60

# K

Kean, Edmund 15
Keate, Dr 16
Kemble, John Philip 15
Kinglake, Alexander 16, 51, 115, 117, 123, 128, 133, 135
Kipling, Joe 146
Kuwasseg, Karl-Josef 60-61
Kyle, Joseph 111

# L

*La Bohème* 39
*La Grande Duchesse de Gerolstein* 35, 56
*La Revue Critique* 53, 65, 89, 108, 130
*La Vie de Bohème* 39
Labouchere, Henry 114
lace 78, *78*, 79, 146
Lady Ludlow Collection of English Porcelain 143, 146
Lallemand, Prof Claude François 20
Lamer, A. C. 79, 81-82, 83
*Landscape with Figures and Goats* 85, *85*
*Landscape with Trees and Cattle* 63, *68*
*Landscape with Watermill* 82, *83*
Largillière, Nicolas de 83
*Le Figaro* 86
*Le Foyer des Acteurs* 33
*Le Roi s'amuse* 21
Le Siècle 33, 131
Ledoux, J.P. 82
Leopold of Sigmaringen, Prince 111
Lepautre, Mme 79, 81
*Les Fleurs* 85
Lévy-Dhurmer, Lucien 146
'lit à la duchesse' 53, 86
Livry, Emma 35
London 14-15
  Arthur's Club 36

Christie's 88-89
conditions in 14
Conduit Street 14, 32
Courtauld Institute 145, 148
Dulwich Picture Gallery 145
Great Exhibition, The 1851 71
Hertford House 71, 120
Houses of Parliament 17
International Exhibition, 1862 87
International Exhibition, 1871 86, 87, 128
Jockey Club 25
National Gallery 77, 145, 148
Royal Academy 59, 63, *67*, 68
St George's Church, Hanover Square 12, 18
St George's Hospital 19
St James's Church, Piccadilly 133
St. Marylebone Parish Church 45
Sir John Soane's Museum 145
social life in 15
South Kensington Museum (later the V & A) 71, 81, 145, 146
Tate Gallery 71
Wallace Collection, The 71, 120, 145, 148
*London Daily News* 114
Louis XIV, King 118
Louis XV, King 36, 46
Louis-Philippe, King 36, 74
Lucas, Hippolyte 131, 135
Lucca, Duke of 73
Lyons, Lord 113

# M

*Macbeth* 129
Maclise, Daniel *22*
Macready, William Charles 15, 27, 30, 107
*Mademoiselle Grabutot* 33
*Madonna of the Pinks* 145
Malmesbury, Earl of 49
Manet, Édouard *54*, *55*, 64, 74, 85, *117*
Maria Christina, Queen 74
Marie-Antoinette, Queen 48, 79
*Marion Delorme* 31
*Marley Hill* *52*
Marley Hill Coal Company (*later* John Bowes

Esq & Partners) 102, 140
Marryat, Joseph 81
Master of Ste-Gudule 73
Master of the 'Virgo inter Virgines' *17*, 72
Maurier, George du *32*, 59, *67*
mechanical mouse *87*, 89
Merlin, John Joseph 88
Michallon, Achille-Etna 83
Miller, Joseph *3*
Millet, Monsieur 136-137, *138*
Millner, Mary (*see* Strathmore, Mary,
Countess of)
*Miracle of the Eucharist 72*, 73
MLA/V & A Purchase Grant Fund 146
Mitchell, John 30
Moltke, Field-Marshal von 56, 111
Monbro *fils aîné* (see furniture) 47, 48, 51, *52*,
*53*, 73, 86
Monet, Claude 145
*Moniteur des Ventes* 79
monkey-puzzle tree (*araucaria*) 2, 134-135
Montalbo, Countess of (*see* also Bowes,
Joséphine) 103, *103*
Monticelli, Adolphe-Joseph-Thomas 79, 85, *85*
Monvel, Roger Boutet de *32*, 36
Morin, Edward *34*, 35
Morin, Prof Laurent-Joseph 35-36, 37, 38, 39
Morisot, Berthe 62
Mündig 18, 25, 106
Murger, Henry 25, 39, 59
Murillo, Bartolomé Estéban 75
Museo de la Trinidad, Madrid 74
*Musique aux Tuileries 54*
Musset, Alfred de 26

N
Napoléon I (Bonaparte) 2, 43, 74, 84
Napoléon III (Bonaparte) 34, 35, 43, 44, 48, 56,
64, 88, 112, *112, 113*
National Gallery of Scotland 148
National Trust, The 140
*Nativity* 72
Negelen, J. M. *24*
*Newcastle Daily Chronicle* 26

*Newcastle Journal* 37
Nieriker, May Alcott 64
Nobleman 56

O
Offenbach, Jacques 35, 44, 56
*Olympia* 85
*On the Sands near Ostend* 84
Orangery, Château du Barry 46, 47, *50*, 51
Orangery, Gibside 4
Orangery, Streatlam 4, 135
Ozy, Alice 34, 40

P
Palladian Chapel, Gibside 4, 11, *101*, 130,
139, 140
Palmer, C.M. 140
Palmerston, Lord 25
Paris
    appearance of 26
    Académie Julien 60
    balloon post 115-116
    Bois de Boulogne 38, 55, 114
    blvd des Capucines 36
    blvd Haussmann 44, *44*
    blvd des Italiens 32, *38*, 40
    blvd Montmartre 27, 28, 38
    British Embassy 120, 137
    Café Anglais 32
    Café de Paris 25, 32
    Cercle de l'Union 25, 32
    Champs-Elysées 63, *65*, 118
    Cité d'Antin 38, 40, 46, 48, 51
    Commune, The *110, 117, 118*, 119-120, 125
    Eglise de Sainte Trinité 127, 130
    famine in 114-115, *114*
    Gare Saint-Lazare 46, 51
    improvements to 43-44
    International Exhibition, 1855 56, 63
    International Exhibition, 1867 56, 87, 88, 89
    Jockey Club 25, 32, 114
    Longchamp *55*, 55
    Musée Jacquemart-André 90
    Musée du Louvre 59, 74, 83, 111, 113, 145

National Assembly 119
National Guard 119
Opéra 56, 103
Palais Royal 26, *26*, 90, 119
Palais de l'Industrie 63, *65*
Préfecture de Police 113, 119, 120
Revolution of 1848 36, *39*, 84
rue de Berlin 51, 52-53, 74, 77, 79, 98, 111, 113, 117, 119, 120, 124, 127, 131, 135, 136, 139
rue Blomet 77, 113, 119
rue de Rougemont 25, 32
Salon 63-66, *65, 66*, 67, 68, 83, 85, 111
Salon des Refusés 64
siege 112-118, 119
social life 54-56
Temporary Gallery, The 77, 113, 117, 119, 120, 130, 134
Tortoni's 32
Tuileries Palace 26, 36, 43, 48, 54, 111, 112, *118*, 119
Paris Salon (*see* Paris)
Pavillon du Barry 46
Pearson, Rev Arthur 16, 101
Pease, Sir Joseph 17, 140
Peel, Sir Robert 113
Pellechet, Auguste 77
Pellechet, Jules 77, 111, 123
Pereda, Antonio de 75, *77*
Pisarro, Camille 46
Planche, Raphael de la, attributed to the Paris workshop of 80
Pompadour, Mme de *89*, 90
Poussin, Nicolas 71, 72, 83
Primaticcio, Francesco, Circle of 72, *73*
Prince Regent (*later* George IV) 81
Proust, Marcel 104
Puccini, Giacomo 39

Q

Quaire, Mme du 115, 117
Quinto, Conde de 74, 148
Quinto, Condesa de 74-77

R

Raban, Jonathan 16
*Racing at Longchamp 55*
railways 46, 77
*Rainbow Landscape 72*
*Rape of Helen 72, 73*
Raphael 145
Renoir, Auguste 54, 65
Ridley Hall 12, 132
Robert, Hubert 82
Rogiers of Ghent 79-80
Roqueplan, Nestor 27-28, 29, 32
Royal Institution of Chartered Surveyors 146
Rubens, Peter Paul 72

S

SS *John Bowes* 45
St Leger 107
Saftleven, Cornelis 17, 72
Saint-Amand, Alphonsine de, Comtesse de Courten (*see* Bowes, Alphonsine)
*Saint Jerome in the Wilderness 72*
Salon, The (*see* Paris)
Salvador Dali Theatre Museum, Figuerás 145
Sassetta, (Stefano di Giovanni *called* Sassetta) *72, 73*
Schleicher, Mrs Anne 116-117
Schneider, Hortense *34*, 35, 56
School of Fontainebleau 72
Scott, John 18, *104*, 106-107, 124
Scott, Owen Stanley 140, 147-148
Scott, Sir Walter 106
Scott, William 18, 104, 107
Seaton Delaval Hall, Northumbria 11
Second Empire 2, 34, 35, 43, 44, 47, 48, 49, 53, 54, 56, 61, 66, 86, 105, 112
Sedan, battle of 112, 113, 120
Shafto, Robert 17
Shakespeare, William 15, 27, 129
Sheridan, Richard Brinsley 15
Shotter Boys, Thomas 14
Silver Swan 88-89, *88*
Sisley, Alfred 46
Smith, Joseph 130, 137, 138

Snyders, Frans 72
Solario, Andrea 72
Solly, Edward 72-73
*Sporting Times, The* 97
*Squally Weather: A Sketch near Boulogne* 63, 97
Standish, Frank Hall 74
Stanhope, Sir Francis 103
Stella, Jacques 72
*Still Life with Cooking Utensils and Vegetables 68*
Stoney, Andrew Robinson (*see* Bowes, Andrew Robinson Stoney)
Stourton, James 145, 148
Strathmore, Claude, 13th Earl of 132-133, 135, 137, 138, 139, 140
Strathmore, John, 9th Earl of 7-8
Strathmore, John, 10th Earl of (John's father) 4, 8, *10*, 10-14, 18, 101
Strathmore, Mary, Countess of (*née* Mary Millner) 7, *11*, 11-15, 16, 18, 45, 99-102;
Strathmore, Mary Eleanor, Countess of (*née* Bowes) 4, 7-10, *8*, 12, 22
Strathmore, Thomas, 11th Earl of 10, 13
Strathmore, Thomas George, 12th Earl of 132
Strathmore family 14, 93, 137, 140
Streatlam Castle *3*, 3-4, 7, 9, 10, 11, 13, 14, 18, 21-22, 33, 50, 51, 52, 53, 67, 72, 73, 74, 76, 87, 93-98, *94*, 99, 105, 108, 111, 114, 117, 124, 125, 128, 129, 130, 131, 135, 139, 140
Streatlam Stud 18, *19*, 107, 124
*Study of Birch Trees* 67
*Study of Poplars* 68
Surtees, Robert 4

**T**

Taglioni, Marie 15, 17
Taine, Hippolyte 65
tapestries 71, 78, 79-80
  *Apollo and the Muses* 80
  *Birth of Samson* 70
  *Life of the Virgin* 80
  *Triumph of Time* 80
*Tears of St Peter 75*, 76
*Teesdale Mercury* 111, 125

*Temptation of St Anthony* 17, 72, 125
Teniers the Elder 72
Texier, E. 27
textiles 2, 78, *147*
  Fashion and Textile Gallery 147
  needlework seat covers 80
Thackeray, William Makepeace *16*, 16, 20-22, *22*, 25, 26, 38, 59, 107
Théâtre des Variétés *27, 28*, 27-40; *37*, 43, 45, 48, 51, 56, 63, 67, 111
theatre in England 15
theatre in France 27, 29, 33, 35;
Thiers, Adolphe 119
Thoré, Théophile 64
Tiepolo, Giovanni Battista 2, *84*, 85
*Times, The* 107, 116, 119
*Tobias Restoring His Father's Sight 75*, *77*
Toulouse-Lautrec, Henri 145
Treitt, Mr 137
Trinity College, Cambridge *16*, 16, 17, 18
*Triumph of Judith* 84
Trollope, Frances (Fanny) 20
Trustees of The Bowes Museum 124, 145
Turner, Joseph Mallord William *100*, 145
Twain, Mark 88
Two Thousand Guineas 107
Tyrconnel, Lady Sarah (*née* Delaval) 11
Tyrconnel, Lord 11

**U**

Uzanne, Octave 35, 49

**V**

Valenciennes, Pierre-Henri de 82-83
Vallayer-Coster, Anne 83
Vandam, Albert 25, 48, 56, 112
Vane, Henry Morgan 51, 103, 116, 128, 130, 133, 135
*Varnishing Day at the Royal Academy 67*
vaudeville 27, 28-29
*Venus de Milo* 113, 120
Vernet, Claude-Joseph 82
Versailles 115, 116, *116*, 119
Versailles Palace, Hall of Mirrors *116*, 118

Victoria, Queen 56
Victoria & Albert Museum (*see* London, South Kensington Museum)
Victoria & Albert Purchase Grant Fund 146
*Victory of the Risen Christ* 74
*View at Ornans* 61
*View of the Fires in Paris during the Commune on 24 and 25 May* 110. *118*
Vigée Le Brun, Elisabeth 46
Vignon, Jules de *112*
Vionnet, Madeleine 146

# W

Wagner, Richard 26, 31
Wales, Prince of (*later* Edward VII) 35, 56
Walker, Isaac, junior 18, 124
Walker, Isaac, senior 19
Wallace, Sir Richard 71, 78, 113-114, 120
Walpole, Horace 7
Washburne, E. B. 113, 116
Waterfield, Giles 71
Watson, J. E. 111, 123, 130
Weeks Museum 88
Wemmergill Hall 11, 12
West Australian 107
Western, E. Y. 127, 129, 130, 132

Wheatley 94
Wheldon, Thomas 15, 17, 18, 19, 20, 22, 25, 28, 31, 32, 36, 43, 53, 105
Whistler, James McNeill 64
Whitewall stables, Malton (*see* also Scott, John) 18, 33, 98, 104, 106, 128
William I, King of Prussia 56, 111, 118
William IV 17
Winsor & Newton 62
Winterhalter, François-Xavier 49, *49*, 112
Witham, Mgr Thomas 93, 128
Wolff, Albert 86
Woodburn, Samuel 72
Worth, Charles Frederick 48, *48*, 50
Wycliffe, John 73
Wyld, William 26

# Y

Young, Eric 75
Yriarte, Charles 25

# Z

Zola, Emile 33-35, 65
Zurbarán, Circle of 75